WAY OUT

in West Virginia

WAY OUT
in West Virginia

A Must-have Guide
to the Oddities and Wonders
of the Mountain State

JEANNE MOZIER

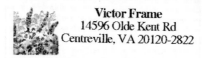
QUARRIER PRESS
Charleston, West Virginia

Quarrier Press
1416 Quarrier Street
Charleston, WV 25301
©1999 by Jeanne Mozier

Book and cover design:
Mark S. Phillips, Marketing+Design Group

12 11 10 9 8 7 6 5 4 3

Printed in the United States of America
on recycled paper.

Library of Congress Catalog Number: 99-60065
ISBN 1-891852-02-7

To my husband Jack,
my personal pilot and
favorite traveling companion.

TABLE OF CONTENTS

FOREWORD

No one ever accused me of being secretive, and I'm not about to start now. The intriguing land and friendly people of West Virginia have stayed hidden from view long enough. I want more people to discover that, sometimes, wild and wonderful can be a little weird.

West Virginia boasts pre-historic Indian burial mounds and 18th century mineral spas. You'll also find vestiges of frontier life, stories of wild and wooly battles of early industrial development and quirky creations of independent — and eccentric — mountaineers. It is a people's state, with nearly two million acres of land set aside for the public in a remarkable system of state parks, forests and wildlife management areas, as well as two huge national forests.

The original notion of an "oddities tour" was inspired by personal experience at two extraordinary events staged annually in West Virginia. Beginning with Fayetteville's Bridge Day and the Berkeley Springs International Water Tasting Competition, I moved to collecting other peculiar attractions of my adopted home state. I put the word out on the Internet and the "mountaineer grapevine". Friends, acquaintances and total strangers were glad to add their own outlandish favorites. The list grew into this book — to be shared with all those who love to color outside the lines.

My own tastes range from the merely unusual to the bizarre. I've made the fantastic and supernatural my environment of choice; *Way Out in West Virginia* reflects that point of view. This book is a searchlight for what's different, unique, individual and odd in a state that celebrates those inclinations. Not all the places listed are out-and-out weird; some are conventional but have strange or distinguishing characteristics. Many are on the National Register of Historic Places or National Register of Historic Landmarks. All are interesting.

Once you've experienced my list of oddities, whether in real life or vicariously through these pages, I invite you to search out more. The directions are easy — look for anomalies like the sign that announced "Donuts and Pepperoni Rolls", or anything that makes you exclaim "gee whiz"; then explore. Keep me posted on what you find; I'm taking suggestions for the sequel.

To paraphrase songwriter Colleen Anderson, let West Virginia choose you. If you do find yourself viewing the mummies in Philippi or listening for messages from outer space at Green Banks, be sure to tell them that Jeanne sent you on this pilgrimage to the edge.

ACKNOWLEDGMENTS

Literally hundreds of people provided information, insight and anecdotes for this book, including folks on the WISe online network, as well as the staff at many Convention and Visitors Bureaus around the state. I am also indebted to unknown people who, over the years, prepared material in local histories and brochures. Two people deserve special tribute — Michael Lipton, my longtime editor at *Graffiti* magazine and West Virginia's paramount pilgrim of the weird; and Topper Sherwood, my friend and fellow writer, who brought me to *Way Out's* publisher.

INTRODUCTION

Wild, wonderful and occasionally weird West Virginia

From churning whitewater in million-year-old rivers to the galactic ears of the 21st century — it's all a trip in "way out" West Virginia.

The matchless qualities of today's West Virginia began in the mists of time — when recurring eons of primeval forces lifted this spot on the planet from the deepest part of a vast inland sea that once covered North America to create the state with the highest mean elevation. Our Alleghenies experienced millions of years of erosion before the Himalayas were even born, making today's West Virginia real estate truly ancient.

Countless shells and watery vegetation from sea cycles have been transformed by relentless geologic pressure over countless ages into the limestone and coal deposits that dominate the present landscape. Marine fossils are regularly discovered on mountaintops. Salt and silica sand resulted from evaporation of a shallow sea period; oil and gas were trapped in eroded sandstone and shale.

Spread out the huge, colorful geologic map of West Virginia and variations in the land are obvious even to the untrained eye — variations "that mean the difference between a gentleman and a bum." The Eastern Continental Divide slices off a strip of the state. To the west, on a great slanted plateau, is the vast majority of West Virginia real estate; ours is the only state located entirely in the Appalachian highlands.

The slice to the east is the edge of Atlantis that slammed against the former inland sea, scrunching it into a rippling sheet of jumbled mountains and careening "hollers." Twists, fractures and distortions are commonplace yet distinguishing characteristics of the Mountain State.

Geology is destiny and the mineral kingdom is a high stakes player in the West Virginia game. The state's human history has been a three century contest of wills between geology and humanity, with the mountains providing obstacles to human constructions as well as endless mineral resources to exploit.

The frontier pattern of independence and self-sufficiency was established early-on in West Virginia, and wild remains closer than you think. When the area was finally admitted to the Union, decades after all its neighbors, it even had "west" in its name.

It was in the step to statehood that fate added another peculiar twist. West Virginia began life as the western expanses of the cradle of American civilization — Virginia. The Eastern Continental Divide served as a marker point for early treaties between English colonists and the tribes of the Six Nations. The Alleghenies were the first mountains to be conquered, and West Virginia was America's first frontier. Then came the Civil War — or the War of Northern Aggression as it's known in various nooks and crannies of the state. Ripped away from rebelling Virginia as political punishment, West Virginia bears the scars of a child of divorce. As the animated Virginia dandy in the prize-winning film *Gilligan's Appalachia* defines the relationship: "you'll be the butt of our jokes forever."

Astrologically a Gemini, West Virginia exhibited the duality of that sign in much of its early state history. There were two Constitutional Conventions, two votes for liberation and a capital city that couldn't make up its mind. First the capital was Wheeling, then it was Charleston, then Wheeling again. The final and current location of Charleston was clinched with the help of two circus clowns in 1887.

Trees, mountains, rocks and rapids are found in abundance in this place where Mother Nature chose to express her wildest imagination. Lacking are the cities. There are no true urban areas, and the state's ten largest population centers don't add up to half a million people. Geology and terrain have conspired to keep the state a perpetual frontier. Like third-world states all over the globe, even the industrial phase was primarily exploitative. Yet West Virginia's arrested development is proving to be a blessing. It precluded the explosive urban growth of the 20th century and made it a safe, friendly and naturally wild place to be as we face the 21st.

Life in West Virginia is not all mountain climbing cows and hand-painted signs advertising DIRT. There is culture galore, a world famous resort, and man-made wonders to admire on a face-to-face scale unmatched in America today. As noted novelist Denise Giardina remarked "For better or worse, there is no place like West Virginia."

HOW TO USE THIS BOOK

Chapters are arranged by category of unique places, events and experiences, independent of their location in the state. Each entry is listed alphabetically in the index, which provides contact information and location. To make the book useful for planning trips, there are indexes of each item by county, as well as general maps and contact information for the statewide system of convention and visitors bureaus. The ultimate information tool is the toll-free number for visitors: 1-800-CALL WVA. When appropriate, items are cross-referenced in the text to other chapters where there is additional information.

Check out our online version: www.wayoutinwv.com

CHAPTER ONE

ADVENTURE DRIVING

D riving in West Virginia is a constant adventure: where every road is a costly engineering marvel, every scenic overlook offers a million dollar view, and every tree could hide a cunning deer poised to leap upon an unsuspecting driver.

Roads twist, turn, climb and dip through relentless mountains and forests. They hug rivers, skim tree-tops, careen along ridges, and reveal plunging vistas. Breathtaking rock formations are down-home mile markers. Congested cities and traffic-jammed beltways are nowhere to be found. Driving through sparkling ice-covered hardwoods and snow-laden evergreens is a routine part of the skiing package.

★ Road signs are literal. Mastering the switchback is a driving necessity for Mountaineers and their guests.

★ Two centuries of creative road building in a state full of rivers and mountains have resulted in a treasure-filled inventory that includes not only innumerable hairpin turns, but also countless tunnels, more than a dozen covered bridges, and the highest bridge east of the Mississippi. *See* "Amazing Architecture" for more on bridges.

"Lay over" roads have a single paved lane down the middle and gravel shoulders to "lay over" if a vehicle suddenly appears from the other direction. This unique highway type is particularly noticeable along the winding, hilly and blind curves in Greenbrier and Pocahontas counties.

My Special Road...

There are skads of special roads throughout the state, and every resident probably has a few favorites.

My husband Jack and I were amazed when we stumbled onto **Smoke Hole Road**, hugging the side of North Mountain and Smoke Hole Canyon for eleven heart-stopping miles. Carved by the South Branch of the Potomac, the rugged 1,421-foot canyon is a forested treasure house of spectacular views, abandoned log cabins, caves and rare rock formations. The narrow gravel road runs through the Monongahela National Forest from SR 28 west of Petersburg to US 220 north of Franklin.

High Marks

All of **Monroe County** earns an A+ for pleasure driving with an edge.

The twenty miles of **SR 3** from the Virginia line — south along the base of Peter's Mountain, through Sweet Springs Valley, past Gap Mills and the turn-off to Hanging Rock, and then on to Union — could fill a daylong driving trip. Way-out scenes along the route include the remnants of Sweet Springs spa, Hanging Rock Raptor Observatory, and Cheese 'n More. You'll also find the oldest church west of the Alleghenies, prosperous farms, flocks of wild turkeys, covered bridges, countless lived-in log houses, the Eastern Continental Divide, and more than fifty historic buildings in the tiny town of Union.

Cutting across the southern edge of the county, the eleven miles of SR 122 from US 219 west to SR 12 are awash in pastoral splendor. Where the two routes join is **Marie Road**. It twists through miles of park-like scenery on the way north to Talcott and the Greenbrier River. Along the way, you'll see the captivating remnants of **Barger Springs**, including a dozen cottages and the pointy-hatted gazebo that still line the road past the once famous springs.

Even the Interstates

The seventy-miles-per-hour posted speed is often more a challenge than a limit on West Virginia interstates. No two mountains are alike — and no engineering solutions are the same — as the four-lane highways curve and twist up, down, around and through these mountains.

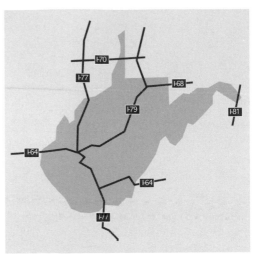

I-77 east of Bluefield boasts the mile-long East River Mountain Tunnel, while **I-70** tunnels through Wheeling. **I-64** is thermal Blue Ridge country — a jumbled swirl and howl of mountain tops — filled with hot and mineral springs' names as the road follows a historic path across the Eastern Continental Divide. Further north, **I-68** cuts through the Divide and is affectionately known as "the tundra" for its predictably hazardous weather.

IN THE KNOW: For conditions on major roads call the Department of Highways: 304-558-2889 or 304-558-3758.

Highland Scenic Highway

One of the first twenty All-American Roads designated by the U.S. Department of Transportation, **Highland Scenic Highway** is the highest major roadway in the state. More than sixty percent of its forty-three miles loom at more than 4,000 feet. Extending from Richwood to US 219 north of Marlinton, the designated highway passes Cranberry Glades and Wilderness, the Falls of Hill Creek and four scenic overlooks. The twenty-two mile Parkway section of the paved, two-lane SR 150 is closed to commercial truck traffic year 'round, and to all vehicles from December to March.

The Badlands

"The Badlands" is the familiar name for the tiny town of **Jefferson**, created as an X-rated haven along gritty US 60 west of Charleston. Substantial car repair shops and industrial buildings are interspersed with motels, adult stores, 24-hour clubs, showbars, "toys for girls and boys" and even a "wet and wild" car wash in an adult mall. Local industrial businesses like the Trojan Building, Onan's, Riley's Tools and Industrial Lubricants seem inspired by the erotic splendor.

Smutty snickers from the back seat fade as the row houses, fast food shops and gas stations of St. Albans replace "The Badlands" along US 60. A graceful girder bridge provides the final distraction before the climactic end of the drive — the **Yeager Monument**, a white-tipped rocket, erect and ready to fire.

QUINTESSENTIAL WEST VIRGINIA HIGHWAYS

In the 1920s — before Eisenhower and the interstates — the federal government strung together primary highways into a system connecting the forty-eight states. In West Virginia, US 60 and US 50 crossed the state east to west in the south and north, respectively, and US 219 linked them together running north/south. All three followed ancient Native American and pioneer trails, with substantial towns strung along their routes.

US 60 is well documented as the historic **Midland Trail**, running 123 miles from White Sulphur Springs in Greenbrier County to the State Capitol in Charleston. Interestingly, the trashy part from Charleston to Huntington (*see* "Badlands") is not included on the detailed map of the Midland Trail Scenic Highway.

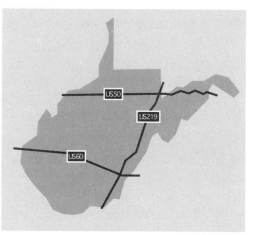

An ancient buffalo trail, the Midland Trail became one of the earliest routes west into the Appalachian wilderness, first as the "old state road" and then as the James River and Kanawha Turnpike. It was used by everyone from George Washington and Daniel Boone to Andrew Jackson and Robert E. Lee. It was designated US 60 in 1924.

Climbing to 3,170 feet at its highest point, the Midland Trail passes by a world class resort, historic battlefields, farm lands, rock formations, waterfalls, wetlands and sinkholes, coal camps and power plants, and repeated breathtaking vistas of the New River Gorge.

US 50 begins near Romney in the east and ends its West Virginia passage in Parkersburg at the Ohio River. Along the way it snakes up and down mountains, crossing ridges and rivers. It was the primary game, tribal and pioneer trail from the Valley of Virginia to the Ohio. French engineering genius Claude Crozet surveyed and blazed the first wilderness road along the route. In the 1830s it was called the North-western Turnpike from Winchester, Virginia to Parkersburg. Farms, deserted roadside motels, a virgin forest, switchbacks, grand vistas (including Saddle Mountain, shown above), and giant log and coal trucks all add to the fun.

US 219 is 150 miles of rhododendron-lined, dip and squiggle road along the western edge of the Eastern Continental Divide, from the Virginia line in Monroe County north to the Maryland border near Cathedral Forest. It was originally known as the famous Seneca Trail, a major artery through the rich hunting lands of West Virginia for various native tribes. High points include breathtaking views; the charming art towns of Lewisburg and Elkins; a hot tub factory outlet just south of Pearl Buck's museum home in Hillsboro; Beartown State Park; Lost World Caverns; Kumbrabow State Forest and the Fairfax Stone Monument. Much of US 219 in West Virginia weaves in and out of the vast Monongahela National Forest.

OTHER NOTABLE DRIVING ODDITIES

★ Once it was a heavily trafficked railroad town. Today, to reach the town of **Thurmond** by car from US 19 north of Beckley, it takes six curving miles of narrow CR 25, crossing and re-crossing river and rail. There are seven one-lane bridges, countless rock overhangs and a single lane, block-long, open-decked bridge that has been "grafted" onto the railroad bridge which makes the final approach to the restored Thurmond station. *See* "Things That Used to Be There" for more on Thurmond.

★ The wooden flooring moves ahead of the car in a wave as you cross the Elk River in Clay County on one of two remaining swinging bridges in the state. The **Elkhurst Bridge** is eight feet wide, 424 feet long. Used daily, it has a weight limit of two tons. From I-79, go south at exit 40 on SR 16 through Clay. At the northern end of the Hartland Bridge, turn right onto the road that parallels the north shore of the river and drive five miles to the swinging bridge. Take the left fork along the south bank of the Elk to get back to SR 16. Don't take the road up the hill; it doesn't go anywhere. A second swinging bridge carries pedestrians across the Hughes River in downtown Cairo.

COURTESY TRAVEL BERKELEY SPRINGS

★ The true Washington trail follows **SR 9 West** from Berkeley Springs to Paw Paw. It passes one of George Washington's favorite views — the noted Panorama Overlook shown above — then spirals down into the mountain hamlet of Great Cacapon. Crossing and re-crossing the snaking Cacapon River, it ends up 25 miles later along the bends of the Potomac River in Paw Paw.

★ The directions are correct, believe it or not. From US 50, vehicles enter downtown **Clarksburg** through the parking garage at the Second Street exit. There's no fee for passing through.

★ **Coffindaffer cross clusters** — two short blue crosses flanking a taller yellow one — were planted around the world by the late Craigsville businessman, Bernard Coffindaffer. He used his millions from his coal-cleaning plant to hire workers to plant the crosses in response to a vision he had that told him to erect cross clusters throughout West Virginia "for the glory of Jesus Christ." One count has 249 of the clusters set in varying West Virginia landscapes. Response to Coffindaffer's visionary inspiration was, and is, often controversial.

★ **Dingess Tunnel** in Mingo County was built as a mile-long railroad tunnel. It later became a paved, one-lane road, with fog so thick that cars often meet, headlight-to-headlight, inside. Used daily, the tunnel is off SR 65 near Laurel Lake. Another former Virginia Railway tunnel is used for one-way auto traffic to Guyandotte Campground north of SR 97 on the upper waters of R. D. Bailey Lake.

★ **US 250** follows a ridge-skimming path for twelve to fifteen miles south of Moundsville. As other ridges gambol alongside like puppies, the road reveals million-dollar views at every turn.

MOUNTAIN BIKING — RIDE LIKE THE DEVIL

Countless miles of trails and old logging roads through nearly endless public lands make it seem like mountain biking was invented for West Virginia. Huge uphills and thrill-ride descents twist and turn through forested mountains, skirting gorges and cutting through inspired geology. In addition to the numerous forest trails, there are over 300 miles of former rail beds that have been transformed to rail trails. The state's tourism division also sponsors pro-am road bike racing with its **Team Go Mart West Virginia**.

At least a half dozen full-service outfitters are busy with bike rentals and guided tours in the Mountain State. World-class mountain bike races are routine events. Some mountain biking pros are relocating here because, reportedly, West Virginia riding is very Euro.

The **North Bend Rail Trail** runs through ten tunnels and over more than four dozen bridges and trestles on its seventy-two mile route from Parkersburg to Wolf Summit. One tunnel, Silver Run, is reputed to be haunted. Another two tunnels lie next to the trail and are available for exploration. Negotiations are underway to add the few remaining miles that will take this section of the American Discovery Trail from the riverfront in Parkersburg to downtown Clarksburg. The Trail is basically flat with a few modest elevations. Like the B&O Railroad that it replaced, the North Bend Rail Trail goes through the middle of Cairo. Once a booming oil town, today tiny Cairo is a perfect trail stop with shops, services and restaurants.

The **Greenbrier River Trail** is 76 miles of beautiful vistas and historic relics running along a mostly level former C&O railbed from Caldwell north to Cass. The trail parallels US 219 and the Greenbrier River, the longest free-flowing river in the East.

The trail is legally held in a state-owned "rail bank." The tracks are gone and the trail consists of hard packed dirt, limestone chips or railroad ballast along the entire route. The Greenbrier River Trail has two tunnels, thirty-five bridges and an antique bank safe along the way. Accessible at various points, a horse or biker can ride the trail in two or three days; walkers should count on five or six.

For more on mountain biking in the Mountain State, try **1-800-CALL WVA**.

FLY THE EMPTY SKIES OF WEST VIRGINIA

West Virginia is paradise for general aviation. The mountains are the right altitude for single engine planes, air traffic is low, and controlled airspace is limited. Snaking rivers, surreal rock formations, mountains worn by time or chewed up by mining, and farms in hollows and on hillsides all guarantee that the scenery is never boring. Abundant forests filled with hardwoods make fall a paisley of brilliant colors. Thirty-eight public use airports are spread across the state, and most are close enough to walk to attractions and towns, although it's easy to hitch a ride from friendly airport folks. There are more than a hundred private strips, virtually all unlisted on any maps.

My pilot husband and I have flown to Bridge Day, enjoyed homemade pie at Fairmont, and hung out with hospitable controllers in their tower at Clarksburg. Government pork brought an oversized airport to Elkins, and the secret government bunker at The Greenbrier did the same for Greenbrier County. *See* "Truly Incredible."

The airport in Charleston was built on three leveled-off mountain tops in 1947. Only the building of the Panama Canal moved more earth. It was rededicated in 1985 as **Yeager Airport** to honor West Virginia's aviation hero, Brigadier General Chuck Yeager, the first man to fly faster than the speed of sound.

WILD RIDES COMING SOON!

The millennium plan for the southern tier coal counties will bring thousands of ATV riders, mountain bikers, hikers and horseback riders careening along 2,000 miles of twisting timber and coal roads at their varying speeds. Trailhead centers are planned to offer access to historically notable communities in the region and seeds are being planted that will grow into outfitters, restaurants and the other businesses of tourism.

Named for the world famous feud based in the area, the **Hatfield and McCoy Trail** promises to be rain forest lush and teeming with game, in radical contrast to dry western trails. Hundreds of ATV riders have participated in demonstration rides using the initial 300 miles of the trail.

CHAPTER TWO

AMAZING ARCHITECTURE

Wealth in West Virginia has tended to be transitory, never staying long enough or within the state's boundaries to fund grand and lasting metropoli. It did trickle down to create workingman towns and small cities. The state's relative isolation during the development-crazed years of the past generation or two have allowed working artifacts to flourish, not yet eliminated by the bland sameness of national franchises. When you find them, intact historic districts usually retain both the architecture and the social fabric of the original communities. However, in some towns you'll also find a few provocative, new buildings scattered among the antiques.

Must-see Historic Districts

★ **Victorian Wheeling** is a treasure trove of six historic districts and more than 900 townhouses built between 1837 and 1891. Every decade of Victorian style is represented. Stained glass, brick, stone, tile, wood, chandeliers and even the nails were crafted in Wheeling.

★ Parkersburg's jewel is the **Julia-Ann Square Historic District**, dominated by post-Civil War 19th century homes, still splendidly lived in today. The district is an easy morning walk from the historic Blennerhassett Hotel.

★ Tiny **Union** in Monroe County has twenty-nine antebellum structures on two main streets within its six-block downtown area.

Shepherdstown's **German Street** thrives with blocks of working artifacts — 18th and 19th century commercial and residential buildings now housing many thriving businesses. The tiny Shepherdstown Library, and the narrow street that forks around it, are the center of both the town and a preservation controversy.

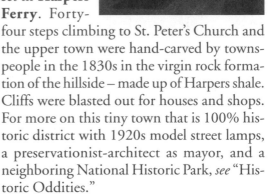

Lived-in armory houses of the 1830s and '40s dot Washington Street in **Harpers Ferry**. Forty-

four steps climbing to St. Peter's Church and the upper town were hand-carved by townspeople in the 1830s in the virgin rock formation of the hillside – made up of Harpers shale. Cliffs were blasted out for houses and shops. For more on this tiny town that is 100% historic district with 1920s model street lamps, a preservationist-architect as mayor, and a neighboring National Historic Park, *see* "Historic Oddities."

Best of the New

"We see it as a three-dimensional textbook," said Bobbi Hill, guiding force and executive director of the brand-new **Museum in the Community** of Hurricane. "The building teaches about architecture. We don't hide anything, we enhance it."

Inspired by Japanese folk houses, everything about the large, single-story building is conscious. It may be the most perfectly designed structure in the state. Exposed pipes are painted green, the universal design color for water pipes. There are electrical switches and wiring exposed behind transparent covers so all the "innards" can be seen. Mounted meters measure the amps and volts when the switch is thrown. One corner of the striking interior roof structure has identifying labels on the soffit and fascia, and signs point out varying angle sizes in the roof lines. The entire structure is built on an eight-foot grid which is constantly reinforced by design features.

The acoustics are perfect and the open central courtyard is graced by a Sassi Harel stone fountain. Designed to be active space, the museum also has classrooms and flexible exhibit areas.

INDUSTRIAL STRENGTH BEAUTY

Martinsburg is a railroad town and the sixteen sided **B&O Round-house** is its defining characteristic. Sandwiched between the railroad tracks and Tuscarora Creek on East Martin Street, the west round-house was a pioneer in the use of cast-iron skeletons, and is the only one of its kind remaining. Inside, an enormous clear space expands under an umbrella design of concentric beams, spoke-like rafters and slanted columns anchored to the floor. Trestles were built in the round-house machine shop, loaded on flatbed cars and taken to other parts of the rail line. Turntable mechanisms for the trains remain in the center of the floor. A string of small window slits around the circumference of the round roof make fanciful patterns of illumination.

The adjacent frog and switch shop used wood trusses and metal tension rods to span a 100-foot roof with no columns. Sections of the floor are still paved with unusual wooden bricks.

The ten-acre complex of three buildings and a ruin is crammed with fine workmanship and detailing in the buildings, bridges and aquaducts.

Because the roundhouse is fenced in, however, the tantalizing view of early industrial style comes through a fence or by standing on the restored porch of the Caperton train station.

There's dramatic social as well as industrial history embedded in the roundhouse complex. The first national railroad labor strike in the United States was initiated there in 1877, when 1,200 brakemen and firemen seized the Martinsburg depot, stopping all freight. The original roundhouse (1843) on the site was destroyed by Stonewall Jackson in 1861 and rebuilt in 1866. The accompanying engine shops were built the following decade.

Twin Splendor

Henry Davis and his son-in-law Stephen Elkins were an industrious pair. Both made their fortunes by bringing the railroad to Elkins — and then taking the coal and timber out. Both served as Senator from West Virginia. And both built mansions on the bluff overlooking the town. Today, **Halliehurst** and **Graceland** are architectural gems restored to original Victorian perfection, and open to the public on the campus of Davis & Elkins College.

In 1890 Senator Stephen Elkins built Halliehurst and named it for his wife, Hallie Davis. The fifty-six room Rhineland castle was designed by New York architect Charles Mott. There are towers and turrets, floor to ceiling sash windows opening onto rambling wrap-around porches, hipped slate roofs, and a spectacular view of the town below. Massive fireplaces with marble and wood mantles include one in the library decorated with handcarved signs of the zodiac.

Named Secretary of War in 1890, Elkins soon filled his new home with visiting presidents, cardinals, and millionaires. Today, the building houses college administration and public rooms. During Augusta Heritage workshops in the summers, knots of musicians gather to make porch music. Spread out along the porches' splendid expanse, they are protected from hearing each other by a quirk of Victorian architecture.

The huge third floor ballroom, once used as a gym for high school basketball games, now houses the Darby Collection.

Halliehurst's Ice House still stands. Each winter from 1890 to 1923, ice was cut from a pond on the estate and stored in the cylindrical stone structure to be used during the summer. Circular floors with an open core allowed the ice to be cut downwards from the top level. The eye-catching building stayed idle and empty until converted to a coffee house and pub by the college in 1967. The witch-hat towers and leaded glass windows of Halliehurst's Gate House still stand guard at the entrance to campus.

See Graceland in "Unusual Places to Stay", Darby Collection in "Remarkable Collections" and Augusta Heritage in "Art Wonders."

BUILDING WITH COAL

The only three coal buildings in the United States — and possibly the world — are in West Virginia.

A gift shop and a residence built of coal stand side-by-side in White Sulphur Springs just down the road from The Greenbrier Hotel. **The Coal House** shop offers visitors a free piece of coal, hoping to prevent souvenir stalkers from chipping away at the buildings.

The oldest and largest coal building, the **Williamson Coal House**, is located in Williamson and houses the Tug Valley Chamber of Commerce. Built in 1933 from donated materials, labor and cash, it used 65 tons of locally mined coal, and was designed by H.T. Hicks, who also designed the town of Welch.

To build these structures, cannel coal, the only type that can be shaped without fracturing, is cut into blocks and shaped with a hatchet. Mortar is colored with lamp black and the finished structure is coated with a clear shellac.

MOST TRAVELED PUBLIC BUILDING

John Brown's brief insurrection of 1859 ended when he and his small band of men were besieged and captured in the armory fire engine house along the Shenandoah and Potomac Rivers in Harpers Ferry. Renamed **John Brown's Fort**, the building traveled to the 1893 World Exposition in Chicago. It was returned to a site on Murphy's Farm near the edge of Harpers Ferry, relocated to Storer College on the hill, and then moved back to its current location across the street from its original site. Open to the public, it has one more move to go before it's home for good.

OLD JAILS, NEW USES

Bluefield Science Center is housed in the Old City Hall, a neo-classical structure built in 1924. The former jail cells have been painted shiny white and transformed into childrens' activity "cells" including "brain cell," "pencell" and "photo-cell."

Also "buy & cell," "foss-cell," and "cass-cell."

Fayetteville Visitors Center has shackled inmates passing through to occasionally-used cells in the former county jail — an impressive stone structure built in 1907. Don't ask them for restaurant recommendations.

Pence Springs Hotel was an elegant, 1920s resort later turned into a women's prison. Once again a desirable hotel, jail cells remain for viewing on the third floor. Owner/restorer Ashby Berkeley grew up on the grounds of the prison where his mother worked as a guard. Women confined in the third floor cells often refereed children's ball games played in the courtyard below. Poetic graffiti remains from the cell's last occupant in 1981: "When the gate slams shut, no one can hear you scream." For more on Pence Springs Hotel, *see* "Unusual Places to Stay."

Blue Ridge Bank in Martinsburg was once the Berkeley County Jail. Originally hoping to keep criminals in the Victorian structure, today the concern is keeping them out. The original brownstone trim looks like nailed boards, an architectural fancy that works for past and present purposes.

The Greenbrier. As befits one of the world's preeminent hotels, the Greenbrier once served as its most elite prison. For 201 days in 1941 and 1942, more than 1,600 diplomats from Axis nations were detained at the Greenbrier with their families while awaiting repatriation. These satisfied inmates left more than $65,000 in gratuities for the excellent service of the Greenbrier's staff, and depleted the Greenbrier shops, spending the American dollars they were not allowed to take home. For more on the Greenbrier, *see* "Truly Incredible."

Inmates were removed and a tour developed in the shell of **Moundsville Penitentiary**. *See* "Tours and Trips Not to Miss" for the gory details.

Eccentricities and Anomalies: More Architectural Nuggets

The brooding Gothic presence of **Weston State Asylum** dominates more than a square block along the West Fork River in downtown Weston. No longer in use, it is the largest hand-cut stone building in America. The fanciful roof lines, distinguished white clock tower and sweeping lawns make it ideal raw material for restoration to a more light-hearted use. The first financial transaction of the newly created state of West Virginia was the borrowing of $60,000 to pay for the construction. The loan was repaid.

★ **Camp Washington Carver**, the first African-American 4-H camp, boasts the largest chestnut log structure in the United States. The **Great Chestnut Lodge** is 110 feet long and built with 534 logs — corpses harvested from the chestnut blight. Built by the WPA during 1939 to 1942, it is irreplaceable. Those giant chestnuts are gone forever.

★ **The Opera House** in Marlinton opened in 1909, and is one of the oldest reinforced concrete structures in the country. It is currently under renovation as a cultural center.

★ **Our Lady of the Pines** always has its door open. The smallest church in the United States can seat twelve. All of its fixtures are handmade. Part of the memorial park includes the smallest mailing office. There are other miniature post offices, schoolhouses and churches around the state, including the child-sized Little House in Shepherdstown. Except for Christmastime when the Little House is open, visitors must bend over to take a peek in its windows.

★ **Star House**. A star cut-out in the gable of a gingerbread Victorian on Union Street in Hinton was a symbol for the hobo community during the Depression — anyone needing a meal could come here to get one.

★ **The Round Barn** of Mannington was built as a dairy barn and home in 1912 for $1,900, and today is a prize-winning restoration project and museum. The barn was built with a spring-fed watering system that the cows could turn on and off. Natural gas deposits on the farm are still used to heat the barn. A Shaker invention first built in 1826, round barns purportedly kept the devil from hiding in the corner. A privately-owned octagonal barn can be found outside Ravenswood.

★ **Natural gravity railyards**. Coal flowed downhill from the rich Pocahontas fields to naturally stop at the weigh station along the railroad in downtown Bluefield.

★ **Itmann's** ornate company store with an elegant arched portico was cut from native stone by Italian stonemasons from 1923-25.

★ **McDowell County Courthouse** in Welch sits atop granite steps leading up the hill. The impressive four-story, ivy-covered granite building also boasts a tower.

★ **West Virginia Wesleyan** in Buckhannon is a movie-set college campus. Built in 1890, the twenty-three modified Georgian brick buildings occupy an eighty-acre square with Wesley Chapel — the largest in the state — at its center.

★ **Huntington Museum of Art** has additions and studios designed by Walter Gropius, founder of the Bauhaus School. His famous clerestory windows bathe the rooms in natural light.

★ The **Upper Market House** of Wheeling's Centre Market is the only cast-iron columned market house in the country. Built in 1853, and in continuous use since, its fifty-four hollow Doric columns are set so that every other one acts as a down spout for the roof.

★ The Queen Anne style **Cooper House** on Main Street in Bramwell has a copper roof, as well as a doghouse built into the outside chimney. The house, with one of the first indoor swimming pools in the state, was built in 1910.

★ **The Ramsey School**, the oldest in the city of Bluefield, is built on the side of a hill. Its seven entrances on seven levels earned the school a mention in *Ripley's Believe It or Not.*

COURTESY TRAVEL BERKELEY SPRINGS

There are bigger and more splendid structures in West Virginia, but the collection of stone towers and battlements overlooking the historic spa town of Berkeley Springs earns the title of castle. Constructed of stone and visions of England in 1885, **Berkeley Castle** was built as a summer cottage and tribute to love. The Castle is open daily to the public, but shines particularly in October and November, when it is dressed in the morbid wit of the season and is home to an intriguing ghost tour.

BRIDGE FANS REJOICE

Technically, rivers are geologically trapped water, and West Virginia has an abundance of them. Their relentless path through the mountains has led to the building of some remarkable bridges. Some are like old erector sets, some are sleek and new concrete. Some are stone-covered double barrel culvert bridges spanning tiny creeks, while others carry superhighways across rivers.

★ The **East Huntington Bridge** looks like a giant harp resting on its side as it spans the Ohio River. It was the first cable-stayed bridge in the country to use triple strength concrete.

★ Built across Opequon Creek outside Martinsburg in 1832, the stone arches of **Vanmetre Ford Bridge** support the oldest intact bridge in use in West Virginia.

★ The **Wheeling Suspension Bridge**, built between 1846 and 1849, was the first bridge over the Ohio River. An innovative design by Charles Ellet Jr., it was also the country's first long-span, wire-cable suspension bridge; for many years, it was the longest in the world. When set in motion by high winds in 1854, the bridge deck was destroyed and later rebuilt. It is the most significant remaining pre-Civil War bridge in the United States, and is a National Civil Engineering Landmark.

★ At more than 3,000 feet long and 876 feet high, the **New River Bridge** on US 19 in Fayette County is the world's longest single arch steel bridge and the highest bridge east of Mississippi. Designed using

computer-aided methods, the steelwork was so accurate that when the arch halves were joined no metal shims had to be used.

COVERED BRIDGES

A central European design used to protect hard-to-replace wooden bridge timbers allowed hundreds of covered bridges to become an invaluable part of West Virginia's nineteenth century turnpike system, before railroads and automobiles made them virtually extinct. Today, sixteen such bridges remain. Here is a complete list of covered bridges in the state.

1. **Barrackville** crosses Buffalo Creek on US250/CR32 at Barrackville in Marion County. 145' long.

2. **Carrollton** over Buckhannon River has a sidewalk inside. Built in 1855. Drive CR 36 through it, one mile from US 119 south of Philippi, in Barbour County. 140' long.

3. **Center Point**. Built in 1888. Crosses McElroy Creek on SR 23 twelve miles north of US 50 in Doddridge County. Historical Society restored and owns. 42' long.

4. **Dents Run**. Built in 1889 and restored in 1984. Last one standing in Monongalia County. Just off US 19 and CR 43 near Morgantown. Open but not used for traffic. 40' long.

5. **Fish Creek** east of Hundred. Still used by traffic on CR 13 off US

250. Built in Wetzel County in the early 1880s. 36' long.

6. **Fletcher**. Still in use over Ten Mile Creek near Wolf Summit on CR 5/29 north of US 50. Built in 1891 in Harrison County. 58' long.

7. **Herns Mill**. Still in use on CR 40 (Muddy Creek Mountain Road) over Milligan Creek. Built in 1884, it is located west of Lewisburg in Greenbrier County. 53' long.

8. **Hokes Mill**. Still in use over Second Creek on CR 62 off US 219 south of Ronceverte in Greenbrier County. 81' long.

9. **Indian Creek**. Built in 1898 by a pair of teenage brothers. The bridge sits off US 219 six miles south of Union, just beyond Salt Sulphur Springs. Walk the old road down and through the bridge. Located in Monroe County. 50' long.

10. **Laurel Creek** was built in 1910, and is still in use on CR 219/11 (Lilydale Road) north of Union and Salt Sulphur Springs in Monroe County. At 24 feet, it is the smallest in the state.

11. **Locust Creek**. Rare double intersection truss design. Just off US 219 on CR 31 south of Hillsboro near the entrance of Calvin Price State Forest. Built in 1888, today only foot traffic is permitted. Located in Pocahontas County. 113' long.

12. **Philippi**. This two-lane bridge crosses the Tygart River on US 250. Located in Barbour County. 285' long.

13. **Sarvis Fork**. Originally built in 1889 over Big Mill Creek west of Ripley, it was dismantled and moved in 1924 to its present location over the Left Fork of Big Sandy Creek about 1.2 miles north of Sandyville on CR 21. Located in Jackson County, the bridge is still in use. 101' long.

14. **Simpson Creek**. Preserved in a small park, this bridge is still in use on CR 24/2 near Bridgeport. Take exit 121 off I-79. Located in Harrison County. 75' long.

15. **Staats Mill**. Constructed over Tug Fork of Mill Creek in 1887 and moved 3 miles to the Cedar Lakes Conference Center complex in 1983 as part of a flood control project. Located in Jackson County just off Route 33 near Ripley. Pedestrian traffic only. An outstanding example of a pure, long-truss covered bridge of notable length. 97' long.

16. **Walkersville**. This bridge traverses the right fork of the West Fork

River. Still in use, the bridge is just off US 19, one mile south of Walkersville. Located in Lewis County. 39' long.

Lemuel Chenoweth was the state's most creative covered bridge builder; two of his unique designs are still standing. A mathematical whiz, he adapted and improved the basic Burr Arch Truss principle.

The two-lane **Philippi Bridge**, built over the Tygart River in 1852, was Lemuel Chenoweth's masterpiece. He beat out several engineers to get the contract by standing on his bridge model to prove its strength. Made of yellow poplar, the Philippi Bridge was burned in a freak accident in 1989. West Virginia University rebuilt the bridge as close as to its original condition as possible, using Chenoweth's original plans. The Philippi Bridge is the only two-lane covered bridge still in use today on a federal highway.

Chenoweth also built the **Barrackville** covered bridge in 1853. It has the longest clear span of the seventeen remaining bridges, and allows no vehicular traffic.

TUNNELS

The best way around many West Virginia mountains is through them. Tunnels abound for automobile, train and canal. Most were engineering marvels at the time of their construction.

Tunnelton's two 4,100-foot railroad tunnels were the longest in the world when completed in 1853. The Northern Railroad excursion train ends short of the tunnels, but walking up the tracks can earn a glimpse of the dual entrance.

The Paw Paw Tunnel is the largest man-made structure on the C&O Canal, the latter now a National Park. It took fourteen years of labor unrest, epidemics and bankruptcy to hand carve the mountain tunnel, which was dubbed one of the wonders of the world when it was completed in 1850. The 3,118 foot long, twenty-four foot high tunnel was built to avoid six miles of Potomac River bends. Lined with six million bricks, the dry, intact structure is open year 'round for walkers and bikers along a well-maintained towpath.

A free standing stone railroad tunnel cut through solid rock in 1906 stands to the west of SR 54, north of Mullens in Wyoming County.

Just Plain Weird

Easily visible from across the Kanawha River at the State Capitol, the crown atop the new science building at the University of Charleston is mystifying to the casual observer. It's hard to imagine any explanation that could satisfy the universal reaction of "Why?" Perhaps the crown was necessary to provide the tinny tone to its chimes.

See "Things That Used to Be There" for more on Bramwell and Harpers Ferry.

CHAPTER THREE

ART WONDERS

Based on standard head counts, West Virginia is rated 100% rural. Yet it is a natural magnet for artists, with more arriving every day. Museums and galleries are well-established, and share the artistic landscape with artists' home studios tucked away in hollows and along streams.

The art may be quirky — one of the state's two symphonies is conducted by the tiny, all-in-black ex-wife of a former governor; or traditional — pickin', quilting and flat foot dancing. Most unexpectedly, it may be sophisticated — internationally recognized contemporary artists whose work is at home in European galleries, Japanese shops and New York stages.

PASSION ON THE POTOMAC

The setting for the **Contemporary American Theater Festival** (CATF) is all wrong. Gritty plays that reflect "ear-to-the-ground" trends of modern society belong in cities, not in a bucolic hamlet along the Potomac. A resident troupe of equity actors spends eight summer weeks taking the risks that new plays involve. It seems a little out-of-place at Shepherd College, which doesn't even have an academic theater program.

The price is wrong too. A CAT card for the full repertoire — all four plays plus other art events — costs less than a single ticket to a Broadway show. The seats are better in Shepherdstown, the play is often a world premier, and an after-show drink almost certainly brings you face-to-face with some of the cast.

Then there's the passionate imp who founded CATF in 1991 so that he could influence the future of American theater by producing and commissioning new plays. As long as it's new and provocative, Ed Herendeen loves it. He is awash in passion for new American plays and recognizes contemporary truth everywhere. When Herendeen mentions the play he commissioned on John Brown, he's not envisioning a Civil War thriller; he's describing today's lurid headlines of Tim McVey, militias and modern fanaticism.

CATF is unique in other ways as well. Contemporary puppetry is taken seriously and included as a full-partner in the repertoire of four summer plays. For eight weeks in June and July, CATF creates a casual and unpretentious artists' colony where actors hang out in the town's one or two pubs, play darts with folks and bump into each other all over town. American literary icon, Joyce Carol Oates, spends the summer in Shepherdstown, working on her cutting-edge plays before taking them public.

Even destiny gets involved. Herendeen discovered a play he thought was a CIA thriller written by an Oregon playwright. It turned out to be the story of an unsolved and dramatic crime in next-door Martinsburg. The cops who investigated the original crime drove a few miles down the road to be in the audience on opening night.

It is an odd and wonderful twist that turns the oldest town in West Virginia into a crib for the newest theater work in America.

At the Feet of a Heritage Master

Augusta Heritage Festival should have a warning label: "Beware, addictive!" You'll keep coming back for more. More companions, friends, high moments of creation with hands, feet, voice or musical instrument. "This has changed my life," is a routine comment.

Augusta is the biggest and oldest traditional heritage workshop series in the world. Dancers adore it. For traditional and blues musicians it's a chance to work with a legend for a week in small classes, then jam through the night. Hands-on folks do everything from make instruments and build stone walls to hunt and cook herbs. Lots of teens come with their parents and legends include the 12-year-piper who entranced the 25th anniversary session.

Augusta Heritage Arts Workshops began on the campus of Davis and Elkins College in 1973 with an earnest dedication to the conservation and teaching of traditional arts. A cluster of little old ladies were concerned that the traditional mountain crafts they practiced would die out. They lured one hundred people to Elkins from all over the country for the first five-week summer session.

In 1981, one-time volunteer Margo Blevin was hired. She broadened the scope of the program, made it self-sufficient and propelled Augusta onto its path of internationally-revered cultural icon. Margo noticed that the folks there for the crafts wanted something to do at night, so music offerings were expanded and evening concerts and dances were born. Blues mini-classes turned into nightly jams, then became Blues Week. She departed from the Appalachian emphasis to add Irish Week, Cajun Week and Swing Dance Week. The resulting unique pattern that blends music, dance, crafts and folklore is well illustrated by a recent Augusta catalog listing more than 200 different classes.

Clustered in five week-long intensive workshops, classes are small and very structured. The classes last all morning. Afternoons offer more classroom work or gatherings of the whole group with guest artists, cultural presentations, or special workshops. Evenings are filled with concerts, jam sessions, craft showcases and dances in the outdoor pavilion. A public dance concludes each week-long session.

More than 2,600 students, instructors and musicians pass through the summer-long program. Master artists come from all over the world to teach, and students range from beginner to expert. Scholarships are given to talented youth and within ethnic communities to help keep the traditions alive.

People-connecting at Augusta is made easy by traditional dancing and playing which includes everyone, and by dorm housing centered around the class and performance spaces. Folks come to learn. When they leave with a fulfilled yearning for cultural connection and the joy of creating, they come back. A few turn pro and a second generation is well established.

The **Augusta Heritage Center** perpetuates the "moment" of the workshops and continues the work throughout the year. There are concerts, field recordings, videos, and CDs. An incredible documentation process and archive collection is presided over by noted folklorist, Gerry Milnes, and housed as the Augusta Collection in Booth Library. *See* "Remarkable Collections."

The Augusta Festival concludes the summer session in mid-August with an open-to-the-public three day celebration of music, dance, poetry, crafts and food in Elkins City Park. Spin-offs from the summer workshops include Spring Dulcimer week in April and the Old Time Fiddlers' Reunion in October.

Timber frame construction by students of Augusta, 1985-7. Materials donated by family of Joseph Kwasniewski.

ANOTHER CARNEGIE HALL

Performers perk up their ears when they receive a call from **Carnegie Hall**. Everyone wants it on their resume. Built for the Lewisburg Female Institute in 1902 as a gift from philanthropist Andrew Carnegie, "the other" Carnegie Hall is the center of artistic and cultural life in Lewisburg. The Greek Revival building was recently renovated and is one of four remaining Carnegie Halls in the world. It hosts an annual program of more than 200 events including classes, gallery shows, concerts, dance, theater and film.

ART CONGLOMERATE

No benefactor in the world gets more for their cultural donation than those who support **Oglebay Institute**. This cultural empire includes theater, fine art, historic buildings and the noted Glass Museum. If Charleston is West Virginia's Washington, then Wheeling must be New York. Oglebay Institute makes that easy to believe.

At the turn of this century, wealthy industrialist Earl Oglebay transformed an ante-bellum farm house into a palatial center for his summer estate — the progressive-method Waddington Farms. The neoclassical structure has been Oglebay's Mansion Museum since 1930, and was the first accredited museum in the state. Its seven tall case clocks are a prominent feature, as are the surrounding Waddington Gardens, with breathtaking flower, water and lighting displays in every season. Lecture tours are regularly available.

The **Stifel Fine Arts Center** occupies another historic home, and is surrounded by formal gardens and manicured lawns. Built in 1910 and donated to Oglebay by the Stifel family in 1976, the stained glass windows, grand central staircase, original Oriental carpet and large rooms make an ideal setting for fine art exhibits that change monthly. The Stifel fortune came from a world-famous calico manufactured in Wheeling for more than a century, and trademarked with a boot. Thanks to Stifel's insistence that the house be fireproof, there is no structural wood in it — only concrete, steel and brick, hidden from view by hardwood paneling, marble and fine plaster.

Other Oglebay Institute art wonders include the newly restored Towngate Theater in downtown Wheeling, and monthly musical performances at the Mountain Moon Coffee House. Towngate recently added regular showings of art and classic films to its programs. The extremely popular Artists' Market draws 80,000 visitors to Oglebayfest in early October.

For more on Oglebay's Glass Museum and the Sweeney Punch Bowl, *see* "Remarkable Collections" and "Superlatives."

ON THE SMALL SCREEN

Award-winning funky videos, often produced by WNPB-public television in Morgantown, are a West Virginia hallmark. Filmmaker Jacob Young became a cult favorite with ***Dancing Outlaw***, a video featuring Jesco White, a Boone County flat dancer and Elvis impersonator. Young followed the bizarre Jesco video with ***Holy Cow, Swami!***, a three-hour documentary on the Hari Krishna community near Moundsville, which was beset by allegations of murder and racketeering. Young's remarkable film includes rare footage of the founding of the Hare Krishnas, as well as interviews with various devotees, public officials and the swami himself. For more on Moundsville's Palace of Gold, *see* "Truly Incredible."

Tom Nicholson, another WNPB filmmaker, captured an offbeat interpretation of West Virginia in ***Gilligan's Appalachia***, one of the world's first docu-comedies. West Virginia-ophile and current resident Bob Denver appears in the film, as does a clay-mation Abraham Lincoln and your author reading the state's future in the stars.

Folklorist Gerry Milnes documents more than thirty West Virginia treasures of folklore, music and stories in *Fiddles, Snakes & Dog Days*.

THEATER MARVELS

The opulent **Keith Albee Theater** in Huntington was built in the late 1920s by architect Thomas Lamb. Intricate detail, baroque ornamentation and Moorish design highlight its majestic lobby. The Ladies Suite on the lower level has four rooms and more space than most modern multiplexes.

Typical of the neighborhood movie houses that once thrived, the **Star Theater** in Berkeley Springs is one of the few remaining. Comfy, overstuffed couches — replacing several rows of seats — are often reserved weeks in advance.

Several other longtime theaters remain active in the state. Built in 1913, the **Apollo Theater** in Martinsburg is the oldest continuously operating theater in West Virginia. A few years earlier, in 1909, one of the country's first movie theaters was opened in Shepherdstown. It later was the first theater in the state with sound. After years of being closed, it reopened in 1992 as the **Shepherdstown Opera House**, showing art and foreign films seven nights a week. The **Capitol Theater** in Charleston was built for vaudeville in 1914. Currently it houses the theater projects of West Virginia State College. Built in 1926, the **Smoot Theater** in Parkersburg remains open for a variety of entertainment.

Cinematic adventure is still available at the rare drive-in. Here's a list:

* ★ **Glen Dale Drive-In:** Glendale, Marshall County; 304-845-2064.
* ★ **Grafton Drive-In:** Grafton, Taylor County; 304-265-2719 (rings at Capri Pizza).
* ★ **Hilltop Drive-In:** Newell, Hancock County; 304-387-1611.
* ★ **Jungle Drive-In:** Parkersburg, Wood County; 304-464-4063.
* ★ **Pineville Drive-In:** Pineville, Wyoming County; 304-732-7492.
* ★ **Pipestem Drive-In:** Athens, Summers County; 304-384-7382 (at Speedway).
* ★ **Sunset Drive-In:** Shinnston, Harrison County; 304-592-0400.

ELVIS LIVES!

Earl Brown, mechanotherapist and Elvis enthusiast, tosses silk scarves to adoring ladies every Friday night at his 1904 **Victoria Vaudeville Theater** in downtown Wheeling. The "Ohio Valley Revue" stars Doc Brown singing Elvis tunes in sparkling duds made to order from The King's original "Aloha Special" pattern. Everyone's invited after the show to hang out with Elvis and other entertainers in the Afterglow Room on the theater's lower level.

SHOW YOUR COWBELL

Started in 1933 on the stage of the Capitol Music Hall and broadcast on famous WWVA radio, Wheeling's **Jamboree** has been tops in the arena of live country music literally forever. Only the Grand Old Opry has been around longer. When the world famous stars yell for sold-out audiences to: "show your cowbell and they'll know you've been to Jamboree," they respond by ringing the signature cowbell given to each one. The practice originated with farmers who would travel to Jamboree and signal their loved ones at home with the distinctive ring of their cowbell.

Capitol Music Hall is a wonder on its own. Built in 1928, it currently houses eight broadcasting radio stations and a shop full of country music gifts. The 2,500 seat main hall retains its original seventy-five foot walls and ornate ceiling, and today has state-of-the-art sound, lighting and projection screens. Jamboree shares the stage with the Wheeling Symphony.

NATIONAL MUSIC BUFFET

Mountain Stage has taken West Virginia's music scene national with a vengeance. The two-hour Sunday evening show, featuring nationally and internationally known musicians, is popular on 115 stations of American Public Radio. Originated in Charleston by Andy Ridenour in 1983 and co-produced by singer songwriter Larry Groce, the show went national in 1986.

Groce avoids categorizing music and selects a sophisticated variety of sounds each week. Weekly guests of varying degrees of fame are backed up by the local Mountain Stage Band. Tradition holds that star attitudes are too silly for West Virginia, so everyone is treated with the same respect and gets to do at least three songs.

The shows are recorded before a live audience at the Cultural Center on Sundays. The *Best of Mountain Stage* and *Women on Mountain Stage* CDs are available at local record stores.

Outdoor Ads Invented

Mail Pouch barn paintings were an advertising gimmick developed by Aaron and Samuel Bloch, the Wheeling manufacturers who invented chewing tobacco in 1879. They named it West Virginia Mail Pouch two decades later, with the slogan "The Real Man's Choice." The tobacco is still manufactured in the same building by the current owners, and the Mail Pouch signs are now federally protected landmarks. Traditionally, the company paid for the paint and the work, and farmers got their barns painted. Today, the barns are vanishing and the signs are often maintained by local artists.

Art Gems

★ Stained glass windows in the ninety-year-old former church building are duplicated in the tile countertop of the **Cathedral Cafe and Bookstore** in Fayetteville. Hand-painted tabletops are all unique. Both are the creative product of Julia Cassells.

*The **Arts Kiosk**, a work by blacksmith Glen Horr, announces the local art scene in Berkeley Springs.*

★ Art is controversial and sometimes just plain weird. The **Yellow Brick Bank's** primary color ceiling, hand-painted by Marion Lewis, evokes strong opinions in Shepherdstown. It was copied from the ceiling of Glenstal Abbey in Limerick, Ireland, which was painted in the 1960s by psychedelic Italians. A giant gold fish sculpture competes for attention. Go for the great food.

★ Cannel coal is carved and shellacked into coal theme knicknacks or jewelry. Readily available in any souvenir shop, **coal art** is the ultimate West Virginia souvenir.

★ The awe-inspiring stained glass dome over the altar in **Mount de Chantal Academy's chapel** in Wheeling was made in the mid-nineteenth century by Rambusch, Inc., of New York City.

★ **Pickin' in the Park** is a free acoustic jam session featuring old time and bluegrass music staged in Elkins City Park every Wednesday, and on the Davis & Elkins campus in winter. Bring your spoons and washtubs.

★ **Artsbridge** of Parkersburg is one of only two successful bi-state arts organizations operating in the United States. It supports a full program of arts events on both sides of the Ohio River.

★ Pick any art scene in the Mountain State and it can eventually connect you to all the others. *Graffiti* is the place to begin. The monthly tabloid bills itself as West Virginia's

*The unique **Peace Totem** adorns the outdoor yard of the Youth Museum in Beckley. Assembled as a community project, it is the only painted work by master sculptor, Mark Blumenstein.*

Entertainment Guide. This title is well-earned, with trademark Noize columns highlighting music scenes from local correspondents all over the state, three pages of performance and exhibit listings, provocative feature articles and the infamous free personals.

★ **Concord United Methodist Church** in Athens glows with a dozen priceless stained glass windows by a mystery artist. Two windows feature the image of a huge eye.

★ The 1000 pound bell hanging at **St. Patrick's Church** in Hinton continues a century-old daily tradition of tolling out the *Angelus*.

★ Dancer Jude Binder has been inspiring Calhoun County with her remarkable **Heartwood in the Hills** school for the arts since 1982.

MURALS

There are lots of murals in West Virginia. Some of my favorites include the town of Mullens' 16 x 90 foot 1923 passenger train on Howard Avenue; another railroad mural can be found in Chicory Square Park, Bluefield. Fire engines in motion decorate the Hurricane Fire Hall on Main Street. Morgantown (shown above) has a missing block of its past painted on a brick wall of its present.

100 BEST SMALL ART TOWNS IN AMERICA

John Villani's popular book, *The 100 Best Small Art Towns in America*, has included four towns from West Virginia in various editions. Berkeley Springs is the champ, appearing in all three editions. It was first joined by Shepherdstown (1994), and next by Elkins (1996). The current edition (1998) matches Berkeley Springs with Lewisburg. The common thread is a vibrant and prominent arts community in each place.

WEST VIRGINIA CRAFTS MAP

It's the ultimate tour of 127 art studios, shops and galleries in every corner of the state, all plotted out on a colorful map. Call 1-800-CALL WVA for your copy.

OTHER ART, OTHER CHAPTERS

The work of nearly 1,200 West Virginia artists and craftspeople can be seen and purchased at **Tamarack**, the art emporium located immediately off the highway in Beckley. Besides the works for sale, scores more are represented in the gardens, architectural elements and furnishings of the building. Some of the dining tables and even the fanciful trash receptacles are individually created art works. For more, *see* "Truly Incredible."

For great once-a-year music and art, *see* "Far Out Festivals and Other Happenings."

.

CHAPTER FOUR

FAR-OUT FESTIVALS AND OTHER HAPPENINGS

T he oddities tour outlined in this book grew from a seed planted at two West Virginia events absolutely unique in the world — **Bridge Day** and the **Berkeley Springs International Water Tasting**.

Annual festivals and events are one-of-a-kind by their very nature. There's always the weather, or the crowd, or some peculiar occurrence that stamps the event as singular even when activities remain the same.

Some of the events in this chapter draw from heritage, others embrace the present with fervor. Sort through the collection, pick, choose and trust that whether it's sipping water or plunging into the rapids, nothing is more fun than a fabulous festival.

I TASTED KIRK DOUGLAS' WATER

After years of worker bee status at the **International Water Tasting** in Berkeley Springs, I was eventually promoted to be a judge at the largest water tasting ever held on the planet. Trained by water-master Arthur von Wiesenberger in the intricacies and subtleties of discriminating among samples of a

COURTESY TRAVEL BERKELEY SPRINGS

liquid that is tasteless at its best, I was ready for the task. It had to be easier than hiding in a back closet defending the top secret list that matched municipal water name with its anonymous number. And, I was able to dress in sequins.

A buzz swept the clutch of judges as we sat on risers, staring into the room crowded with spectators. Zip code 90210 was represented, reported the judge to my right. Von Wiesenberger nodded. It was true. Somewhere among the twenty-five municipal waters set in glasses before me and the dozen other judges was celebrity water from Beverly Hills. A note verified that it had been drawn from the tap in actor Kirk Douglas' bathroom by his son, Peter. Celebrity water! It was a first for the Berkeley Springs competition.

Since the judges taste blind — meaning we know nothing about a water but its assigned number — I had no idea which of the identical looking fluids was the one Kirk used to brush his teeth every morning. I searched for a clue. None of them seemed to have even the slightest hint of a cleft chin, piercing eyes, or the square-jawed look of Spartacus.

I performed the tasting ritual judges are taught each year. Glass by glass I looked for brilliance, sniffed for unwanted aromas, and rolled a sip of each water around my mouth. "The tongue has more than 100,000 taste buds," von Wiesenberger told us. "You need to wake them up, get them all involved." After the fifteenth glass, my taste buds were in a coma.

Taste is rated in three categories: flavor, mouth feel, and aftertaste. Von Wiesenberger's manual of water tasting terminology was the guidebook we used. Did water #24 have the finesse required by a movie star's palate, I wondered? Was it a balanced water with harmonious minerals? Or did it have the "sucking on a wet Band-Aid" taste we all dreaded to find in our unsuspecting mouths? Maybe Kirk's was #16 which seemed to have the breeding — the elegance and thirst-quenching capacity — one would expect to find in Beverly Hills. Surely it wasn't #19, assaulting my nose with a wave of chlorine odor. My face scrunched in sympathetic dismay with my harassed taste buds.

Tasting and rating water was more difficult than I imagined. I couldn't distinguish celebrity water from tap water drawn in Nowheresville.

Tabulators worked to add up ratings from all the judges. Then emcee J.W. Rone dramatically announced the top five municipals, beginning with the fifth place water. If Kirk's water won, would he attend next year's competition; would a host of celebrity waters enter in future years?

Fifth place went to Eldorado water from the Rocky Mountains south of Boulder, Colorado. Ames, Iowa was announced in fourth place, Pittsburgh rated third, and Dover, Delaware came in second.

The winner was on the tip of Rone's tongue. Would Kirk Douglas' bathroom tap provide the world's best tap water? Would Beverly Hills replace defending champion, Atlantic City, or two-time winner, Charleston?

No! Number one was not Beverly Hills, it was Kent, Ohio. Ohio. Home of . . . of . . . Ohioans. I was crushed. Not only had Kirk's water not placed in the top five, but neither had any West Virginia water.

After we tasted our way through still and sparkling bottled waters, I searched out the list that matched name with number. Kirk's water was #20 and placed seventh! I checked my rating sheet to see if I had noticed a special sparkle, a certain greatness to #20. Nope — only a mediocre 32. My eyes raced down the column to check for comments. I froze. Flabby! I had rated Kirk's water as flabby! Lacking vitality. How embarrassing.

No one was watching as I slipped the offending sheet into my pocket. Kirk Douglas never needed to know that I thought the water of Spartacus was flabby.

Note: In 1994, it was a Mountaineer sweep with the top three waters in the world all hailing from West Virginia sources. In 1998, Kirk's water did indeed win, submitted by his provider, the Metropolitan Water District of Southern California.

JUMP, BOYS, JUMP

It was a gorgeous Saturday in mid-October, and the New River Gorge was ablaze in fall colors as we flew along its jagged path into a private airport almost within walking distance of the bridge. We were in Fayette County for **Bridge Day**.

One incredible sight after another paraded before our eyes. The north-bound lanes of US 19 on both sides of the New River Bridge were closed to traffic and served as miles of parking. The closed north side of the world's longest single arch span bridge – 3,030 feet long — was open to legal foot traffic for the only day of the year. Thousands of denim-clad human butts lined up along the edge of the bridge watching more than 300 jumpers hurl themselves off a platform into the rapid-strewn river or onto a nearby sand beach nearly a thousand feet below. Colorful nylon chutes filled the air.

The overwhelmingly male BASE (bridge, antenna, spans and earth) jumpers, rappellers, and rafters in the river are the one-day show of Bridge Day. They come from all over the world to jump from the only major vehicle bridge in the world that allows it on the one day it is permissible. More than 100,000 people — and global television — are the audience. There's also a sideshow of 250 vendors stretched on the bridge roadway offering everything from roadkill cookbooks to Italian sausage sandwiches. Religious groups of all persuasions are out in force. Chanting Hare Krishnas are cheek to jowl with Fundamentalist Christians peddling Bibles.

In 1997, a dozen people set the world record for simultaneous jumps. That same year a five-man Elvis team jumped, dressed all in white. There have been only three fatal leaps since the event began in 1980; the most recent was in 1987.

THERE'S A FULL BALLOON OVER MORGANTOWN TONIGHT

At a signal, twenty large balloons, fully inflated and tethered at Mountaineer Mall in Morgantown, blast their burners and light up the night sky in a choreographed pattern. Thousands of people gasp in admiration at **Nite Glow**, the free opening event of Morgantown's Annual Balloon Festival.

More than forty balloons assemble each year for the three-day festival set at Hart Field, the local airport. Mass ascensions and balloon rides delight the public while balloonists amuse themselves throwing identifiable bean bags at a target balloon in the challenging "Hound and Hare" chase. Surrounding landowners are hospitable, spreading a white sheet as a welcome mat and presenting champagne to balloonists who land. Not only does the event provide dazzling photo ops, it has also inspired more than a decade of beautiful promotional art. The Balloon Festival is usually held on Columbus Day weekend, unless a home football game at West Virginia University interferes. The town could not handle both simultaneously.

Electrified in Wheeling

Driving through the arched tunnel of dancing snowflakes was magical, and it was just the entrance. Millions of lights in more than a hundred animated displays are the shining center of **Oglebay's Festival of Lights**. The city of Wheeling joins in with nearly 300 giant snowflakes and 200 twinkling trees. Started in 1985 and now the nation's largest light show (not counting the daily lighting of Las Vegas), the Festival of Lights draws more than 3,000 buses and a million visitors. Folks are welcome to drive themselves around 300 acres of hillsides, golf courses and a lake to see the well-designed collection of beautifully lit folk icons.

Cinderella's coach races towards the castle, while mice frolic around a pumpkin in a display that took two years to make. There are toy soldiers that march and salute, and a boy who waters the ground where flowers then grow and bloom. The Funny Fisherman perpetually catches and loses fish in Schenk Lake, and dinosaurs roam over a football field-sized dell. The poinsettia wreath and candle display is the tallest light sculpture, reaching sixty feet.

New displays are added each year and others are retired. They are all fabricated by industrial arts students at Wheeling Park High, who have worked with festival designers since the beginning. From November through February, the lights are on from dusk to 11 p.m.

Midnight Madness

24 Hours of Canaan is only half over at midnight on Saturday. To the pleasure of thousands of spectators, hours of break-neck riding up and down torturous mountains in the real dark of West Virginia lies ahead for more than a thousand riders. The grueling mountain bike race over the state's most rugged terrain was the first 24-hour team relay race in the United States. Bikers come from all over the world, and professionals race for a $30,000 cash purse alongside teams made up of friends or casual groups. Rules related to age and gender determine whether each team is a four or five person team; the total field is limited to 400 teams.

An opening sprint to their bikes and the mountainous 24-hour course are loosely based on the famed Le Mans auto race.

There are numerous legends about Canaan races, including the one where a local team set out to prove their hardiness by using a single-gear bike. As an added attraction they used only one pair of racing shorts, which the concluding rider would strip off and hand, along with the bike, to the next rider.

WEIRD AND UNUSUAL DOINGS FOR EVERY SEASON

★ At midday on January 1, nearly an hour of weird floats and zany folks parade down Washington Street from the General Lewis Inn to Church Street in downtown Lewisburg. There's a grown man in a diaper and a $2 bill for everyone. Otherwise, reports of the annual **Shanghai Parade** are vague and content is spontaneous, making it the most inexplicable of West Virginia celebrations.

We do know that it has been a Lewisburg custom for most of the past 120 years to parade along Washington Street on New Year's Day. Whether it represents the ultimate "day after" event or a tribute to the new beginning is all in your point of view. Post-Christmas caperers and dudes dressed-to-kill both figure in speculation about the origin of the custom, and newspaper reports from the nineteenth century always used the plural — Shanghais. Today, as in the past, there is no need to sign up in advance. Paraders are self-invited and simply fall-in for the march.

★ West Virginia has long been a major manufacturing center for marbles. Three manufacturers remain today: Marble King in Paden City, Champion Agate in Pennsboro, and Mid-Atlantic Glass in Ellenboro. Millions of marbles a week are made and sold all over the world. The **West Virginia Marble Festival** in Cairo features trading, a shooting contest and contemporary marble artists.

★ **Luminaria**. On the last Sunday before Christmas, 2,500 candles in paper bags line a mountain road north of Bruceton Mills going to old time Salem Church. Lit by parishioners at 4 p.m., the illumination lasts most of the night.

★ **Fasnatch** is a Swiss pre-Lenten Mardi Gras bash and ritual where Ol' Man Winter is burned in effigy at midnight in Helvetia. The Hutte Restaurant and friends cook Swiss treats for days. Masked merrymakers parade through the tiny town with lanterns and end up in Star Band Hall for music, dance and yodeling.

★ The traditional mountain music competitions, dancing, and crafts of Charleston's Vandalia Festival take back seat to its **Liars Contest**, where scores of folks compete for the Golden Shovel award. The tallest tale may feature anything from a favorite hound dog to magical trains and talking fish.

★ Each year, the Saturday before Columbus Day finds more than a hundred living history volunteers re-enacting the tumultuous **Presidential Election of 1860** on the streets of Harpers Ferry National Historic Park. Local electors make speeches and stump for their candidates up until the balloting at day's end. In case you've forgotten the results, Abe Lincoln won, but not in the area today known as West Virginia.

DISTINCTIONS

★ Arden Cougar is a worldwide celebrity thanks to ESPN, which broadcasts the **Webster Springs' Wood Chopping Festival** every Memorial Day weekend. He deserves the honor, having won the festival's world championship of wood chopping forty-four times! The folks in Webster Springs can't get enough of competition — the state championship turkey calling contest is also staged during the wood chopping fest.

★ It's the ultimate insiders event. Join Robertson Associates' private cavers group just once and you can attend the **Old Timers Reunion** forever. As many as 3,000 attendees from all over North America and beyond stake out a big field on the Tygart River near Dailey every Labor Day weekend for the world's largest cavers convention. Bare breasts decorated with day-glo are a favorite spontaneous exhibit for folks who spend their spare time in dark caves.

★ Buckskinners in 1840s attire decorate the state **Flintlock Championship** in Hurricane on Labor Day weekend.

★ The **Summersville Bluegrass Festival** brings thousands of music fans from all over the United States and about a dozen foreign countries to Nicholas County. Everybody parks their RVs and hauls out their lawn chairs at the small Nicholas County farm for a four day blast rated as one of the biggest in the East. Everyone who's anyone in bluegrass is on the playbill. The music continues each day from 9 a.m. to midnight, and then the real fun begins at the jams.

⋆ **The State Fair of West Virginia** has the usual display of prize-winning sheep and carnival rides. In addition it offers the only opportunity to watch harness racing in West Virginia. As unusual as the giant vegetables are the parking arrangements. Guaranteed by a land grant that stipulated parking will always be free, the 1,000 acre fairground hosts a temporary city of nearly 1,500 camper units averaging four people each. It's a captive audience for the nine-day event.

⋆ **Mountain State Arts and Craft Fair** is rated the best traditional fair in the nation. Spread over a hundred acres at Cedar Lakes near Ripley, works by more than 250 juried craftspeople and artisans make for great shopping. There are craft demonstrations, traditional entertainment and mountain food. The fair is held for several days during the July 4th holiday.

⋆ The **Gauley River Festival** concludes the three-week Gauley Season, with the country's largest whitewater marketplace along with food and music. *See* "Fast Living".

Funky Food Festivals

⋆ Edeline Wood of Parkersburg had a wild food party using recipes from Euell Gibbons and invited him to attend and speak. He did and returned annually for years until his death in 1975. Gibbons considered West Virginia the wild food garden spot of the world. Ms. Wood created and still runs the National Wild Food Association in his honor.

The Natural Wonder Wildfoods Weekend held at North Bend State Park in mid-September is the outgrowth of Ms. Wood's party. People come and forage under a botanist guide, help with the cooking, and eat the truly wild entrees in the cooking contest and feast. The list of foods demonstrates how foraging can be spun into epicurean. There could be chocolate-covered ground cherries and wild greens quiche competing with rattlesnake salad and squirrel. Venison mincemeat muffins, turtle stew, milkweed bud casserole, barbecued groundhog, quail supreme, bear casserole, and sumac lemonade have all been on the menu.

⋆ For nearly six decades thousands of folks have descended on Kingwood, in Preston County to celebrate the area's former chief crop

— humble buckwheat. In the process, they eat 20,000 sour buck-wheat pancake meals and six tons of home-ground whole hog sausage, all served with syrup and applesauce. It's the ultimate in all-you-can-eat. All the ingredients are produced locally including the buckwheat, still ground in season at Hazleton Mill. Not related to the cereal family, buckwheat can be eaten by those with wheat allergies.

The **Buckwheat Festival** also has a lamb dressing competition. Entrants are not dressed to be eaten; they are dressed-to-kill with fashionable bonnets, capes and other attire. There's even a real-life buckwheat fairy tale. The first Buckwheat Queen and King, meeting at their coronation in 1938, fell in love, married and lived in wedded bliss for nearly fifty years.

★ The weirdest native food of all is celebrated at the **Feast of the Ramson** — a tribute to ramps, the pungent, early spring relation to lilies and onions. Proclaiming itself Ramp Capital of the World, Richwood has hosted the granddaddy ramp dinner feast since 1937. Elkins more recently established the day-long **International Ramp Cook-off**, a culinary showdown hotly contested by the town's half-dozen chefs and assorted amateurs. Each cook is given ninety minutes to prepare their dish, without electricity or prepared ingredients, while anxious tasters watch. A gallon of each dish is required for public tasting. Presentation counts, so entrants are often costumed to complement their dish. Cash prizes are awarded. Community ramp dinners are also held in Helvetia, Clay, Core and many other spots around the state.

★ The rules of disposing with roadkill became a hot political issue in 1998. West Virginia legislators with too much time on their hands spent weeks debating a bill that allowed folks to take their roadkill home and eat it. Next they'll be requiring expiration date tags for roadkill left behind. No one in Marlinton cared. Their **Roadkill Cook-off** always features wild game and a parade of logging trucks.

A ROMAN HOLIDAY

Rated one of the best heritage events in the United States, the **Italian Heritage Festival** in Clarksburg is West Virginia's most extravagant celebration. Organizers scour the state for young beauties of Italian heritage and make them princesses for a week. There are pepperoni rolls galore, a pasta cook-off, beer and wine in the streets, and continuous free entertainment from two stages featuring famous Italian-

American performers and opera. As the state's most notable enclave of Italian-Americans and the homeplace of Oliverio's (*see* "Local food") you can bet the food and fun are authentic.

BEARDS

He's a huge hit every year at **The Honey Festival** in Parkersburg and year 'round at his honey-producing Thistledew Farms. Steve Conlon is the man with the most exotic beard imaginable — bees! Steve lures the bees by strapping their queen in a tiny basket to his sturdy chin; the rest follow. He reports fewer stings from the beard demonstration than from his general work around the bee farm.

COURTESY STEVE CONLAN

Babes judging beards always draws a crowd and nearly fifty contestants at the annual **Apple Butter Festival** in Berkeley Springs. The facial hair contest renders such notoriety that contestants have been known to work from one year to the next to win. One local park bum wore his blue ribbon around for two weeks. This is genetic politics at its best.

IT'S A HAUNT AT HALLOWEEN

Halloween brings unique hauntings all over the state, from a coal mine and theater in Beckley, to a castle in Berkeley Springs, a hotel in Bluefield, and a cave in Lewisburg. Ghosts come and go, so check with the visitors centers in these areas to find out times and locations of seasonal hauntings.

CHAPTER FIVE

FAST LIVING

The commonplace image of West Virginia tempo is relaxed, if not downright slow. The fastest movement that comes to mind is the banjo picker's fingers or the clogger's feet. In real life, there's more speed than that in the mountains and along the rivers. There's bona fide fast living.

A Ph.D. in Speed

Sounds of squealing tires and roaring engines accelerating through the multiple gears of twenty Ferraris ricochet around the two and a half mile, ten-turn **Summit Point Raceway** in Jefferson County.

Three days later, the two-lane asphalt highway track in the woods is the site of Accident Avoidance School. The following week, Advanced Driver Training addresses students wanting to drive safely at high speeds and under threatening circumstances. The training programs emphasize realistic techniques and provide ample opportunity for students to practice under both controlled conditions and the watchful eyes of top-notch trainers who ride along. During the standard day of school, five and a half hours are spent driving the car. Various intelligence and law enforcement agencies train their workers in the courses to protect them in high speed chases and terrorist attacks.

Brandishing a Yale Ph.D. and a championship Formula One racing career, Bill Scott is Summit Point's energetic center of speed and action. His anti-terrorist training includes role playing in nearby towns, while consumer courses encourage owners to bring their own cars — like the ever-popular Camaro — and learn to drive at top road speed, spin-out safely and make the always handy J-turn at 60 mph.

Although Summit Point is more a participatory than a spectator track, it does host an array of open-to-the-public races including vintage motorcycles, go-karts and formula cars. On a big day, 5,000 people can watch races that may include celebrities like Paul Newman or Tom Cruise, both of whom are occasional drivers at Summit Point.

Scott's high speed empire has room for other slower, but still exotic activities. Thirty acres adjacent to the raceway are planted with hundreds of apple trees on trellises. The unusual types Scott prefers are stored a few feet away in, according to Scott, "the best storage building in the United States". The apples are then sold directly to nearby urban areas: look for the Summit Point sticker on specialty Galas, Nittanys and Mountaineers in many gourmet markets.

The Summit Point Raceway garage houses the motorized symbols of Scott's diverse interests — a rare pair of gleaming red Porsche diesel tractors.

MOTHER NATURE'S RUSH

White water rafting is a top echelon adrenaline sport, and West Virginia has the best white water in the east. Many experienced rafters rate the **Gauley**, West Virginia's longest river, as the best two-day white water trip in the world. With gargantuan boulders and rapids named Pure Screaming Hell and Heaven Help Us, the Gauley lives up to its reputation.

Nine rivers provide a 200-mile commercially rafted area, with a full range of all six levels of rapids during the white water seasons of spring, summer and fall. The New and Gauley Rivers are paramount among these with tossing waters, matchless scenery and history. Both are part of the largest federally protected watershed in the eastern United States.

The huge **New River** watershed provides enormous water volume that squeezes through the narrow canyon creating big, roller coaster waves as the river falls 750 feet in fifty miles. The Gauley River is second in difficulty among the nation's rivers, with 100 rapids — fifty major ones — in a twenty-six mile stretch that drops nearly 700 feet.

For white water rafters, nothing tops the **Gauley Season**: a twenty-two day stretch beginning in mid-September when the Army Corps of Engineers stages its annual "draw down" of water backed-up by the huge Summersville Dam. One million gallons of lake water gushing through the Summersville Dam tunnels each minute create an irresistible, three-week wave of turbulence across more than a hundred rapids. White water enthusiasts flock to ride rafts and kayaks — sometimes twice a day — on the nearly inaccessible Gauley River. It's strictly for the experienced.

Since the high water rafting releases prevent fishing on the Gauley during that period, white water outfitters compensate the fishermen by stocking the river with an additional 1,000 pounds of trout.

White water is a multi-sensory experience with roaring sounds, drenching wetness and heart-pounding anticipation. There are stretches of placid drifting surrounded by scenic wilderness and coal camp remnants. The wild **Cheat River** has holes called hydraulics, breeders of whirlpools that capsize rafts. At its best during April, May and June, the Cheat has thirty-eight rapids in eleven miles.

All the rivers offer hidden waterfalls, churning rapids, and rock-strewn channels, so be prepared for white water sports. In spite of **Class VI River Runners'** well-deserved claim of gourmet lunches, white water rafting is not for cream puffs. Lodging for overnights along the rivers is primitive, and the rapids require real paddling.

Inflatable kayaks, known as duckies, are sufficient for the mild rapids and quiet pools of the Upper New, and provide an easy way to see the gorge close-up.

Guides are an indelible part of the white water experience. They are expert pilots, often well-versed on the history and ecology of the river, and overflowing with rafter jokes.

Summersville Lake, created by the dam, is a hotbed of water sports, unexpected in a state known for its mountains and boasting only one tiny natural lake. Avid divers seek out the 3,000 acre man-made lake for its crystal clear water with visibility up to sixty feet, rocky cliffs, underwater boulders and water caves. A dive shop and jet skis round out the water sports menu.

Inaugurated in 1968, today's white water industry in West Virginia has nearly forty commercial outfitters offering everything from kayaking clinics to rafting trips for the handicapped. Since adrenaline junkies are seldom satisfied with a single, life-stretching experience, most of the rafting companies also provide rock climbing and rappelling.

For more about the New River — possibly the oldest in the world — *see* "Mother Nature's Wonders."

MORE SPEED

★ **Jet Boats at Hawks Nest**. Fast living at Hawks Nest State Park begins with a walk down into the dizzying view of the New River Gorge from the outer deck of the lodge. A two-minute aerial tram ride takes adventurers down to the dock where the twenty-one foot jet boat — the Miss M. Rocks — floats on the river, waiting to take off under the railroad/walking bridge. For thirty-five minutes, water-sprayed passengers speed upstream along the rocky cliffs of the gorge, pockmarked with beehive ovens where local coal was coked.

Rick, the gravelly-voiced boatman, narrates colorful tales of the river, and points out wooden boxes posing as fishing camps all along the barest edge of shoreline. Dragonflies pace the boat as it slows to turn at the Fayette Station rapids under the world-famous New River Gorge Bridge. Soaking up passengers' awestruck glances, the second highest bridge in the United States arches gracefully against the sky above the river.

★ **Rivers** is one of a dozen or more rafting companies that ply the waters set aside for commercial white water rafting. Among their attractions is the **Red Dog Saloon**, a built-for-partying center festooned with hundreds of trophy underwear dated by river ride. The namesake red dog sleeps on the bar.

★ **Summerfest** brings high-powered craft from all over the country into Huntington in July to race along the Ohio River for the national speedboat title. The National Power Boat Association stages its national championships during odd-numbered years at Bluestone Lake in Hinton during the State Water Festival in mid-summer. More than 500 drivers in modified stock speedboats and hydroplanes scream over the lake at speeds in excess of 90 mph.

★ Dirt track car racing enthusiasts go to **Pennsboro Speedway** in October for the Dirt Track World Championship and its $50,000 prize. Not far away in Mineral Wells, WV Motor Speedway offers one of the world's best dirt tracks.

GUNS

What's a wild state without weapons? Defensive firearms training is available from **Take-in Creek** in Beckley and at the **Summit Point Raceway**. A combo cycle and shoot package can be found in Lewisburg with a day of biking on the Greenbrier Trail and a day of shooting on the move and from a vehicle at the **Savannah Lane Shooting Association's** Defensive Handgun Course.

POOL PARLOR MEMORIES

Traditional urban neighborhood night life is well represented by **The Strand**, a longtime Charleston eatery and beer joint with a back room famous for its extensive collection of billiard tables and legendary card games. Pool-shooting legislators rub elbows with construction workers and lawyers while the historic aura of gambling and deal-making hangs like old Mose's cigar smoke in the room.

A sibling if not a twin of The Strand is **The Met** in Morgantown. Even the crusty owners could pass for family. The pool hall occupies the same basement area in the Metropolitan Theater that was built for it in 1924, with the same dozen tables — one billiard, eleven pool. Long-time owner, Bill Bonfili, tells poignant stories of old, nearly blind West Virginia University alums clambering down the steep stairs on their walkers, opening the door and saying, with relief, "Nothing's changed since I wasted my youth here." Open from 11 am to 3 am, the Met begins to get busy around 9:30. Beer and pool are its only products; WVU students and faculty are its primary denizens.

CHAPTER SIX

GREAT PLUMBING

Mother Nature sets the pace with natural plumbing wonders, especially the network of thermal and mineral springs found along the eastern spine of America in West Virginia. The springs bring up the source water and nearly a score of rivers on both sides of the divide hustle it out to sea. Rivers or creeks run under and past most cities and towns.

These numerous springs inspired man-made plumbing marvels that include historic and contemporary spa towns and resorts.

THE PURSUIT OF BATHING

The presence of the only monument to presidential bathing gives a hint. The official name of the town around the warm mineral waters of **Berkeley Springs** clinches it. George Washington and his cronies named the town Bath when they founded it in 1776 to serve as America's first spa. The town remains Bath today, though the world knows it by the post office name of Berkeley Springs. Real place or state-of-mind, the purpose remains unchanged through history and pre-history: to bathe in and drink the waters.

The water George Washington came to drink and soak in is unchanged — warm, clear and lightly mineralized. It serves as the drinking water for Berkeley Springs, is bottled commercially and available — as Lord Fairfax prescribed — free to the public, from a fountain under a nineteenth century spring house in **Berkeley Springs State Park**. Thousands of people come regularly from near and far to take the waters — home with them. Selling plastic jugs is a profitable sideline for the Park Foundation.

COURTESY TRAVEL BERKELEY SPRINGS

The variety of bathing options and treatments available today would stagger old George, who made do with large hollows scooped from the sand, lined with stone and screened from view by woven brush. His bathtub monument along the west ridge of the park honors this historic fact, minus the woven brush screens.

By the end of Washington's nearly fifty years of visits to Berkeley Springs, he would have bathed in a wooden bathhouse built in 1784. Today, thousands of people a year re-enact history when they slip into four-foot deep tubs filled with the slightly buoyant, warm mineral waters heated to a cozy 104 degrees. All this indulgence takes place in the nine private bathing rooms of the **Roman Bath House**, built in 1815 on the same spot as the original bathhouse. Interested in recouping the costs of a modest renovation of the Roman Baths, the state park encourages bringing a friend — or even two.

The bathing in Bath doesn't end in historic chambers....

Across the park, there are soak tubs and more Roman Baths in the **Main Bathhouse** built in 1929. The west ridge of the park between the two bathhouses is lined with wild versions of the baths. There's a long channel with tiny waterfalls, where kids love to wade during summer concerts; and big pools, including one with sinking sands where the springs bubble free.

Trace the waters under the streets and bridges throughout Berkeley Springs and other exotic plumbing is revealed. There are luxurious pink baths at **The Country Inn's** spa with a panoramic view of the town. Other private spas and inns have whirlpool baths filled with the same refreshing springs water. The often controversial town seal, created in the 1870s, features a barely clad lady sitting at a spring. There's even a Madonna in a bathtub-based grotto at the Catholic Church across from the springs.

The 19th century park bathkeeper, old John Davis, believed that the chief end of man was to bathe. While soaking in the waters is still the most direct way to experience Berkeley Springs, there are new pleasures that John Davis never imagined. The historic spa town now boasts three times as many massage therapists as lawyers. Bodywork treatments are provided by trained practitioners, ranging from Reiki masters to the exotic Chinese-Malaysian owner of Atasia Spa, who has given more than 10,000 massages in the Thai technique he learned from a personal master in the noted Wat Po Buddhist Temple in Bangkok. Mud wraps and aromatherapy round out the exotic menu at Berkeley Springs year 'round spa feast.

FIRE HOSES AND AN OPULENT POOL

It's the incomparable light that makes the first impression. Gold and white and exhilarating, light streams through the billowing white fabric covering the glass dome over the pool and ricochets off topaz mosaics and tile floors. The brightly decorated lounge filled with white rattan, tropical prints and exotic vegetation loves the light.

When built at **The Greenbrier** in 1911, the Roman-inspired indoor pool with its arches and pillars was one of the largest in the world. The 142-foot pool remains the dominant feature of the **Mineral Baths and Spa** building and the entryway to the recreational spa. Designed as a luxurious "European Cure in America" just in time for World War I, the spa retains the continental flavor of an exclusive clinic.

My spa experience began with a white-clad attendant scrubbing me down with seaweed and a loofah mitt. Then I was guided to the Swiss shower and Scotch spray area where I was battered by multiple shower heads and hosed down by another attendant in white. In the next area I was rubbed with moisturizing cream, wrapped in hot towels and left to marinate in preparation for a massage. "The Greenbrier trains us," explained the masseuse when I asked about her traditional Swedish technique. No reiki, energy-balancing subtle treatments at the Greenbrier.

The traditional sulphur water is available for drinking outside at the distinctive dome built over the spring in 1830, and inside the hotel in the spring room — not that many people drink it these days. Since 1913, drinking water for the hotel has been piped in from Alvon Springs twelve miles away. Both waters are available for baths in the spa.

The Greenbrier began with a miracle cure for rheumatism in 1778; and today its spa offers an *a la carte* menu of treatments ranging from aftersun sulphur baths with calming oils and lotions to sea mud packs, paraffin wraps and aromatherapy. There's even a unique **Greenbrier Diagnostic Clinic** — preventive care at a bargain price of only $3,055.

For more on The Greenbrier, *see* "Truly Incredible."

PLUMBING WONDERS OF SHEPHERDSTOWN

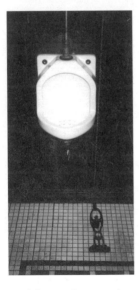

Shepherdstown is a shining star of eccentric plumbing. Some of its plumbing marvels are natural, like Town Run, which surges along the main street over drops sufficient to drive the founder's 18th century grist mill. The mill is still standing today and boasts the largest and oldest overshot waterwheel in the world.

Other marvels are man-made. Each of **The Bavarian Inn's** extensive collection of private whirlpool baths can easily accommodate two. There are piles of large eggshell-white towels and a toiletry basket with body cream, appreciated after a long soak. If the municipality would decrease the chlorine in town water, the Bavarian baths would be perfect.

*Odder than the Bavarian's bidets is the area's only working foot-flush urinal found at **O'Hurley's General Store**. It's a unisex bathroom, ladies, so check it out.*

The European-born owners of the Bavarian provided bidets in nearly all the rooms. This continental indulgence with a strong hygienic argument was a mystery to me. Without instructions, I was forced to follow logic and found it worked. After repeated usage in a brief overnight stay, I added bidets to my list of treatments, like massage, that feel good and are good for you.

DROPLETS

At 3,860 feet, the outhouse at the Raptor Lookout on **Peter's Mountain** *offers the best view in the state.*

Water is available from the original antique fountains in the halls at the **General Lewis Inn**. *For more on the Inn, see "Unusual Places to Stay."*

★ Sulphurated and void of bacteria, **Pence Springs'** water can sit on a shelf for a year without treatment. The springs' current owner, Ashby Berkeley, proclaims it the "best water in the world" and dispenses it at

his Pence Springs Hotel and at the legendary Sunday flea market held on the grounds.

Long favored by wandering animal herds, the springs were first tapped in 1872 when Andrew Pence sank a thirty-foot hollow gum log, attached a spigot and began selling bottled water. By the time Pence added a hotel in 1897, the spring area was tiled and he was selling a couple hundred cases of his water each week. In 1904, the water won a silver medal at the St. Louis World's Fair, and was sold nationally in ginger ale and root beer through the '20s. Historically, the water has been noted for assisting poor digestion.

★ The 65 degree water of **Capon Springs** was long-known to native tribes, and was discovered by colonial settlers in the mid 1760s. While its origin may be unknown, the mineral content of the water is well-known: calcium bicarbonate predominates, with a rare touch of lithia. It is an alkaloid spring similar to Vichy, France or Carlsbad, Germany.

In a familiar pattern, a town — complete with a small boarding house and cabins — sprang up soon after the founder of Capon Springs brought his wife to be cured. The fame of the water spread and Capon Springs evolved into one of the most fashionable of the 19th century spa resorts along the Virginia/West Virginia border. In mid-century there was a large bath colonnade with forty bathrooms and hot and cold plunge baths. Today, bathing is limited to the outdoor pool; and water fountains scattered around the green walkways deliver the famous spring water directly to guests' lips. For more on Pence and Capon Springs, *see* "Unusual Places to Stay."

THE ULTIMATE IN BATHING PLEASURE

Many West Virginia lodgings are rustic and take advantage of the rugged outdoor beauty of the state. But there are sybaritic pleasures to be found, especially those of the bath.

Nothing is more luxurious than a whirlpool bath in the room. More than a hundred lodging spaces in every corner of the state offer in-room jacuzzis or whirlpools for those who want no bathing suits, no time limits and no sharing with strangers.

★ **Highlawn Inn** of Berkeley Springs takes its cue from the world famous warm mineral waters in the park down the hill. This Victorian empire — run by the queen of West Virginia B & Bs, Sandra Kauffman — boasts two rooms with whirlpool baths, a house with a whirlpool room bigger than most bedrooms, and the most elaborate bathroom in the state.

Highlawn's secluded Carriage House has a pink whirlpool bath framed in dark green tin panels from the ceiling of a turn-of-the-century building downtown. Molded with arm rests, there's no struggling to stay upright in this tub. A wall of windows and a pair of French doors set on the oblique separate the tub from the bedroom. Adjacent to the tub is a pedestal sink and marble-topped long English washstand with tiled backdrop. The enclosed toilet area flaunts a whimsical triangle window, cut like those on an outhouse door.

★ **Warfield House**, at the foot of the grounds of Davis & Elkins College, boasts the best example of an intact Art Deco room in the state — a shiny black marlite bathroom trimmed in chrome. The Oak Room down the hall has a faux black striped marble whirlpool tub that barely causes a ripple in the Victorian decor.

★ Three honeymoon cabins at **Smoke Hole Cabins** along the river go all the way with heart-shaped jacuzzis in front of a roaring fire and satin sheets on the beds.

★ Choosing a jacuzzi with the best view is a close contest between the top floor suite at **Hilltop House** and the palatial Presidential and Royal Suites on the top floor of an Alpine chalet at **The Bavarian Inn**. Separated by just a few miles, both contestants look out on the majestic Potomac River. The Bavarian also offers river views and whirlpools in more than thirty other rooms.

★ Drawing from their own prized springs, **Coolfont Resort and Spa** offers whirlpool baths in thirty-one chalets of various sizes.

★ The super suite in **Stratford Springs'** Waddell House has a large fireplace and jacuzzi tub.

★ The two-person whirlpool tub at **Country Inns and Suites** is conveniently located next to the bed and within view of the television.

★ **Bonnie Dwaine B&B** offers five rooms with private whirlpool baths; while the **Historic Charleston B&B** has one in its Bridal Suite. **Hutton House** places honeymooners in Corrine's Room where the whirlpool bath has gold fixtures and shelves for knickknacks.

★ Six rooms in the contemporary log **North Fork Mountain Inn** have private jacuzzis. The vacation cottages at **Creekside** have jacuzzis and a view of Indian Creek. Harman's **North Fork Cottages** have jacuzzis and rock fireplaces.

★ The three-room suite in **The Manor B&B** overlooking Berkeley Springs has a small jacuzzi and the noted waters. Down the block, **Maria's Inn** added three deluxe rooms each with whirlpool baths.

★ Chain motels are fast becoming whirlpool centers, with Super 8 boasting whirlpools in most of their West Virginia locations. Others with jacuzzi suites include: South Branch Inn, Expressway Motor Inn and two AmeriHost Inns in Parkerburg; and Howard Johnson Express Inn and Shoney's Inn in Beckley. The only in-room jacuzzi in Morgantown is found at the Comfort Inn. The large tub is conveniently reached from both the bathroom and bedroom side.

Private Tubs in the Great Outdoors

Seven riverside log, fieldstone and redwood cottages at **Cheat River Lodge** have seven-foot outdoor hot tubs where soakers can fish from the river. **Mill Creek Cabins** heat their five whirlpool tubs with two wood burning stoves. Other cabins or chalets with private, outdoor hot tubs abound in the New River Gorge area, including **Country Road Cabins** and **Ace Adventure Center's** A-frame chalets.

O'Briens Cabins near Berkeley Springs keeps old-fashioned claw foot tubs on the outdoor decks of two cabins. No whirling motors, just soaking in silence.

For more on springs and bathing, *see* "Things That Used to be There."

For Your Viewing Pleasure

Once a stag bar, **Wimpy's** pool hall added a ladies room but kept a glass door on their single-urinal men's room.

CHAPTER SEVEN

HISTORIC ODDITIES

For more than 10,000 years, humans have lived within the boundaries of today's West Virginia. Quirks of history have linked U.S. presidents, revolutionaries, rebel spies and labor leaders with West Virginia. The state itself is a historic oddity, the only one formed at gunpoint from the lands of another state.

THE ANCIENTS

Giant skeletons, enormous burial mounds and mystery carvings are found at nearly a hundred primitive sites in West Virginia, remnants of civilizations that reigned long before the pyramids were built in Egypt. With few exceptions, these ancient wonders were disregarded by early white settlers.

The larger of these burial mounds evidently had sufficient sacred juice to keep the invading white man at bay long enough for the mounds' worth to be appreciated. Countless smaller ones, however, were leveled by farmers and town builders. A century ago the Smithsonian Institute documented fifty Indian burial mounds in the Mountain State — one of the largest groups in America. The mounds were built somewhere between 2,000 and 3,000 years ago. Today only a few remain, including the largest conical earthen mound of its kind, **Grave Creek** in Moundsville.

Grave Creek is big and impressive, being 300 feet in diameter and sixty-nine feet high. It is composed of 60,000 tons of earth – all moved by hand more than two millennia ago by a people known to the Indians as "the old ones." Today archaeologists call them Adena. Originally a forty-foot moat surrounded the mound. Although eighteenth century natives never mentioned the old ones' size, archeologists postulate that they were smaller than modern man. However, evidence of seven-foot-tall giants was found both among mound skeletons as well as etched in stone.

Excavations conducted at Grave Creek twice during the nineteenth century turned up a crematory, complete with burials ranging from full and partial cremations to the burial of bones or disarticulated flesh burials. Only a few whole skeletons were found, along with the shell jewelry, weapons, tools, robes, tobacco pipes and food containers buried with them. Also uncovered was a mysterious sandstone tablet etched with runic figures, undeciphered to this day.

Between excavations, local residents treated the mound as a geographic feature worthy of no more respect than the mountains some chewed up for coal. In 1858, a county fair and racetrack operated at the base of the mound. The top was leveled off for a saloon. Soon after, like a macabre joke, the brooding hulk of Moundsville Penitentiary was built within spitting distance. For decades, the warden and his inmates maintained the ancient mound.

Today, there is a museum housing artifacts and telling the story of the mound builders as we know it. Visitors can climb on stone steps that spiral up the mound to the stone obelisk and low stone wall at the top. Back down on the flatland, they can visit Marshall's Dairy Bar across the street where an old man — a daily denizen of the place — told me he had been up the mound once as a child.

Cresap Mound, an Adena site with petroglyphs, is about six miles down the Ohio River from Grave Creek.

At thirty-five feet high and 135 feet in diameter, the **South Charles-**

ton Mound is second in size only to Grave Creek, and has a similar recent history including horse races held at its base in the 1840s. Built near the Kanawha River, it was first identified in 1803, and excavated by the Smithsonian eighty years later. A giant skeleton surrounded by a dozen others was found along with the requisite artifacts.

The South Charleston Mound is now a small park marked by *Burial Attendants*, a modern sculpture by Cuthbert Smith. Stone steps spiral up the mound to a circle of stone at the top, where you can look down on a decidedly non-sacred scene of major industrial plants. Other burial mounds are found nearby at Sunset Memorial Cemetery in Spring Hill, Shawnee Golf Course in Institute, and the South Charleston High School campus.

Continuing the tradition of a mound as entertainment, present-day **Camden Park**, the amusement park outside Huntington, is home to the third largest mound in the state. A twenty-foot high conical Indian burial mound lies alongside the vintage roller coaster and bumper cars. It has never been excavated, although at one time the top was flattened and it was used in the early 1900s as a concert bandstand for the park.

The **Romney mound** remains true to its original purpose and is the center of the Indian Mound Cemetery at the western edge of town. It shares top billing with the country's first Confederate monument, which was erected in 1867. The seven-foot mound was never excavated.

Oak Mound in Harrison County is twelve feet high and was never excavated.

There are other archaic sites including **Ben's Run** in Tyler County, one of the most extensive Indian fortifications remaining in the United States. Two parallel circular walls of stone and earth are several miles in length and enclose an area of more than 400 acres. In the mid-1960s, a large village site was excavated near **Buffalo** revealing a plaza, stockade, houses and ceremonial buildings. Today, industrial development is threatening to overrun the site.

The site of the reconstructed mansion on **Blennerhassett Island** formerly was occupied by one of the earliest sedentary villages in the region, dating to about 1000 A.D. Later villages grew to have as many as 1,000 inhabitants who existed on a simple agricultural way of life supplemented with deer and fish.

Petroglyphs are identified at twenty-seven recorded sites in sixteen counties in West Virginia. Some of the most significant in the eastern United States have been found along the Guyandotte River in the small town of Salt Rock, Cabell County. Symbols or figures rubbed or pecked into sandstone with flint, petroglyphs are used like runes by shamans to embody information and magical technique. Images found in West Virginia range from birds and serpents to suns, bear tracks and abstract symbols.

The most controversial of the petroglyphs is the seven-foot **Maiden of the Rock**. Found on the roof of a natural stone shelter overlooking a small valley in Putnam County, the huge slab has been removed to a mini-park in downtown Hurricane. Although authentic points, stones and tools were found at the site, and the figure matches ones found in other locations, some claim that three Putnam County teens etched — or at least embellished — the figure in 1925.

For more on the extensive collection of ancient artifacts housed at the Blennerhassett Museum, *see* "Remarkable Collections."

CORNSTALK'S MONUMENT AND HIS CURSE

When colonial settlers poured along the rivers and over the mountains into the western wilderness of Virginia, grabbing land wherever they moved, the Shawnee resisted. They laid claim to the lands that are now West Virginia as their ancestral home and hunting grounds. **Cornstalk** (Keightughqua) was one of the great Shawnee chiefs.

The geopolitics of the time made the Shawnee and the English allies against the Americans who were moving west. After an early career as a warrior, Cornstalk saw the merit in compromise and worked to avoid fighting until 1774, when marauding settlers near Wheeling murdered Logan, a friendly Mingo chief.

Reluctantly, Cornstalk abandoned his peace attempts and led nearly 1,000 Shawnee and other warriors to engage an equal number of Virginia militia. They met in a fierce day-long battle on a thumb of land between the juncture of the Ohio and Kanawha Rivers. Hundreds of Indians and Virginians were slaughtered in the hand-to-hand combat. It was the biggest Indian battle to take place on West Virginia soil, and one that Cornstalk knew would be the most important the Shawnee would ever fight.

Though Cornstalk led his men away undefeated, he would not live to fight again. Three years later, when Cornstalk went to warn Americans of an Indian attack, he was captured and brutally murdered. The Shawnee retreated west and the Battle of Point Pleasant marked the end of the Indian wars in West Virginia and the Ohio Valley.

Legend has Cornstalk cursing Point Pleasant with his dying words. Twentieth century activities linked to the curse include reported UFO activity and the collapse of the Silver Bridge in 1967, when forty-six people died within sight of the historic battlefield.

Today, the two-acre **Battle Monument State Park** is dominated by an eighty-four foot granite obelisk honoring the fallen Virginians. A smaller monument was erected to Cornstalk and later the State Park placed restrooms nearby — hardly a way to relieve the curse.

Cornstalk's daughter, **Aracoma**, comes alive in an outdoor drama bearing her name which is performed every summer at **Chief Logan State Park**. Aracoma married Bolling Baker, who shed his white identity and became a Shawnee chief. Both are buried in Logan County.

Geography guaranteed that Point Pleasant would always be noticed. Along the river side of the battlefield is a plaque planted in 1749 by French explorer Joseph Celoron de Blainville recording that he had "re-established tranquility in some Indian villages." Twenty years later, Benjamin Franklin proposed the formation of the 14th colony, Vandalia, with its capital at Point Pleasant.

TECUMSEH

Like Cornstalk, **Tecumseh** was a great Shawnee warrior chief with ties to West Virginia. Legend has it that in 1806, in a spot overlooking Tenshwatawa Falls at **Holly River State Park**, Tecumseh provided information about an impending solar eclipse, which he had gained from a white friend so that Tecumseh's medicine man brother could demonstrate his power.

FIRST CITIZEN

George Washington was America's premier land developer, and modern-day West Virginia was his favorite piece of 18th century real estate. His footsteps criss-cross the state from the Potomac to the Ohio rivers.

America's best prepared teenager, George began his career at sixteen, surveying the western lands of his native Virginia. Two years later he used his salary as a surveyor to purchase 550 acres along Bullskin Run in Jefferson County. It was 1750 and the beginning of George's life-long investment in the land that would become West Virginia. He acquired 30,000 acres in "West Augusta" for his service in the French and Indian War. Twenty years later he patented nearly 5,000 acres that embraced the sites of today's towns of St. Albans and Dunbar. In 1775, he patented 125 acres on the Kanawha River upstream from Malden. This land contained a bituminous spring (oil and gas), making George a pioneer in West Virginia's mining industry, which developed a century later.

Many farms still follow the boundaries Washington set while surveying the Lost River and Capon Valley area from 1748-52. In Wayne County, he named a creek Twelve Pole because it was twelve poles of rods wide. He surveyed land above the Ohio River at Parkersburg for the Henderson Hall land grant signed by Patrick Henry, then governor of Virginia. While in this area, which he called "the Ohio River Crowded with Islands," he surveyed and hunted on those notable islands. The telescope he used for surveying the Kanawha Valley is on display in the State Museum, while other artifacts are housed in the **Washington Western Lands Museum** at the great bend of the Ohio near Ravenswood.

From the beginning, Washington focused on filling the western wilderness with prosperous industry and communities. He supported early iron smelting and hired inventor James Rumsey to design locks for navigating the Potomac River. He also foreshadowed the Morgantown Chamber of Commerce when he met with Morgan Morgan's son at the Pierpont home in 1784 to discuss the feasibility of a trade route through the area to the Ohio River. Rating Harpers Ferry as the "most eligible spot on the river" (the Potomac) for one of two federal gun factories, Washington lobbied hard for his district; and the famous armory was built there.

As a young officer in the French and Indian War, Washington marched his militia through Hampshire County and ordered a string of forts to be built along the South Branch in 1755 to protect the frontier. **Fort Ashby**, in Mineral County, still stands. The area returned the favor and provided beef to feed Washington's soldiers during both the French and Indian War and later at Valley Forge.

Washington could even rank as West Virginia's first white water rafter, having run the rapids of the Potomac near Harpers Ferry.

Although most of the land he owned was west of the mountains, it was today's Eastern Panhandle that captured his heart. During an early buying spree, Washington and his brother Lawrence acquired tens of thousands of acres in Jefferson County. The area elected him to his first political office in the Virginia House of Burgesses. Brother Charles inherited much of the acreage and established **Charles Town** in 1786, with streets named for family members. Today, Washington-related sites are everywhere, including a half dozen homes open for occasional tours and a cave marked with his signature. His first purchase — Rock Hall Tract — is now the location of **Hillbrook Inn**. Almost eighty Washington family members are buried in the **Zion Episcopal Church Cemetery** (1852) in the center of Charles Town, including at least three George Washington namesakes.

Washington raised numerous troops from the Eastern Panhandle and a historic rumor claims that he once considered Shepherdstown for the nation's capital.

His bathtub monument in the state park highlights the intimate relationship Washington sustained with **Berkeley Springs**. According to his journals, "ye fam'd warm springs" was the first West Virginia stop on his earliest surveying trip into Lord Fairfax's wilderness in 1748. He returned to the rough spa town with his family several times over the next two decades, and highly prized his large tract of land west of town along the

Gat Caperton reenacts George Washington's first visit to "ye fam'd warm springs" in 1748.

Potomac. He would ride daily to Prospect Peak and used the panoramic view to fuel his dreams of a way west. When Lord Fairfax's domain was "liberated" in 1776, Washington's family and friends established the town of Bath around the springs, and George bought two prime lots. After the Revolutionary War, he resumed his pre-war habit of "taking the waters" at Bath and contracted with James Rumsey to build him a summer house there. Two wooden shacks resulted, hyped during the 20th century into "the first summer white house."

WASHINGTON FAMILY HOMES

Washington's brother Lawrence died young in 1752, and left his considerable acreage to various family members. Five homes built by this famous family still stand today in Jefferson County. Only one however — **Harewood** — is an original Washington family home that still houses Washington family descendants.

Samuel Washington built **Harewood** of native gray limestone in 1770 from his brother George's design. It has a family graveyard on the property. The mansion is well-known as the site of the wedding of James and Dolly Madison. **Cedar Lawn** was built elsewhere on Harewood's property in 1825.

Charles Washington built **Happy Retreat** in 1780 on the southern edge of the town named for him. In 1820, two young Washington brothers married two sisters and built two mansions — **Blakely** and **Claymont** — facing each other across the North Fork of Bullskin Run. Today, Claymont Court Mansion is a bed and breakfast, the largest of the Washington homes and the only one open to the public.

In 1840, Colonel Lewis William Washington expanded the eighteenth century house named **Beallair**. In 1859, John Brown took him from the house as a hostage and robbed him of George Washington's sword.

GEORGE'S CAVE

The signature is faintly carved in a back room — G. Washington, 1748. Although there's doubt about its authenticity, the signature was noted as early as 1833 and two similar signatures appear in Virginia caves.

Tradition has it that the large three-room cave was the first Masonic meeting place west of the Blue Ridge. Samuel and John Augustine Washington were among a group of Masons who bought the cave in

1773. In 1844 a major Masonic celebration was held in the cave. For a few years in the late 1920s, the cave was a commercial venture complete with a free tour for every hot dog purchased. Today, permission is needed to squeeze past the barred door and descend the stone stairs into the spacious main room with its flowstone mounds. Stooping is required to enter the back room where an alcove houses the famous signature.

CLEOPATRA OF THE SOUTH

Told at age ten that she was too young to attend a party her father was throwing, **Belle Boyd** countered by riding her pony into the ballroom of the house in Martinsburg that serves today as her museum. Belle's willful and impulsive nature earned her a prominent place during the Civil War, one of the few women to grace the history of that period.

When Union forces captured Martinsburg in 1861, Belle's mother was manhandled by a blue-clad soldier as she tried to defend her Confederate flags. The eighteen-year old Belle promptly shot the man, thus beginning a career that would find her in and out of jail, condemned and lauded as a Rebel spy.

Repeatedly, Belle used her considerable charms to wheedle information from Union soldiers, which she then turned over to the Confederacy, once saving Stonewall Jackson from a Yankee attack. Sent on a mission to London, Belle was captured at sea. She wooed the U.S. Navy Captain who was her captor, promising to marry him if he defected with a book of information. He agreed and the pair had a big wedding in London. After another round of arrests and releases, former Captain Harding and his wife Belle took to the London stage, a career that Belle continued even after their divorce. She eventually performed in America with her second husband, an actor half her age.

Though the portrait of Belle Boyd that hangs over the museum's mantle shows a fierce looking brunette with a prominent nose, her lifetime of exploits attests to a seductive power the popular press captured when it labeled her "Cleopatra of the South."

Today, Martinsburg attorney Laura Rose portrays Belle Boyd at various regional events. Her attention to detail includes historically accurate undergarments for her ball gown and a red-haired husband who willingly plays Belle's Confederate beau, J.E.B. Stuart.

THAT WHEELIN' FEELIN'

Big Bertha's Gentlemen's Club near the Capitol Theater on Main Street is a pale shadow of the vice and gambling heyday that the city of Wheeling enjoyed for nearly a century. A wide-open river town perched on a major route west, Wheeling's back room poker games were standard fare in city saloons at the turn of the century, as was the well-established red-light district. During World War I, Wheeling became known as the city of nightclubs. It boasted the only totally open book-making parlors between New York and Chicago, and the only burlesque theater in the state. For a lot of young men heading on trains out to war, "that Wheelin' Feelin'" was a favorite memory.

Beginning as a bootlegger during Prohibition, **Big Bill Lias** rose to become the Wheeling crime boss for a scene that included gambling casinos, bordellos and gang wars. When the federal government seized his assets for back taxes in the 1950s, they ended up with his racetrack — and hired Lias back to run it! By the time the scandal hit Congress, Lias was the third highest paid federal employee, close behind the President and Chief Justice of the Supreme Court.

UNUSUAL PLACES WITH NOTABLE HISTORIES

★ In 1855, Thomas Friend carved three huge wine cellars from a stone mountain near Dunbar, reportedly once owned by George Washington. For six years they served as the site of a thriving wine making industry. After that they were never used again, possibly because the true purpose of the cellars was to serve as way stations on the Underground Railroad. Restored in 1981 as the centerpiece of a 316-acre city park, **Dutch Hollow Wine Cellars** are one of only two such cellars east of the Mississippi. The heavy wooden doors on the cellars are locked at night and re-opened early each morning, ostensibly to avoid nighttime boarders.

★ Discovered in 1704, it is rumored that Thomas Jefferson found the bones of a dinosaur on his 1791 visit to the cave. Mined by the Confederates for saltpeter, the third largest cave in the United States was large enough to shelter a thousand soldiers one winter, and is filled with their Civil War graffiti. Thirty-seven of Robert E. Lee's saltpeter hoppers also remain in the cave. **Organ Cave** is named for the forty-foot limestone formation in the cave that emits beautiful music when struck with a hammer.

★ **Fort Mill Ridge Trenches** are among the best preserved Civil War earthworks in existence. Still four feet deep in places, the trenches run for nearly a half-mile along Mill Creek Mountain, just west of Romney.

★ **Bunker Hill Mill** is the only one in the state with dual water wheels. The old stone building was reconstructed in 1875 on a 1738 mill site.

★ **Fortification Hill** in Barboursville has a long history of uses ranging from an Indian campground and courthouse to a Civil War battlefield and the site of Morris Harvey College. Today it is West Virginia's only state veterans' home.

★ Lord Fairfax considered the western limit of his land to be the headspring of the Potomac River. In 1746, one of the oldest markers in the United States was set at that spot. That marker, the **Fairfax Stone**, was used to establish the state boundaries of Maryland, Virginia and Pennsylvania as part of the Mason-Dixon surveying mission. In 1767, the western terminus of that famous line was set on Browns Hill, northwest of Morgantown.

MORE WEIRD HISTORICAL FLASHES

★ Anticipating continued growth, in 1901 town fathers of Union placed the **Monroe County Confederate Monument** in an empty field south of town. In 1998, it is still an almost empty field, and the twenty-foot native blue limestone statue remains in the middle of nowhere, surrounded by grazing cows.

★ Robert E. Lee's horse, **Traveller**, came from a farm in Greenbrier County. Lee first saw the horse near his camp during the Sewell Mountain campaign in 1861, and bought the horse from Major Thomas Brown of Charleston for $ 200.

★ An obscure Wisconsin politician, **Joe McCarthy** got his start when he addressed a Wheeling Republican group and first announced his list of alleged Communists in the U.S. State Department.

★ Two municipalities in what would become the state of West Virginia were incorporated on the same day in 1762. Both **Shepherdstown** and **Romney** lay claim to being the oldest town in West Virginia.

★ The small town of **Alderson**, split by the Greenbrier River and CSX Railroad, has population in three counties: Greenbrier, Monroe and Summers. Memorial Bridge links the two sides of town and was built in 1914. Today the bridge is open only to foot traffic. It is the longest earth-filled reinforced concrete arch bridge in the state.

★ **John W. Davis** of Clarksburg is the only West Virginian to run for U.S. President — so far. A prominent attorney who ranks with Daniel Webster in arguing the most cases before the Supreme Court, Davis ran as a Democrat in 1924 against Calvin Coolidge.

★ **Charleston** was finally selected as West Virginia's capital through both the oratory of 21-year-old Booker T. Washington and the generosity of two clowns, who allowed Charleston leaders to travel with the circus and speak for their position. In 1921, major explosions from truckloads of guns and ammunition seized during mine wars and stored in the State Capitol attic caused the building to burn down.

★ Widely known through folk tunes, the steel-driving **John Henry** was memorialized in 1972 by a larger-than-life statue in a small park above Big Bend Tunnel in Talcott, where he allegedly challenged the track-building machine a century earlier. The 6,500-foot tunnel was carved through the mountain from 1870 to 1873 for the C&O railroad; a twin tunnel was added later.

★ In 1995, famous television and movie actress Mary Tyler Moore purchased a red brick home built by her great-great-great-grandfather, Conrad Schindler, Jr., on German Street in Shepherdstown. She turned it over to Shepherd College for use as a scholarly research center on the Civil War and named it the **George Tyler Moore Center** after her father.

★ Lydia Boggs Kruger reputedly had "a way with a man." According to local legend, she was able to persuade Henry Clay in 1819 to reroute the **National Road** right past her Wheeling home. Today, her stone house is the headquarters of the Osiris Temple.

IN A CLASS BY ITSELF

The only town with its own national historic park, **Harpers Ferry** has a long and notable pedigree, beginning with Mother Nature's attributes. Located at a break in the Blue Ridge, where the Shenandoah and Potomac rivers meet, Harpers Ferry has always been an important stop on the way west, by either boat or train.

George Washington gave Harpers Ferry's destiny a boost when he built a Federal armory there in 1794. Eventually a complex of twenty buildings, the armory was the site of important industrial firsts. The first U.S. military rifle was built there, as well as the first percussion rifle. John Hall was first to perfect the use of machine-produced interchangeable parts on an industrial scale at the armory rifle works on Virginius Island. In 1803, Merriweather Lewis came to the armory to get guns and the unique metal boat frame he took to explore the Louisiana Territory with William Clark.

On the eve of the Civil War, Harpers Ferry was booming. The armory drew the railroad, and both served to make Harpers Ferry the most valuable property along the emerging north/south border. When a radical Ohioan who dreamed of establishing a black republic in the hills of West Virginia seized the arsenal in 1859, he wanted the 100,000 munitions stored there. **John Brown** initiated the spirit of the Civil War with his failed insurrection, and Harpers Ferry was ultimately destroyed in the process. In one of those odd quirks of history, Brown was captured by U.S. Marines led by Robert E. Lee and J.E.B. Stuart.

Two years later, Lee and Stuart were fighting for the Confederacy, and the armory had been burned and dismantled by both sides along with bridges, railroads and much of the town. The largest surrender of U.S. forces until 1942 took place in 1862, when Stonewall Jackson took Harpers Ferry.

The 1870 flood finished the area as an industrial power when it washed away Virginius Island — where a third of the town and much of its industrial infrastructure had been located. Today only the ruins of a pulp mill remain on the island.

The National Park Service restored a dozen buildings, as well as the third of the town along the river front, to their respective condition in 1859 — Harpers Ferry's height of fame and fortune. Today, many of the municipality's 300 residents live in more than 125 historic houses. The town also boasts a charming row of shops, tightly climbing the cobblestoned hill up from the river front; the latter being the lowest point in West Virginia. Summertime tours and living reenactments are replaced in winter by stark views and the solitude to explore museums, exhibits and trails on your own.

Storer College was established in Harpers Ferry in 1867 as one of the earliest institutions for educating former slaves. W.E.B. DuBois held the first meeting of the **Niagara Movement** on U.S. soil in 1906 in the town, drawn by Storer and the legacy of John Brown's raid. The meeting prompted establishment of the NAACP to take aggressive civil rights action.

Closed in 1955, historic Storer College now houses the National Park Service. For more on Harpers Ferry — *see* "Things Used to Be There" and "Amazing Architecture."

TIME WARP

The men-only **University Club** is an antique wood-paneled anachronism in downtown Bluefield's newly restored Science Center.

TREASON

Jefferson County Courthouse was constructed in 1836 on land donated by Charles Washington. Its fame derives not from its Greek Revival architecture or its Washington heritage, but from a historic roll of the dice that made the courthouse the setting for two of America's three pre-World War II treason trials.

Within two months of his capture in 1859, **John Brown** was tried there for his Harpers Ferry insurrection. He was jailed in the building now used for the Charles Town Post Office. Crowds of onlookers watched from a farmhouse as he was hung in a nearby field. Today, the farmhouse is the Iron Rail Inn. The site of the hanging is now a house at 515 Samuel Street. Future presidential assassin, **John Wilkes Booth**, came to town for the trial and gave dramatic readings from Shakespeare in the Episcopal Reading Room.

In 1922, four union leaders and more than 700 miners were indicted for various crimes — including treason against the state — as part of the **Blair Mountain confrontation** between miners and coal company defenders in Logan County. The only trials that ever occurred were the few staged in Jefferson County, including that of **William Blizzard**. Leader of the uprising, Blizzard was later acquitted of treason.

FORGOTTEN INVENTOR

History books credit Robert Fulton with the first successful steamboat, but Eastern Panhandle devotees of **James Rumsey** claim the honor for their guy. Working in Berkeley Springs and Shepherdstown more than twenty years before Fulton, Rumsey was an inventive character who left behind a trail of mill buildings and steam engine trials. He won the support of George Washington for his new method of boat propulsion, and his efforts to protect his inventions led directly to the patent system in the U.S. Constitution.

In December 1787, Rumsey and eight Shepherdstown ladies successfully tested his steamboat on the Potomac River, a short distance from the ford of the river, where townspeople watched. From Shepherdstown, Rumsey went to England with the support of Benjamin Franklin. Rumsey died in London in 1792, literally on the eve of success.

A sleek Ionic column of granite topped with a globe was erected to honor Rumsey in 1915. **The Rumsey Monument** sits atop the cliffs along the Potomac in a small park at the end of North Mill Street in Shepherdstown. A half-scale working version of Rumsey's steamboat, displacing 5,000 pounds, was built in the 1980s by Shepherdstown aficionados who float it about once a year. On weekends during the summer season, the boat can be seen at the Rumsey boathouse behind the Entler Hotel. Another Rumsey exhibit, featuring more than twenty of his patents, is housed in the **Museum of the Berkeley Springs**.

AMERICA'S MOST FAMOUS FEUD

Long, complicated and still debated, the feud between the **Hatfield and McCoy families** was the original example of what tabloid media exploitation can do to fact. The feud spanned nearly sixty years and was entangled in war, politics and labor battles, in Matewan and across the river in Kentucky. It began when the two families found themselves on opposite sides in the Civil War, then continued with lawsuits over ownership of a pig. These disputes resulted in thirteen killings among the two families during the 1880s. Tabloid news coverage of the feud by a *New York World* reporter was turned into a book. Published in 1889, it introduced the hillbilly image to the world.

In 1920, Sid Hatfield was Chief of Police in Matewan. He sided with the miners and locals in a battle against the coal company and their Baldwin-Felts detectives. The old **Matewan National Bank** building in the center of town still has bullet holes in its second floor windows from the bloody shoot-out. This conflict contributed to the miners' uprising the following year at Blair Mountain, and in 1922, Hatfield was gunned down by retaliating detectives on the McDowell County Courthouse steps in Welch. John Sayles captured this bloody chapter in his film *Matewan*.

The original patriarch of the Hatfield clan, **Devil Anse Hatfield**, is captured in an impressive, life-sized marble statue in the family cemetery near Sarah Ann.

Labor History

Federal troops were used for the first time during a labor strike in 1877 at the **B&O Roundhouse** in Martinsburg.

More than forty years later, labor unrest unleashed another military first when General Billy Mitchell directed U.S. aircraft to fire on its own people at Blair Mountain. The five-day battle along a 17-mile front in August 1921 pitted 3,000 deputies and mine guards against 7,000 coal miners led by William Blizzard. The battle and subsequent treason trials prevented the United Mine Workers from organizing in the state for more than a decade. Many artifacts of the battle remain, and many supporters are fighting to keep Blair Mountain from being mined.

In 1907, 361 miners died at **Monongah** in Marion County in the worst coal mine disaster in the United States.

Completed in 1932, the construction of the **Hawks Nest Diversion Tunnel** was the worst industrial disaster in the United States. The deaths of 1,500 miners, lungs shredded by glass-like dust, triggered a Congressional investigation and led to the recognition of acute silicosis as an occupational disease. The miners died cutting a forty foot square, 3.8 mile long tunnel through the almost pure silica rock of Gauley Mountain in order to redirect the New River through the mountain to Union Carbide's power plant on the other side. Today, the tunnel mouth lies hidden behind huge green doors visible from Hawks Nest State Park.

CHAPTER EIGHT

LOCAL FOOD SPECIALTIES & MEMORABLE EATERIES

Locals in certain parts of West Virginia will often tell visitors: "There's a place in (fill in the blank) but it's always closed *'cause nobody eats there.*" Regardless of those reputed wastelands, the stereotypes that people are starving, and state legislation removing the criminal status of picking up roadkill for the pantry, there are unique food treats and world class dining to be found in the Mountain State.

THE STATE FOOD OF WEST VIRGINIA

It's the food that Mountaineers have shipped around the globe, that brings them back again and again no matter where they roam. "It's a valued commodity in my world, traded regularly for housing," said one devotee. Generally available for a dollar, it's a primary food group for struggling artists and students, and the only food I found worthy of a quest. Everyone I interviewed agreed with my choice — **pepperoni rolls** are the ultimate state food of West Virginia.

Giuseppe Agiro invented the taste treat in 1927 as a one-hand, one-bite lunch treat for Fairmont coal miners. His son "Cheech" continues the tradition at the family's **Country Club Bakery**, making about 4,000 of the famous rolls a day for area stores.

From its Fairmont birthplace, pepperoni rolls have spread to dominate a quadrant of the state from Morgantown to Weston. When I asked a sixteen-year-old in Elkins where I could search out a pepperoni roll, she looked at me as if wondering where my home planet was. "In any gas station," she said.

The concentrated geography made my quest for the perfect pepperoni roll logistically easy, balancing the impossibility of identifying culinary champs. Even the knock-off versions found near the cappucino station at every convenience store in the pepperoni district are edible.

Here are my observations after several extensive tasting sprees.

The traditional pepperoni roll is the six-inch torpedo still made today by Country Club — cholesterol-free plain yeast dough rolled around two thick sticks of spicy pepperoni. The bread bakes into twin tunnels around the pepperoni sticks which, in turn, soak the fluffy white bread with their oil, making the inner core the ultimate taste sensation. A packaged dozen of the pepperoni rolls bought at the bakery are an incredible bargain at $5.50.

Most supermarkets in the pepperoni district make their own rolls, as well as stocking one or two boutique brands like Mama Leona's of Dailey. Several convenience store clerks assured me that people do have their favorites. Supermarket and convenience store knock-offs generally use sliced pepperoni, a step down in taste intensity. Sliced pepperoni also lacks the bite quality a stick provides. Cheese can often be found as a component of the core. Not always a tasty addition, the cheese can be a problem when eating the pepperoni roll cold. Agiro, the inventor's son, avoids using cheese because "good cheese melts out."

The bread is generally improved with heating, although I've found using a microwave degrades the pepperoni sticks. However, to serve as quality road or trail food, pepperoni rolls have to be acceptable at body temperature.

The price is right — a bag of a dozen or more fingers for under $2; individual big ones under $1.50. All the bread is basic white and usually undistinguished. Exceptions that I've discovered include the originals from Country Club and the braided dough modification made by **Tari's Café** in Berkeley Springs.

My favorite pepperoni roll breakfast — a bag of three-inch-long fingers with stick pepperoni — came from **Tomoro's**, a family bakery in Clarksburg. It should be noted that this northern tier city with a strong Italian population base also claims to be the pepperoni roll homeplace.

I had the ultimate pepperoni roll experience with a modified version that would disqualify it from consideration by purists. I turned off US 33 onto SR 20 heading into Buckhannon. On the left a sign caught my eye. "DONUTS" read the top line; "Pepperoni Rolls" read the next. Obviously, this was not a chain. I ordered a 99¢ pepperoni roll, not quite certain what I was getting. I jumped in the car and drove off, taking a bite, then another. Incredible! Ground pepperoni, sauteed and put in a large square white bun and layered with spicy cheese. "It's not a pepperoni roll unless the meat is baked in the bread," said one expert with disdain. Whatever it was, I turned the car around and went back for a second one. Later, a certified insider nodded his agreement. "That's the **Donut Shop**, where everyone goes for breakfast," he said about my Buckhannon find.

The pepperoni is chunked in **Colacessino's** overstuffed version, served in a large, crispy roll with homemade tomato sauce, melted cheese and Oliverio's peppers. Only $2.50, it is a meal-sized version of the state food. A family business in the Belleview section of Fairmont for eighty years, Colacessino's evolved from a crammed neighborhood beer joint and political center to a still tiny carry-out and bakery, providing frozen pizzas to stores around town. The traditional footrest and bar countertop remain, handy for waiting while the roll is prepared. It's a busy place and their pepperoni rolls are bought in multiples.

It's not all smooth sailing and thick sticks in the world of pepperoni rolls. The federal government tried to impose meat shop rules on West Virginia bakeries making pepperoni rolls — but after a major battle, the state legislature prevailed and ruled that pepperoni rolls do not require a meat handler's license.

To take your own pepperoni roll tour, stop at every convenience store and grocery chain along I-79 with gourmet stops in Clarksburg, Fairmont, and Buckhannon.

COLEMAN'S FISH SANDWICH

I heard it from everyone in Wheeling: "Wait until you have a **Coleman's fish sandwich**." I scoffed. I had childhood memories of Friday night fish fries that would be hard to beat, but I went to Centre Market, stood in a lunchtime line and ordered a fish sandwich at a bustling stall offering fresh fish as well. Lots of sweet fish, perfectly crisp, fried in canola oil — even wrapped in white bread, Coleman's fish sandwich matched my memories of the best. Another under $3 gourmet treat.

SWISS SPECIALTIES

Kathy Mailloux kneaded bread that would be part of lunch for diners at her mother Eleanor's **Hutte Restaurant** in Helvetia. I had just enjoyed the delectable bread in my homemade sausage sandwich served with tangy hot applesauce and sauerkraut. I also polished off an order of *rostli* — a fried pancake of shredded potatoes.

Helvetian cheese was on its way down to the restaurant, made the traditional way by the three Bolle sisters — Gertrude, Anna, and Freda — all in their eighties. "The cheese usually comes off the hill at noon," explained Kathy between knuckle-wrenching the bread dough. "They core it and bring it in."

Kathy has been cooking at the restaurant for more than thirty years. The center of activity for the tiny town, it's the only restaurant for endless miles around. The wooden tables and other furnishings in the low ceilinged, rambling building belong to local residents. There's a wood burning stove, and church bells ring regularly. For the full Swiss culinary experience, the enormous fifteen item Sunday buffet called **Bernerplatte** should not be missed. Served at 5 pm, Bernerplatte is loaded with items ranging from bratwurst and Hutte chicken to onion pie and curried pineapple.

"You think you're never going to get here, but you will," Eleanor Mailloux tells people as she gives them directions and warns against taking shortcuts. Helvetia is tucked away in the central mountains, surrounded by hemlock and spruce. Settled in 1869 as a Swiss colony, Helvetia once had a population of more than 300, which now has dwindled to about a third of that number.

RAMPS

A native plant in the lily family, **ramps** are the first green shoots of spring, easy to find in forested ravines. They have broad, flat, spear-shaped leaves and a potent onion taste. A type of wild leek, they are an excellent source of vitamin C. Indians dried and ground ramps, using them as a substitute for garlic. Early settlers viewed it as a wonder, fresh and green after a winter of meat and dried foods. For ramp festivals and dinners, *see* "Far-Out Festivals." Ramp lovers, and the merely adventurous, should try the ramp wine made by **Kirkwood Wineries**. It has to be tasted to be believed.

More Menu Items

Snyder's Gourmet Hams in Martinsburg welcomes tasters for samples of their preservative-free, air-cured ham. It's saltier and spicier than most. As a bonus, they add fresh fruit to ham orders.

Frank Androczi makes honey-mead at his **Little Hungary Farm Winery** near Buckhannon, and sells it with a fervor as *Melomel.* Subtitled "Fountain of Youth, Health, Strength and Beauty," Frank claims nearly miraculous health-sustaining results from his elixir.

Oliverio's Italian Style Pepper is another food group introduced by the state's Italian community. Antoinette Oliverio began canning peppers in the back of the family's grocery store in Clarksburg in the early 1930s. Her son Frank turned her specialty into a major business in 1972. Today, the family enterprise hand stems and packs about two million pounds of peppers a year. Oliverio peppers are sold in seventeen states and featured in regional Wal-marts and countless salad bars.

For the best selection and price go to the source. The original store is now **Oliverio's Cash & Carry**, where the full product line is available. Delicacies include spicy cauliflower salsa, peppers in all degrees of hotness; and peppers with a variety of sauces such as portabello mushroom sauce.

Richter's Maplehouse offers the bonus of an authentic maple syrup camp with both modern and antique mapling equipment along with their tasty products, including rare maple cream. Open all year, the camp has special tours during the Maple Syrup Festival, held annually in nearby Pickens, on the third weekend in March.

Parkersburg weighs in with two local gourmet treats: **Mister Bee's potato chips** and **Holl's Chocolates**.

The 20,000 Swiss chocolates Holl's produces in a year are made fresh daily and use only the freshest ingredients. Holl came from Zurich in 1958 and brought recipes still used today for his family's traditional twice-dipped truffles and almond *gianduya*. The rich, deep and indulgently chocolate taste of Holl's candies attests to their pure Swiss heritage. Visit the shop, watch the process, and mix and match a selection to take home.

Mister Bee's chips are light and crisp with subtle flavors. They're widely distributed throughout the northwest sector of the state.

West Virginia trout are found everywhere, from nearly 2,000 miles of pristine trout streams to countless restaurant tables in every corner of the state. Brown, brook and rainbow trout — some domestic and stocked, others wild — show up fresh out of the stream in wilderness frying pans or as trout cakes, smoked trout logs or specialty dishes. Check out the **Elk River Trout Ranch** near Snowshoe, a combination hatchery, fishing stream and Rainbow Grille specializing in home-grown trout dinner entrees. Another tasty choice is the pecan-coated trout at the **Cheat River Inn**.

Bonnie Belle's Bakery in Nutter Fort can produce a cake or cupcake with a computer-generated design in edible food colors. Orders come from all over the East and families are known to have every child's face on a cake in the freezer. Started in 1947, the family bakery makes everything from scratch using original family formulas. Only the digital robotics decorating is new.

EAT HERE!

Trinidad native Errol Bishops relocated his island food haven to one more corner of the Charleston area in early 1999, continuing his claim to fame as the state's main purveyor of Caribbean food. **Island Sunset**, in Kanawha City, is the latest stop for Bishop, who has had successful restaurants in both Washington, D.C. and Baltimore. He came to West Virginia via his bride, Diana, a native of Fayetteville. The authentic and exotic menu includes ginger beer, sweet potato pie, curried chick peas and a sweet puff bread. Parslied potatoes are covered in a tangy island sauce, the orange pineapple chicken is tasty and full-bodied, not sweet, and the jerked chicken is hot and spicy. There's always a buffet for sampling a range of island treats. Errol's original sauces and special spice mixtures are on sale in the restaurant.

Southern Kitchen has been offering Charlestonians homemade pies and comfort food 24-hours a day, year 'round since 1947. The decor features hundreds of chickens of all sizes in everything from metal to ceramic, plus hanging baskets filled with eggs. The waitresses are professionals of the old school, and every customer gets a chicken thank you note when they pay the bill.

Tari's Cafe. Let me admit it up front. Tari's is my hometown restaurant and the more years I log in at her tables the more I am spoiled for virtually everything else. And it's not just me. Ask anybody where to eat in Berkeley Springs and they'll point to the white and green storefronts in a restored turn-of-the-century building, with Tari's name on the door. Folks regularly drive a hundred miles to eat there. People beg to have Tari cater their wedding.

Yes, there is a Tari and she's an inventive genius in the kitchen, obsessed with pleasing her customers. "I love to feed people," says Tari who attributes her encyclopedic knowledge of cooking to her father, Squirrel. His down-home image graces the labels of her bottled sauces, and his homegrown vegetables fill salad bowls in season.

Tari's culinary inventions are seemingly infinite. She developed a dry rub and spicy marinade for Southwest Steak and now bottles the concoction for sale. Other notable dishes include stuffed Italian meatloaf, Ouzo Orzo chicken, Thai noodle salad, scallops Marguerita, the best crab cakes west of the Chesapeake Bay, and a full range of homemade salad dressings, many fat-free. Her soups are paragons of taste. There's delicate Italian wedding soup with homemade meatballs, creamy crab served with a shot of sherry on the side and flavorful baked potato soup. Bean soup is on the menu daily, satisfying vegetarians from near and far. Old fashioned ice cream sodas are available, along with her braided pepperoni rolls.

As if savory food weren't enough, the servers at Tari's are polite, fast and just a little sassy.

The ultimate tribute to Tari's universal appeal comes each year in June when a busload of nearly a hundred international patent attorneys — mostly Japanese — end their annual pilgrimage to Washington with a trip to Tari's. The first year they just dropped in unannounced; now they make reservations and take over the restaurant. Tari serves them mostly southern favorites including greens, jambalaya, stuffed cabbage leaves and barbecue. She always adds four dozen nightcrawlers to the menu so they can fish at Cacapon State Park.

The bottomless bowls of **Undo's** pasta are a food-lover's magnet in the old Italian neighborhood of Benwood just south of Wheeling. Red checked oilcloth covers the tables and the building is flanked by a Garabaldi's Lodge and a dead end industrial wall. This is the original Undo's, complete with Undo himself, shuffling around offering patrons a taste of the house wine in plastic glasses. Incredible bread — little pizzas with garlic and oil as well as breadsticks — is served with an individual butter pot over a flame for dipping.

Car hops have been the mainstay of **Stewart's Original Hot Dogs** in Huntington since 1932. Once a job only for boys, today's curb service is provided by girls as well. Not much else has changed — it's the same location, same family and same secret sauce on the hot dogs. Stewart's supports other Huntington businesses using Logan hot dogs and Heiner's buns (*see* "Tours Not to Miss" for Heiner's.)

Another longtime hot dog stand serviced by carhops is on SR 10 in Stollings, in Logan County. **Morrison's Drive-In** also features a secret hot dog sauce, along with crispy onion rings and the redheaded Sally Wall, who's been carhopping there since 1955. (Get there quick, Sally's considering retiring now that she's seventy.)

At **Bugsy's**, distinctive sauces, fresh green salads, cutting edge decor and professional waiters with a touch of punk draw discerning diners to the heart of downtown Wheeling. Symphony maestra Rachel Worby prefers the table sheltered by the looming Statue of Liberty that greets all comers.

The tram ride down from the rim to **Mountain Creek Restaurant** in Bluestone Canyon at Pipestem Resort is a beginning as unusual as the food. No one starves in a state park but they're usually not known for gourmet treats — except at Pipestem's exclusive dining room in the gorge. The unique menu includes quail; grilled pork filets with a tangy spinach and tomato-based sauce served with grilled sweet potato; West Virginia trout with grapes, almonds and brown butter; and man-sized slabs of prime rib and filets, all served before a wall of windows overlooking the Bluestone River. We loved the misnamed enchilada appetizer which was, in fact, wild mushrooms wrapped in phyllo dough, baked crisp and served with roasted pepper cream. It was so good, we paid the ultimate compliment and ordered a second one after our meal. Individual round loaves of sourdough bread were first rate and a tiny scoop of peach sorbet was presented to clear the palette between courses.

A reminder of Clarksburg's railroad heyday, **Julio's** is tucked away on the corner across from the train station. There are no menus or prices, only waitresses who recite the mostly Italian offerings.

Installing the famous Greenbrier staff as the management of Tamarack's food court — **"The Taste of West Virginia"** — was an inventive and tasty deci sion. Lunch and dinner are served daily, cafeteria style. From the dozens of lunch choices, Jack chose real sliced pork barbecue with no fake smoke, sweet and sour cole slaw, and new red potatoes in country style chunks. I indulged in chicken pot pie with big chunks of chicken, a thick sauce and pre-made herbed crust that perched atop the bowl. As a bonus to our $10. lunch, we coincidentally sat at a table whose top was made and designed by Berkeley Springs' jewelers and longtime friends Carol and Jean Pierre Hsu. For more on both Tamarack and the Greenbrier, *see* "Truly Incredible."

On the way to Peter's Mountain hawk observatory in Monroe County, we stocked up for lunch at two Mennonite-run food shops, **Cheese n' More Store** and **Kitchen Creek Bakery**. The first store was remarkably neat with bags of nuts, candies, spices, hard-to-get ingredients, and an array of cheeses. Across the road is the bakery with a full supply of breads, cookies, rolls and pies, all made by smiling, red-faced women with little white hats.

Authentic down-home food hides behind the facade of **Clingman's Meat Market**, a run-down grocery that's been a main street landmark in Lewisburg since 1945. **Gwen's Kitchen**, or Gwen's, is famous for biscuits and gravy at breakfast and two offerings at lunch — with meat for $2.50, without for $2. The food is simple, served across a Dutch door from a stove full of pots of mashed potatoes, vegetables, apple sauce, and Gwen's famous home made rolls. Local businessmen, farmers and students crowd into the few tables by the window and a few more in back for lunch. The lunch line forms at 11 am, and most of the food is gone by 1 pm. Gwen greets everyone at the door, inquiring of strangers their name and place of origin. It's a one-of-a-kind experience with the atmosphere of West Virginia in the 1920s and 30s.

It takes more than sixty trained chefs to turn out 4,000 meals a day in season at **The Greenbrier**. Most of the chefs have been trained at the resort's own Culinary Training Program, the first of its kind in America. The freshly printed dinner menu on the day of our visit included a list of traditional favorites, and our choices proved to be exceptional, with both the duck l'orange and filet mignon rated as the best ever.

As superlative as the food was, it paled in memory next to the bread lady, an ancient crone who surely had served Robert E. Lee during his regular visits, and was extending her life by drinking the famous spring water. Whatever her story, we watched entranced as she hobbled continuously around the huge room with its scores of tables, poised to drop a roll on the plate of any individual sending her the appropriate brainwaves. She never spoke, not even a whisper. In fact, we were not certain she even breathed.

The Main Dining Room with its dress code for dinner is not the only place to find world-class food at The Greenbrier. **The Golf Clubhouse**, nicknamed the Casino, is famous for its luncheon buffet, and the **Greenbrier Cooking School** elevates tasting to a high art.

Historically, food has been a holy grail at the Greenbrier. In 1858, the 1,200 seat dining room in Old White was the largest in the United States. A splendid dinner in 1908 persuaded the C&O Railway chief to buy the Greenbrier. Over the years, twenty-six U.S. Presidents have dined there, along with countless celebrities, royalty and other politicians.

The Greenbrier continues to make all its own breads, pastries and 26,000 pounds of chocolates each year. The resort's largest soup kettle makes 125 gallons fresh each day. Dinner and breakfast come with a stay at the Greenbrier; it's a dining opportunity not to be missed.

Food was the beginning for **The Bavarian Inn**, and continues as the centerpiece today. Although owner Erwin Asam no longer cooks daily as he did when the restaurant began, he does keep his spoon in the soup, tasting and suggesting adjustments to his team of chefs. The kitchen complex is designed for handcrafting superb meals for hundreds of guests a day. A bakery produces first-rate apple strudel and signature Black Forest cake; a special meat room is used for "fabricating" custom cuts of meat.

The standard menu includes popular German staples like red cabbage, herring and the full-bodied **jaegerschnitzel** — hunter's veal loaded with mushrooms in a bacon-flavored sauce. Tiny red potatoes are often cut to look like mushrooms, then roasted; and mushroom melanges appear in appetizers like **Shwammerl-wildpilze** — portabellos, shiitakes and white caps in a brandy sauce over a flaky puff pastry. Table-quality white wine contributes to the rich taste of most meat dishes as the liquid of choice when chef Jeff McGee deglazes the saute pans, loosening taste morsels. Asam's attention to detail even has the kitchen using only homemade veal stock in its veal dishes.

In addition to the year 'round German and Continental specialties, the Bavarian Inn's menu features a fall and winter "Game Festival." Although venison and other game must be certified and can be found from only a handful of suppliers, Asam offers a wide range of exotic choices, from wild boar and marinated rabbit to roast pheasant with champagne kraut. Our late March dinner menu listed as spring specialties three different asparagus dishes and shad roe. In summer, chef McGee adds vichyssoise and cold fruit soups to his repertoire. Excellent service is provided by a bevy of fresh-faced dirndl-clad waitresses and red-vested waiters who watch each table to deliver various courses at exactly the right moment.

The **Red Fox Inn** at Snowshoe has been listed by *Fodor's Travel Guide* as one of the top twenty-five restaurants in the United States, in part because of their unique menu filled with wild game native to West Virginia. With two versions — one for winter and one for summer — featured items on the menu includes wild boar, elk, venison, pheasant, duck, quail and trout.

It was a new culinary experience for Martinsburg in 1997 when **Asian Gardens** opened with an extensive traditional Japanese menu. There's sushi, a range of noodles and three types of seating: traditional low tables on a two-step platform with pillows, Western tables, and a dozen high stools at the sushi bar.

CHAPTER NINE

MILLION DOLLAR VIEWS

I f views were bankable, West Virginia would top the charts of wealthy states in this country. It is impossible to list all the vistas that make a casual traveler on a winding road gasp in wonder. Million dollar views of rolling hills, rivers, distinctive mountains or extravagant rock formations can be found in every corner of the state. Each season dresses the view differently. Frozen forests are winter fairylands, red bud and a million shades of green color the spring, while summer begins with mountain sides of rhododendron in bloom. Fall is always a five-star occasion with endless hardwood forests ablaze in golds, reds, oranges and yellows.

Water vapor is the accessory of choice in many panoramas. Columns of fog rise along ridges and rivers; miles of clouds roll along the base of mountains; and mists fill river canyons and veil mountain tops.

But the views must be viewed to be appreciated. No words can describe the ridges and peaks fading into the hazy blue horizon or the gilded light that seeps through thick forests.

There's no need to hype Mother Nature in West Virginia. There is, however, a need to protect her from those business interests that are trying to flatten the state — eating mountain tops and then spitting out the refuse to fill in the valleys. So, when it says Scenic Overlook — do. It's always worth it and you never know how long it will last.

THOMAS JEFFERSON'S FAVORITE

Many of the million dollar views are ancient and were certainly appreciated by tribal residents for thousands of years. Among the earliest historical praise by a colonial is a rapture written by **Thomas Jefferson** in 1783. He wrote the passage about the view from a very high piece of land above the Shenandoah River at Harpers Ferry, now known as **Jefferson Rock**.

It reads: "The passage of the Potomac through the Blue Ridge is perhaps one of the most stupendous scenes in nature. On your right comes up the Shenandoah having ranged along the foot of the mountain a hundred miles to seek a vent; on your left approaches the Potomac in quest of a passage also. In the moment of their junction, they rush together against the mountain, rend it asunder and pass it off to the sea."

Jefferson continued to exclaim about the rock-strewn Shenandoah and the cliffs upstream along the Potomac, proclaiming it all to be "worth a voyage across the Atlantic . . . to survey these monuments of a war between rivers and mountains which must have shaken the earth itself to its center."

Robert Harper, who, in 1748, first staked out the place that now bears his name, called the meeting of the rivers "The Hole." Carl Sandburg seemed to agree, although more poetically, nearly two centuries later when he wrote, "Harpers Ferry is a meeting place of winds and water, rocks and ranges."

Today the view of the Potomac Watergap from Jefferson Rock includes a railroad tunnel carved through a mountain, and the steeple, buildings and streets of Harpers Ferry National Historic Park. Painters and photographers flock to the scene.

The hike to Jefferson Rock from Harpers Ferry is an easy one, but if indoor comfort and good food are what you like with a view, visit **Historic Hilltop House**. The century-old stone inn provides a view of three states and two rivers, from the Potomac side. Six foot windows open in the gracious old dining room for a clear view. The abundant food drew the first visit by a president and vice president when Clinton and Gore dropped in for an unscheduled lunch on Earth Day 1998. They join a list of famous visitors to Hilltop including Woodrow Wilson and Mark Twain.

More Historic Endorsements

Blackwater Falls is another scenic marvel that has a long history of effusive travel prose. The most popular travel writer and illustrator of the 1850s was Porte Crayon, a pen name for David Hunter Strother. Strother was a native of Martinsburg and owner of a hotel in Berkeley Springs. He was particularly taken with the area in the central mountains, which he called "the Land of Canaan."

Saturated images of the river and falls and detailed pencil sketches are found throughout Strother's travelogue of a visit to Blackwater. He described "a headlong current unceasingly fettered with masses of drift and monstrous boulders" and "massive jets and sheets from a common center falling in graceful curves into the black pool below."

"The stream makes a wild leap into the abyss of life," wrote Strother about the river's transformation into what the nineteenth century visitor knew as the Great Falls of the Blackwater.

The falls remain as magnificent today but are much easier to reach than in Strother's day. A sturdy boardwalk from the **Blackwater Falls State Park lodge** offers several vantage points of the sixty-three foot plunge of the river through a deep and rugged canyon. The water glistens in the sun with a nearly black sheen, the result of natural tannins and iron compounds. In spring, the densely forested canyon is covered with blooming rhododendron; in summer, it's lush and green. The roaring of the falls and the spray of their water give the views added dimension. For more on Porte Crayon, *see* "Remarkable Collections."

Romance trumped scenery in an eighteenth century tale involving George Washington's nephew and an overlook near Berkeley Springs that is still rated one of the best views in the east. Originally called Cacapon Rock, and then Prospect Rock, today it is known as **Panorama Overlook**. This scenic spot was a favorite destination for George Washington when he visited Berkeley Springs to "take the waters." According to his own account, George's nephew Laurence Augustine rode to Cacapon Rock from the springs in 1796. From the summit he expected to see "one of the wildest, sublimest [sic] and most interesting views of mountain country, interspersed with cultivated valleys and rivers, which our country afforded." Young Laurence's rapture at the "solitary hamlets with their circling columns of dense smoke and two beautiful rivers" was instantly swept away by the lovely fifteen-year-old Polly Wood, who was with another party of riders enjoying the view. After a feverish courtship, the two were married the following year and remained happily in love until Laurence died in 1824.

The panoramic scene of mountains, valleys and the joining of the wild Cacapon River with the more stately Potomac continues virtually unchanged from Washington's time, except for the paved mountain road curving down to the still solitary hamlet of **Great Cacapon**. A cliff of fluted Tuscarora sandstone hovers above the contemporary restaurant that faces the overlook.

Birds on the Wing

Hanging Rock Raptor Observatory perches at more than 3,800 feet somewhere near the middle of a fifty-mile ridge of the Eastern Continental Divide called Peter's Mountain in Monroe County. In addition to the hawks and occasional bald eagles who cruise the area, the view from the top is a panorama of timeless animal trails, now roads, winding sinuously through neat Monroe County farms. Virginia is to the east; a retreating horizon of West Virginia mountains extends to the west; and the rock spine of the divide extends north and south to either side.

Open daily except Sundays, the area affords hikers a chance to enjoy an exclusive picnic site in a small frame building with benches and a table. We feasted on Mennonite taste treats from the two shops in Gap Mills — pepperoni rolls and caraway cheese — the day we made the forty-five minute hike into the observatory. Volunteers record more than 200 hawks a day during migrations in September.

We climbed 1,230 feet on North Mountain to giant Oriskany sandstone outcroppings on a boulder-strewn peak populated by giant black turkey buzzards. Spread at our feet was the rolling countryside of Hampshire County. Winds swept the cliffs and the birds rode the waves. The rocky perch known as **Raven Rocks** is part of the Ice Mountain Nature Conservancy. *See* "Mother Nature's Wonders" for more on Ice Mountain.

NEW RIVER VISTAS

The ancient **New River** cuts its way through tree-covered mountains that rise over a thousand feet on either side, creating a spectacular gorge with miles of stunning views. The views are enjoyed by the folks hiking, driving or rafting the gorge and the river's once inaccessible length. The fifty-three miles designated as a National River include deserted mining towns, bridges, rock-strewn rapids, and sheer sandstone cliffs dotted with beehive ovens — along with basic raw beauty. **Canyon Rim Visitors Center** offers different perspectives, including a boardwalk down to an overlook of the New River Bridge. Further upstream, **Grandview Visitor Center** is famous for a riotous spring rhododendron display. For more on the New River Gorge, *see* "Mother Nature's Wonders.'

The southern view from today's **Hawks Nest Overlook** along the New River Gorge includes cliffs covered with hemlock and rhododendron forests, and a railroad bridge carrying eighteen to twenty trains a day. The view to the north is of the boulder-strewn riverbed of the New, its water now dammed into Hawks Nest Lake. Most of the flow has been redirected through a tunnel to a power plant on the other side of the mountain. The rock outcropping, prominent long before the dam, was once named Marshall's Pillar for the noted Chief Justice who visited in 1812. Nearly 1,300 feet high, the overlook can be reached by Cliffside Trail from the lodge or by a short loop trail off US 60.

The same vista is particularly stunning in the morning with clouds hanging low over the river and mountain peaks protruding above them. Stairs from the lodge to the observation deck seem to plunge into the gorge.

Sandstone Falls, the largest falls on the New River, spans the river eight miles north of Hinton, dropping ten to twenty-five feet. The best view is from above; a boardwalk leads to river-level views.

THE BEAUTIFUL RIVER

Known to Indians and early settlers as "the Beautiful River," the **Ohio River** provides countless endearing river views. There are twenty lock and dam structures along West Virginia's stretch of the Ohio, as well as abundant river traffic, mostly tugboats shepherding long barges of coal, oil and chemicals. Only the Mississippi River is busier.

The **Robert C. Byrd Locks and Dam** on the Ohio River in Mason County is a multi-million dollar view — $224 million to be exact. In 1938 the Gallipolis Locks and Dam, the largest roller dam in the world with eight rollers, was built in the same location. The Army Corps of Engineers renovated the dam and locks in 1992, rededicating them to West Virginia's Senator. The "workings" of the complex are located on a river island with its own bridge and a flock of geese hanging out on the lawn. The observation deck at the visitors center is open daily.

Priceless Panorama

East River Mountain Overlook at 3,500 feet barely surpasses the collection of mountains that surround Bluefield in all directions. Most impressive, however, is what's underground — the incomparable twenty-four foot high seam of the Pocahontas Coal Field.

Bluestone Canyon and a jumble of densely forested mountains populate the spectacular vistas at Pipestem State Park. Prime vantage points include the **Pipestem Observation Tower** at 3,000 feet, as well as decks around the lodge and the tram down into the Canyon.

The best panoramic cityscape in West Virginia can be seen from the **Point Overlook Museum**. It includes three counties, two states, twelve miles of Ohio River and bridges, and downtown Wheeling.

Looking due east at the first line of the Blue Ridge, the orchards and farms of southern Berkeley County spread out left and right below the pull-off at **Bucks Hill** — the intersection of SR 45 and 51. It was April and the daytime colors were red bud and peach blossom pink. That night as I headed back across the mountains there were clear skies overhead, a huge bank of cumulus clouds hovering over the mountains, and a dazzling light show of flashing lightning bolts illuminating the clouds from behind. I stopped at the overlook to watch Mother Nature show off. It was a popular choice — at least a half-dozen cars were already there.

Sheer cliffs, enormous boulders and the wildwater of the Cheat River as it pours through the gorge 1,200 feet below are the stars of a spectacular view in **Coopers Rock State Forest**. That the view is enjoyed from a dramatic sandstone overhang is a bonus for the crowds of people who visit each year.

Saddle Mountain has been a landmark since prehistoric times, visible from the mountaintop overlooks along the game and hunter trail that is now US 50. Geologically, it is a wind gap abandoned by the stream that originally defined it. Legend claims that Abraham Lincoln's mother, Nancy Hanks, was born on the east side of Saddle Mountain in 1784.

Another timeless landmark, marked on the oldest of Appalachian maps, is the pair of 900 foot rock chimneys known as **Seneca Rocks**. Curves in roads for miles in all directions reveal glimpses of them protruding from bare rock upthrusts of North Fork Mountain. Porte Crayon described them in the mid-nineteenth century as "the loftiest and grandest specimen of the peculiar rock work to be found" in the North Potomac Valley.

There's a panoramic valley view of the surrounding Seneca Creek area from the steep but walkable trail on the west side. A true summit with only one way up — to climb it — the narrow top offers an exclusive view. There are horseback rides from Yokum's Stables to the top of the trail and folks have ridden to the top to get married. My personal favorite is the airborne view. We would circle Dolly Sods and Spruce Knob, the tallest peak in the state, then fly around the pair of rocks and wish we dared fly between them.

When the first climbers reached the summit in the late 1930s, they found an inscription dated 1908, reportedly made by a surveyor working in the region at the time. Few climbers followed the pioneers and from 1943-44 American soldiers were trained in mountain climbing on the rocks by Scandinavian troops.

Today, several hundred folks a year go through the original **Seneca Rocks Climbing School** attached to John Maxwell's Gendarme Store. In session from April through November, the classes range from three-day basic to mountain rescue courses. With the growing popularity of indoor walls and gym climbing, would-be mountaineers need the school to remind them that in addition to better views, climbing real rocks is harder. All technical equipment is provided by the school.

The **Gendarme Store** also serves the great rock, selling equipment and offering a social center. The rough-sided outbuilding porch is usually cluttered with climbers or their remnants and posted with notes about hazards on various routes. The interior is jammed with esoteric equipment needed to climb.

For more on Seneca Rocks, *see* "Truly Incredible" and "Mother Nature's Wonders."

CHAPTER TEN

MOTHER NATURE'S WONDERS

O ver countless millennia, nature's forces have made West Virginia a one-of-a-kind place, a state in constant homage to natural quirks and deviance. There are arctic ecosystems too far south, ancient mountains surrounding even more ancient rivers, and wilderness unmatched east of the Mississippi.

Trees cover 75% of the state's area, including nearly 1.5 million acres in federal and state forests. The Monongahela National Forest alone is larger than the entire state of Rhode Island. West Virginia has more species and subspecies of birds — nearly 300 — than any other area of its size in the world. West Virginia's nickname could be The Tree State or The Bird State as easily as its current moniker, The Mountain State.

And then there's the weather. In winter, the weather ecology can change in the space of a few hundred feet — up, down or sideways. Other than the flooding dangers inherent in 30,000 miles of rivers and streams — many flowing through narrow confines of canyons and gorges — there are no threatening weather occurrences, but there are oddities. The west side of the mountain slopes along the Eastern Continental Divide rack up sixty inches of rain a year, while the other side, lurking in a rain shadow, can muster up only half that amount.

THE OLDEST NEW

The **New River** and the fourteen-mile gorge it carves through 330 million year-old Nuttall sandstone are Mother Nature's overachievements in West Virginia. Geologists agree that the mysteriously named New River is, in fact, second in geologic age only to the Nile. Some white water devotees contend the New is older. Age may explain the river's rather deviant path. The Eastern Continental Divide is a natural barrier that runs along the top of the Alleghenies. Rivers rising to the east of the Divide flow into the Atlantic Ocean; those to the west flow into the Gulf of Mexico. Except for the New. It rises east of the Appalachians in the Carolinas, then cuts through the mountains to empty its water into other rivers that end up in the Gulf of Mexico.

Travel flaks hype the **New River Gorge** — which is up to 1,300 feet deep and a mile wide — as the Grand Canyon of the East, although its cliffs are tree-covered. Inaccessible until the late nineteenth century, the deep cut of the gorge ultimately led to its exploitation, by giving lateral access to the area's rich coal seams — another prerogative of geologic age. Its "salt sands" also produce oil, gas and brine.

Railroads followed the natural pathway of the gorge and opened it to mining in 1873. Booming coal camps quickly filled the area. In less than a century they were gone, leaving behind quaint ruins and cliffs, pockmarked with beehive ovens carved from the rock, which had been used to turn coal to coke on the spot.

Today, fifty-three miles of river, cliffs and gorge are protected as a National River. The river is ranked Category 1 by the U.S. Fish and Wildlife Service for its abundance of unique and irreplaceable aquatic species. Great blue heron abound alongside rock climbers who flock to 1,400 documented rock climbing routes.

The National Park Service's **Canyon Rim Visitors Center** explains all these rarities, as well as offering a close-up view of the river, gorge and world-class bridge from a sturdy boardwalk.

GOLDILOCKS WELCOME

When I began soliciting suggestions for way-out wonders in West Virginia, one response dominated — **Beartown State Park**. We immediately scheduled a trip to the Pocahontas County wonder and were able to proclaim the suggestions right on target. Beartown is unique.

The 110 acre state park is well disguised. The entry road begins at the black and white log Mt. Olivet Church and then passes an undistin-

guished collection of houses and farmland. Even the initial stretch of park boardwalk gives few hints of what's to come: the remarkable assemblage of house-size boulders and astonishing rock formations broken from the sandstone cap of Droop Mountain. Hemlock and rock cap ferns bathe the area in iridescent green, complementing the pervasive quiet as the boardwalks meander around the rocks. A half-hour walk takes you in, through and out of the wind- and rain-eroded rock city, with different views at every twist and turn.

Whether bears actually hibernated among the fanciful rock formations or not is a disputed point, but the notion gave rise to the name. Beartown State Park was established by Mrs. Edwin Polan of Huntington, in memory of her son Ronald, a student employee of the state parks who was killed in Vietnam in 1967.

Bizarre Botanicals

West Virginia boasts the most varied flora and fauna in the United States, including more than a hundred species of trees, virtually all hardwoods; thirty-six species of orchids; and more than 2,000 wild plant species. **Panther State Forest** in McDowell County is touted as the most biologically diverse area in the state.

Virgin stands of timber with trees hundreds of years old are rare anywhere on the planet, but even more so in West Virginia, which was virtually denuded of trees by timber companies during the past century. The unique feel of virgin stands — weighty, old and pure — can be experienced in two locations in the state.

Gaudineer State Forest owes its fifty acres of old growth red spruce to a surveyor's mistake in 1859. Incredibly tall and straight, some of the trees are over 300 years old. A scenic walk just off the road offers a breathtaking panorama of the surrounding mountains and forests, with nary a bit of human habitation to be seen.

The ultimate forest primeval is **Cathedral State Park**, a registered natural landmark just off US 50 east of Aurora, and the only stand of mixed virgin timber left in the state. Its 130 acres include virgin hemlocks — huge, straight blue-green giants with lacy needles. Very accessible, you can drive through Cathedral or walk along a forest floor where rhododendron and ferns are the only underbrush.

Though glaciers came to West Virginia's front door, they never made it into the state. The arctic climate they brought along, however, left behind vegetation that still thinks it's north of the fiftieth parallel. The 750 acres of spongy bogs in the high Alpine bowl that make up **Cranberry Glades** kept the atmosphere cool enough to seduce rare glacial plants from leaving after the Ice Age. This misplaced tundra includes the southernmost extent of many arctic flora, including reindeer moss. Barrier-free boardwalks criss-cross this national natural landmark, and tags identify exotic plants like the carnivorous sundew and snake-in-mouth orchid. Fifty-five square miles of this back country was declared the Cranberry Wilderness in 1983, permanently off-limits to cars and commercial activities. As we drove out of the Glades, a bear cub ran in front of our car, confirming that abundant cranberries serve as a bear magnet.

The treeless heath barrens of **Dolly Sods** at 2,600 to 4,000 feet are home to glacial plant life and lots of woodland creatures, from hawks and bobcats to beaver and flying squirrels. The southernmost habitat of snowshoe hare is also found among Dolly Sods' 10,000 acres. Happily, motorized vehicles and bikes are not.

The original spruce and hemlock forest, with its thick humus floor, was grazed and logged to destruction, then burnt down to the rock. Further humiliation rained on the area along with artillery from World War II practice runs. Most of the bombs left behind have been removed. Today, the eerie windswept high plains support boulder fields and wind-stunted vegetation, as well as abundant blueberries and cranberries. Natural landmarks are scarce, so hikers and berry pickers must remain alert.

North Fork Mountain lies on the rain shadow side of the Eastern Continental Divide, making it the driest place in the state with grass balds like the Smoky Mountains. Extensive dwarfed pine barrens are the southernmost trace of red pine and include a virgin stand at Pike Knob. Clumps of arctic vegetation and rare animals have also been discovered. Westerly winds on the summit of **Spruce Knob** create one-sided red spruce stands; at 4,860 feet, it's the highest point in the state.

The southernmost extent of the great spruce forests that once covered America were found in the high country around **Canaan**. At one time the forest floor was so dense that there was hardly room to walk on the more than eight-foot "duff" layer of shed vegetation. Tragically, the area was lumbered and burned away in a generation. Today, the spruce forest is once again flourishing, replanted by the Civilian Conservation Corps in what many believed was an impossible project.

The **Pipestem bush** has hollow stems that were used by Indians and early settlers to make pipes, and gave its name to Pipestem State Park. Identified by this name only in books of West Virginia flora, the bush is technically *spirea alba*.

The worldwide standard for yellow apples is the **Golden Delicious**, which originated from a chance seedling of a tree on Porter's Creek near Odessa in Clay County. The mother tree had been found in 1905 by the Mullins family, who turned it over for development nearly a decade later to Paul Stark of Stark Brothers Nursery. The big, yellow and delicious fruit that Luther Burbank later called "the greatest apple in all the world" received the apple world's premier medal — The Wilder — in 1919, the only yellow apple to ever do so. After producing apples for nearly fifty years, the mother tree is now remembered by a plaque at the site.

West Virginia's most famous contribution to horticulture, the Golden Delicious, was superior to an earlier yellow apple also found in the state. The **Grimes Golden** apple originated in 1802 in Brooke County. Today, the notable beginning is marked by a watering trough in a Wellsburg park.

Too Hot / Too Cold

Historic reports claim ice was cut year 'round at **Ice Mountain**. On my trip to the rare and sensitive cold-producing mountain slope along the North River in Hampshire County, I found the chill to be far less dramatic. I stuck my hand into a cold vent that looked like an animal burrow surrounded by clusters of misplaced arctic flora — bunchberry and Siberian prickly rose, both in their southernmost locations. It felt like good air conditioning. No core samples have ever been taken and no one knows why the area is cold producing.

Ice Mountain is a Nature Conservancy area. Twice a month, the group conducts an appealing hike among poplars, fossils, ferns, blue cohosh, rhododendron, cucumber magnolia and witch hazel to the banks of the river and the cold vents (see photo at right). The hike continues up to Raven Rocks. *See* "Million Dollar Views."

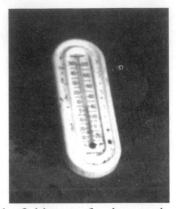

Another story of peculiar natural cooling comes from the southern coalfield city of **Bluefield**, which bills itself as "nature's air conditioned city." Demonstrating that the title is more than hype, Bluefield serves free lemonade anytime the temperature is over 90 degrees. The gimmick began with Lemonade Lassies in 1939 and has continued ever since, in spite of the grueling summer of 1952 when lemonade was served free twenty-four times! What did not continue after the first attempt in 1937 was the giving away of free hotel rooms. Once it got too hot at the same time a state convention of Odd Fellows was in town.

On the other end of the heat spectrum is Wyoming County, noted for **Burning Rocks**, where warm air melts ice and snow in winter.

Goings-On Underground

What's beneath the surface in West Virginia has often been more valuable than what's on top; this includes rich deposits of coal, oil and gas. In **Wyoming County**, there are three acres of coal for every acre of surface. The unimaginably rich, nearly 1,000 square mile **Pocahontas coal field** has a twenty-four foot high coal seam, rather than the twenty-four inch seam customarily found throughout the state. This makes it the highest known coal seam in the world!

Of greater recreational interest are the state's **caves**. Limestone deposits along the eastern edge of the state led to a region riddled with caves, with more than a thousand in Greenbrier County alone. Many are long and large because of the unique uninterrupted quality of the limestone deposits. Today, spelunkers count more than 3,500 caves in West Virginia, with wild ones being discovered every day.

Gandy Creek disappears into a cavern for about a mile near Spruce Knob Lake. The surrounding area, known as the **Sinks of Gandy**, is filled with sink holes and caves that can be explored, although the land is privately owned. There are reports that a Native American ghost in full war dress occasionally appears around the caves.

Lost River goes under Sandy Ridge near Wardensville, and comes out two miles on the other side of the mountain as the headwaters of the Cacapon River, which then travels 100 miles north to empty into the Potomac.

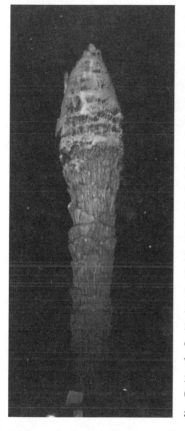

A commercial cave in Greenbrier County, **Lost World Caverns**, is home to several unique features. In its former incarnation as the wild Grapevine Cave, the huge, multi-room cavern was known worldwide through the tabloid press as the original home of "bat boy." The world also focused on the cave and its star rock formation — the half million year old War Club, a stalagmite twenty-eight feet tall with a base diameter of two and a half feet — when two guys named Bob decided to stalagmite sit in 1971. Bob Addis of Parkersburg built a platform attached to War Club and sat for fifteen days, twenty-three hours and twenty-two minutes for what he claims is the Guinness World Record. His partner, Bob Lehman (the first, not the second Bob in "Bob & Bob's", *see* below) would bring Mexican food to his partner from Clem's Diner in Lewisburg. The Greenbrier High School band came to play and enjoyed the great sound in the cavern.

Although the cave was not discovered until 1942, cave bear bones over 10,000 years old were found in what is now Lost World Caverns. Registered cavers can still drop 120 feet by rope through the natural entrance.

Bob & Bob's International Headquarters is an enterprise of cavers serving cavers, with the largest catalog of caving equipment available. They fill mail orders from all over the world for thousands of items including lights, helmets and the patented adjustable seats from the Gendarme Store in Seneca Rocks.

At the turn-of-this century, workers digging post holes for a livery stable in the heart of downtown **Charles Town** made an incredible discovery: the limestone underpinnings of the town George Washington's brother built were riddled with caves. The workers also discovered a sixty-foot deep, three acre lake. Opened in the 1930s as a tourism destination, boat rides were given on the underground lake. Today the entrance is hidden, riveted beneath a metal plate on the floor behind the lunch counter at the Liberty Street Cafe. The tiny blue building — and it is assumed, the underground expanse — are owned by the town.

Underground caves also riddle the limestone foundation of **Lewisburg**. Yell into the giant street grate at the corner of Court and Foster Streets and you'll hear the sound echo through the huge cave below.

There are neither boardwalks nor staircases in a wild cave. **Scott Hollow** is a developed wild cave in Monroe County. Discovered in 1984, Scott Hollow has over twenty miles of passages — through the black voids of the Mystic River — that have been mapped. The current owners have built a very unique trap door structure over the cave entrance. Open around the clock, cavers can take the wild entrance by dropping through a culvert under the trap door. There's a large metal door on the basement level for those choosing to walk in. Guided trips lasting four to five hours can be arranged.

Read about Organ Cave in "Historic Oddities." *See* "Superlatives" for information on Smoke Hole Caverns and Seneca Caverns.

NATURE CHUNKS

There's not much water in West Virginia, and most of it is geologically trapped in springs, rivers and streams. There are ten man-made lakes in the state, but only one natural lake. It's actually a two-acre sinkhole in the limestone rock of Hardy County named **Trout Pond** for the great fishing.

Part of a shallow sea millions of years ago, **Bluestone Canyon** is named for the gray-green shale readily visible along the road in the bottom of the canyon. Geologically, canyon walls rose around the river, which drops 1,700 feet in its seventy-seven miles. Indians called it Big Stone River because of the boulders found throughout its riverbed.

The canyon road is the morning walk of choice for guests at Mountain Creek Lodge. A tiny fawn trailed me for a mile or so along the road, and then back to the lodge where it stood waiting on the lawn. When I opened our balcony door and told Jack it was there, the fawn looked up to find my voice.

At the **Falls of Hill Creek**, Mother Nature had promotional help from humans. Hill Creek drops over rock layers of sandstone and shale in three waterfalls as it passes through a narrow gorge. Three quarters of a mile of maintained boardwalks, steps and four overlooks make it easy to appreciate the sight. In summer, even the light is saturated with green. The lower falls at sixty-three feet is the second highest in the state.

Just east of Bramwell is **Pinnacle Rock**, a 364-acre state park built around a 2,700 foot remnant of an ancient geologic fold. Climbing a rugged stone staircase nearly to the top, one is rewarded by a panoramic view of the swath of mountains along the Virginia border and Jefferson National Forest.

Eight rivers flow out of the mountains of **Pocahontas County** heading in all directions. No rivers flow in. The eight are: the Greenbrier, Elk, Cheat, Tygart Valley, Gauley, Cherry, Williams and Cranberry.

Few explorers from George Washington on have missed describing the amazing stretch of the Ohio River as it winds its way south from Paden City to Parkersburg. In less than 100 miles, more than forty islands litter the river, ranging from less than an acre to more than 400 acres.

Many have sandy beaches. There is only one bridge — from St. Mary's to Middle Island — that connects the Ohio River islands to the mainland, and none connecting them to each other. Their prized wildlife ecosystems include bald eagles, peregrine falcons, beaver, mink, muskrat and over thirty species of freshwater mussels, including the endangered pink mucket and fanshell. Fifteen of the West Virginia islands are currently part of the **Ohio River Islands National Wildlife Refuge**.

Seneca Rocks guarantee West Virginia's mention in the annals of geologic wonder. However, the 10,000 climbing pins left in the ancient 900 foot cliffs — which map out 375 major climbing routes — suggest a lessening of the great rocks' great karma. For more on Seneca Rocks, *see* "Million Dollar Views" and "Truly Incredible."

WEIRD APPARITIONS

Catch the moon about midnight at the 165 acre **Lake Sherwood**, and the reflection of the water looks like a giant cliff. The illusion often has an accompaniment of hoots and howlings, which break the predominant sound of you sucking air. **Hopkins Vista** is nearby, with mysterious sounds from Second Creek, shooting stars and few lights. It's an ideal spot for UFO landings.

CHAPTER ELEVEN

REMARKABLE COLLECTIONS

The magnificent obsession that marks great collections is well represented in West Virginia. Some evolve from the history and industry of the place, while others are driven by individual hunters and gatherers.

A sparkling sample of contemporary collectors was the inaugural exhibit at Hurricane's **Museum in the Community** in May 1998. Among the automobiles, string holders and Pez dispensers was a small but colorful array of *Graffiti* editor Michael Lipton's more-than-eighty-item electric guitar collection. Lipton's quote could be the universal theme for all collectors. "If I had a twenty dollar bill and saw a twenty dollar guitar, I'd buy the guitar and know I'd have it longer than I would have had the twenty."

Whether the motivation for collecting is buried in childhood memories or devotion to a particular facet of life, it all adds to the treasure store of things worth keeping.

ANCIENT WONDERS

Seventy display units — hand-built wood and glass cabinets more than six feet tall — line more than sixty feet of wall in the basement of the Blennerhassett Museum. The cases were built in the late nineteenth century for the **Native American collection of Thomas Stahle**, a music teacher and amateur anthropologist who immigrated to Parkersburg from Germany just after the Civil War.

Stahle interpreted as well as collected, telling stories section by section. He developed the displays and hand-lettered the explanation of each. There are extensive samples of musical flutes, toys, whistles, hematite cosmetics and "paints," drills, cutting tools, pipes, ornaments and more. A pair of 5 x 3 inch shell masks with etched facial features stand out among the thousands of rare artifacts.

Stahle's collection was inspired by the very rich deposit of Native American artifacts buried on Blennerhassett Island, some of which date back nearly 14,000 years. Other local collectors donated their finds to his work. The Blennerhassett collection is also home to the **Cedar Rocks petroglyph**, which was found near Wheeling. This arrangement of human and animal forms surrounding an abstract geometric pattern is a rare portable petroglyph, carved into a 3 x 2 foot sandstone slab rather than the more typical exposed bedrock.

See "Historic Oddities" for more on Native American sites.

X-FILES FORESHADOWED

For more than twenty years, Clarksburg was a major center for UFO devotees, thanks to world-famous UFO expert Gray Barker. Today his work is featured on more than thirty websites, and the **Gray Barker UFO Collection** is open to the public in Clarksburg.

Born in Braxton County, Barker's life was changed forever in 1952. That's the year when sightings of flashing lights in the sky, glowing objects and the mysterious "Flatwoods Monster" were turned into a story for *Fate* magazine. Barker pursued his writing, becoming well known in the flying saucer world of the 1950s and 60s, writing and publishing *Saucer News*, and later, the long-lived *Saucerian*.

As an astrologer, I have lots of friends in the UFO community. I was intrigued by West Virginia's connection, and set out to see Barker's collection at **Waldomere** in Clarksburg. Waldomere is the pre-Civil

War, Greek Revival mansion housing the Harrison County Public Library and the Barker collection. Librarian David Houchin was reluctant but knowledgeable as he unlocked the door to the Gray Barker room. Barker's assemblage of publications and papers have been part of the special collections of the library since his death in 1984.

A card catalog guided me through thirty-five drawers of Barker's files and notes, a journey that included forged letters, references to his persecution by "Men in Black" – the first known use of the phrase — and bogus saucer films. The model saucer allegedly used by Barker to falsify photographs is in the collection, along with the typewriter he chopped up and hid in a stone wall to avoid an FBI probe. Most of his published works are there, including: *They Knew Too Much about Flying Saucers*, *Book of Adamski*, and *Secret Terror Among Us: Silver Bridge*. More than 500 books and copies of seventy-five magazines and periodicals line two walls of the room, with titles ranging from the *Fortean Times* and *Flying Saucer* to *Saucer Space & Science* and *Star Log*.

Barker supported himself, as I do, operating a movie theater; he ran Lovett's Drive-in for thirty years.

UFO activity tends to be reported from numerous people in the same geographical area; one such area is the Indian mounds of the Ohio River valley. Point Pleasant was a hotbed of activity in the mid-1960s, with scores of UFO sightings as well as the appearance of the mysterious "Mothman" in 1966. In December 1967, the collapse of Point Pleasant's Silver Bridge, and the resultant deaths of forty-six people, brought the town to the attention of the world. Seeking meaning in tragedy, some linked the bridge collapse to Mothman and UFO activity, while others pointed to Indian Chief Cornstalk's curse.

West Virginia has a cottage industry in UFO films, including *Whispers from Space*, an independently produced documentary which questions Barker's belief in the saucer phenomena he exploited, and Bob Teets' *West Virginia UFOs: Close Encounters in the Mountain State*. Mothman is documented in *The Mothman Prophecies*, a book by John Keel, and there is even an "official" Mothman website (*see* Index).

WEST VIRGINIA GLASS MOTHER LODE

The world's largest punchbowl (*see* "Superlatives") is one of more than 3,000 pieces of Wheeling glass identified and displayed at **Oglebay Institute's Glass Museum**. In an adjacent room, nearly 200 pieces of Wheeling-made china and porcelain are housed in elaborate cases from a downtown jewelry store. The prized feature of the collection is not glass, but a "hologram" of glass chemist, William Layton, Jr. Stand in front of the display and the seated Layton will explain how his father, working in Wheeling, revolutionized the glass industry in 1864 when he added bicarbonate of soda to the mix of sand. Layton's change in formula resulted in a substance that was cheaper, easier to manipulate, and resulted in better, clearer glass.

Glass from the major Wheeling companies — Ritchie, Sweeney, Hobbs, Brockunier, Central and Northwood — is the collection's main focus. The collection, plus glass studios where visitors can watch glass artists at work, is housed downstairs in the Carriage House Glass Center. Upstairs, the glass is for sale.

JOHN HENRY IN WOOD

I had no idea what I would find when the volunteer at the Summers County Visitors Center suggested I go upstairs and see the **John Henry carvings**. On the second floor I found a large room, empty except for a long table against one wall. Sitting on the table were 120 hand-carved wooden figures. Not even the figures' lack of display could limit the primitive power of the art.

Charlie Permelia was an injured coal miner from Lester, West Virginia. Completely self-taught, Permelia spent eight hours a day for seven and a half years carving foot-tall versions of West Virginia's legendary steel-drivin' man and his mates. The figures and train cars are carved from fifty-six kinds of wood — black and white walnut, ash, cherry, chinquapin, buckeye, sassafras, basswood, magnolia, paw paw, bamigallian, spice wood, cucumber, sourwood, tamarack, red brush, arbor vitae and more – all depicting John Henry and his friends "workin' on the railroad."

ROADSIDE ATTRACTION

It snuck up on us as we drove east on US 50 in Preston County. The long, low wooden building was a traditional roadside stop of the 1930s and 40s, with a sign stretching across the front listing at least fifty items sold inside. We had no plans to stop. We did not need a cider operating press, sorghum molasses or ammo; nor did we need tomahawks, auto supplies or fertilizer. Then we saw the spinning twenty-foot-tall metal waterwheel and dozens of wheeled antique farm implements parked behind the fence.

There is no charge to wander among the scores of old machines at **Cool Springs Park** — no interpretation or signs either. A rare steam tractor is parked with a half dozen other antique tractors; a block of railroad track supports three cabooses and a freight car. Peacocks and emus share the park with the rusted metal.

Songs and Sketches

Over 1,000 individual collections assembled since 1933 are housed in the **West Virginia and Regional History Collection** at West Virginia University, making it the state's most extensive collection. Here are countless political and historical papers, including those of the "loyal" Virginia government, as well as Civil War diaries. It also contains the largest collection of West Virginia photos and newspapers in the state. All are on microfilm.

Gems include the **Chappell Collection**, more than 2,000 songs and tunes recorded originally on aluminum disks and now transferred to nearly 700 tapes. Assembled by Lewis Watson Chappell, these are the first sound recordings of American folk songs, and were recorded in the field between 1937 and 1947.

More than 500 sketches and some paintings by David Hunter Strother comprise another prized collection. The celebrated nineteenth century illustrator and author — pen name: Porte Crayon — was a household word in America due to his work in *Harper's New Monthly Magazine*. The **Strother Collection** includes dozens of illustrated travelogues for *Harper's*, Civil War recollections, and a ten-part series — *The Mountains* — which focused on the rural character and folkways of the new state of West Virginia. Strother was a native of the state and lived most of his life in Berkeley Springs, where he and his father before him were innkeepers. He chose the North and became an Adjutant General in the Civil War. Strother used woodcut drawings to illustrate his travelogues.

The Pale Blue Army

Along with spaghetti and comfortable guest rooms named for archangels, Peg Perry serves up icons, statues and paintings of the Divine Mother at **Maria's Garden** in Berkeley Springs. The restaurant entryway has a stone wall set with an image of one of the first Mary apparitions — Our Lady of Guadeloupe in 1531. The grotto in the outdoor garden was a natural for a shrine according to Perry. "I always associate niches with the Madonna," she said.

At Maria's you'll find more than a hundred images of the Virgin Mary, as well as private stories of wondrous meetings, roses growing in winter, and whirling statues.

POWDER HORN BONANZA

From 1910 to 1940, Elkins builder **H.M. Darby** compiled a "magnificent conglomeration" of prehistoric and early American artifacts, which he assembled and deeded to Davis & Elkins College in 1941. After nearly thirty years in various attics, the college began to preserve and research the collection in 1969.

Darby was not a traveler. He called himself "a dealer in curios" and his letterhead announced "Darby's Pre-Historic and Early Pioneer's Art Museum." He collected through advertisements and people who brought him various pieces. He kept meticulous records of the uses, history and price of all the objects in his collection. Fate dealt Darby's ghost a blow when the years of being stored in random attics around the college led to the loss of documentation for countless pieces in the collection. For decades, Dorothy Lutz has worked to reconstruct the information, carefully tracking down clues as to the use and source of various artifacts. Researchers and scholars come from all over to see the collection, and to help Lutz with the work of identification. Today, only a quarter of Darby's enormous collection is displayed at Graceland and Halliehurst, the twin mansions of Elkins. The collection's stewards are looking for more display space.

The **Darby collection** of more than 200 colonial powder horns is one of the largest in the world. While it is doubtful that anyone has recorded the full extent of the collection, there are also more than 5,000

Indian points and primitive stone tools dating back nearly 10,000 years. Countless thousands of other artifacts range from tobacco mills, numerous lamps, early American tools, magic cult objects and bizarre relics, to ordinance, pistols, swords and kitchenware.

COLLECTIBLE BITS AND PIECES

You'll recognize Jack Moody's **War Memorial Museum** in Nitro by the rare World War I Renault tank sitting outside the small building. Inside are historically significant artifacts from virtually every American conflict beginning with the Indian wars, as well as archival material from the town's fantastic beginning. Nitro was built by the U.S. Government in ten days as the site for a gunpowder plant; it was named for one of the ingredients — nitrogen tetroxide. Among hundreds of rare artifacts at the museum are the gun used to assassinate Archduke Ferdinand and start World War I, a pistol used by Jesse James to rob a Huntington bank, and a gas canister from a Nazi death camp.

A favorite of visitors to the West Virginia State Museum are Emmiline and Alexander, the stars of **Professor Hechler's Flea Circus**. The well-dressed fleas are on display in a colorful circus car exhibit. When alive and in their prime, the quarter inch-long creatures could pull nearly 700 times their weight. Their stunts included hauling carts and wagons, jumping through hoops, dancing, juggling and leaping nearly a foot in the air. The famed New York performers came to West Virginia in 1906.

Coke collectibles and iced coke in vintage bottles are prime attractions in Romney's **Coca Cola Bottling Works Museum**.

The mother lode for coal research is found on the second floor of the Craft Memorial Library in Bluefield. Thousands of photos, tools, rare books, coal camp scrip, blueprints, oral histories, films, and diaries make up the vast collection of **The Eastern Regional Coal Archives**.

The museum collection at **Homeopathy Works** in Berkeley Springs, housed in original Victorian pharmacy cabinets, rivals that of the Smithsonian. Authentic nineteenth and early twentieth century machines for manufacturing medical remedies stand ready for examination under the bust of Samuel Hahneman, eighteenth century physician and inventor of homeopathic medicine. Owner and collector, Joe Lillard, has designed and published an informative timeline of homeopathic development that is mounted in the exhibit and is available for sale. Machine buffs will enjoy "Thumper" — one of two "helio Korsakoff potentizers" in the world.

West Virginia's State Archives are a treasure trove for genealogical researchers, with hundreds of volumes of state, census and military records as well as county, community and family histories.

The restored birthplace of novelist **Pearl Buck** showcases her eighty-five books, including some signed and first editions. Some of her books are for sale in the gift shop. Buck was the first American woman to win the Nobel Prize for Literature. Built in 1858, the white frame **Stulting House** was always known to Pearl as her mother's house.

Scholars travel from all corners of the globe to examine the folk music treasures in **The Augusta Collection** in Booth Library at Davis & Elkins College. The collection includes more than 2,500 sound recordings, as well as a growing number of videotapes of performances of the material, generated during the annual Augusta Heritage program. Histories, interviews, field recordings and photographs from Gerry Milnes' field work for Augusta are included, along with tapes from early West Virginia Folk Festivals and the Mars family gatherings.

On two floors of a restored Victorian schoolhouse in Wheeling, tens of thousands of vintage toys — including one-of-a-kind store samples — are lovingly displayed at the **Kruger Street Toy and Train Museum**. Many are from the nearby Louis Marx Company, which closed in 1980. The guides at the museum are as fascinating as the toys.

Parkersburg's place in history as the first producer of oil and gas in the United States is documented in an extensive collection of equipment, documents, maps and stories at the **Oil and Gas Museum**. An inviting pile of metal and machines including giant wheels and pumps are housed in the yard next to the brick museum building.

Henderson Hall — a three-story Italianate mansion with an intriguing silhouette — was a center of social and political life for nearly two centuries. The original Federal portion was built overlooking the Ohio River in 1836; the mansion was added just before the Civil War to make a total of twenty-nine rooms. The house, still occupied by descendants of the original family, retains all of its contents, and is open to the public for limited tours. The rare clocks, rosewood piano, silver and china, twelve-foot gilt mirror and other unique pieces are not antiques; they are the daily furnishings of successive residents. Fortunately for modern visitors, the Hendersons kept everything from dresses to portraits to correspondence from everyone they knew — and they knew everyone important at the time. There is a cherry stair railing that runs continuously from the first to the third floor; the floors are all the original wood. The major change in the house was the addition of electricity early in this century.

Huntington is home to several diverse collections.

The **Herman Dean Firearms Collection** has its own room at the Huntington Museum of Art. Hundreds of items range from early pistols and powder horns incised with maps to a breechloading rifle made by John Hall of Harpers Ferry. There are outstanding examples of decorated weapons including both pistols and a Kentucky flintlock rifle.

Between the extensive collections of both the Huntington Museum and Marshall University, Huntington can also lay claim to the state's largest collection of art books. The **Museum of Radio and Technology** in downtown Huntington is the largest radio museum in the East, with hundreds of old radios from the 1920s to '50s and a radio station studio from the 1950s. The gift shop and its posters and reproductions are Nirvana for radio buffs.

The **African-American Heritage Family Tree Museum** near Hawks Nest State Park showcases a large collection of rare photographs from black coal camp communities.

Leland's Small World in Alderson is a gaudy collection of carousels and mechanical toys of all sizes in a hot pink storefront attached to an auto parts store. Open by chance.

Thousands of rare and unique artifacts are displayed in **Wymer's General Store Museum** in Wheeling's Artisan Center. More than 10,000 pieces from Wheeling's past include a complete salesman's sample of every type and size nail made by LaBelle Cut Nail Factory, decaled pottery steins and Marx Toy Company figures. Other items are part of an 1880s general store.

The **West Virginia State Farm Museum** just north of Point Pleasant houses some interesting taxidermic oddities — a two-headed calf and General, the world's third largest horse.

CHAPTER TWELVE

SHOPPING TREASURES

Power shopping is all in your point of view. For some folks, the hand-painted sign on a roadside market in the mountains outside Elkins announcing COLD BEER • TANNING • LOTTERY covers all the bases. For the more discriminating, there are unique products, historic shops, notable buildings and unparalleled bargains.

HIGH FASHION

Stylish women in West Virginia are proud of getting a knock-out look at knock-down prices. They tell more stories about **Gabriel Brothers'** bargains than about five-figure designer gowns.

A foxy Lisa Starcher Collins was the hit of an arts gathering with her dazzling layered look, head-to-toe from Gabe's for $13. Rosalyn Queen wheedled a photo with the Pope in Rome thanks to her Gabe's bargain suit. Lined black satin mini-skirts with a Donna Karan label at $5 each outfitted the entire staff of a small town restaurant at a cost less than dinner for two. The price tag on my Enzo Angelini leather bag read $248; at Gabe's it was $12.99. Nothing is ever more than $100; often ten dresses can cost less than $300. Women fly in from all over to shop.

Even better than the price tags are the challenges of the hunt.

New batches of low priced close-outs and irregulars in men, women and children's clothing appear daily in twenty-one Gabriel Brothers' stores in five states. In true bargain-basement style, there is minimal order and selection is limited.

It takes practice and skill to work Gabe's for the ultimate bargain. Practitioners boast of daily pilgrimages and hitting five Gabes — Parkersburg, Fairmont, Clarksburg, Morgantown and Washington, PA — in a single day-long power shopping surge. Regulars know to guard their bargains while collecting them and to check each item thoroughly. Individual items may be flawed or damaged, and there are no guarantees. Even at $7, the glittery designer sweater I bought was no bargain when I put it on for the first time and discovered one sleeve was six inches shorter than the other.

This palace of cut-rate clothes shopping sprang from the ambition of Z.G. Gabriel, a Lebanese peddler operating from a truck in Pennsylvania. In 1961, Gabriel and his sons settled into their first store, the downtown building now housing the West Virginia Brewery in Morgantown. Gabriel Brothers' has always been a family store with good stuff at good prices for the area. They bypass wholesalers, dealing directly with store liquidators, who now often seek out Gabriel Brothers' because of their good reputation.

It's still family owned and operated, but currently there are two businesses, caused by a family split in the mid-1980s. Brothers James and Arthur became Gabriel Brothers and kept the West Virginia stores. Today, their nine children and more than 2,500 employees operate the family clothing store chain. Stores are open daily except traditional holidays. Hours are a standard 9 am to 9 pm.

Buying at the Source

Jackie Kennedy Onassis was one of **Cabin Creek Quilts'** first customers. She bought the quilts from VISTA volunteer James Thibeault, who in the early 1970s went on the road, selling the quilts from the non-profit cooperative he had developed. Cabin Creek Quilts was born in the tiny town of Malden, with the help of Thibeault and six elderly ladies. Today Cabin Creek Quilts is a world famous name and the largest quilting cooperative in the United States. Women who once practiced quilting as an economical way to use fabric scraps are now recognized for the artistry of their work. The price tags on the quilts have increased: with prices from $10. to $25. before the co-op, today's retail prices sometimes top $1,000.

A visit to the 1838 pink Hale House in Malden — rescued by the co-op and made Cabin Creek's home in 1991 — is a visual as well as a shopping treat. Dozens of colorful quilts hang full length on moveable racks, story-telling tapestries hang on several walls and one room is filled with fabric ornaments for under $5. The **Jacqueline Kennedy Onassis Quilt** — begun as an honorarium two days before she died — was finished in two weeks and is now part of the permanent collection.

A producer of fine china for more than a century — since 1907 in West Virginia — **Homer Laughlin** created inexpensive and colorful **Fiestaware** in 1935. Fiestaware became the firm's best selling line and one of the most collected in the world. The retail outlet at the factory has a large seconds room where a rainbow of Fiesta bowls, pitchers and plates are stacked in huge bins for sale at extreme discount. Selection and availability of specific pieces or colors change daily and there is always the chance that limited batches of new items will appear from the factory. During our visit, I was able to buy a collector friend a new design — a small Fiesta pitcher that was a clock. More than 25,000 china patterns have come from Homer Laughlin, many custom-made for noted clients, including The Greenbrier. A third of all dinnerware ever sold in this country has come from its kilns, and it was the first totally lead-free pottery in America.

A large showroom was built in 1921 to rival those of Europe. Today its ceilings, covered with ornately carved ceramic tiles cast at Homer

Laughlin, arch over broad walnut shelves filled with displays of the company's many patterns and pieces.

For more on touring the factory, *see* "Tours Not To Miss."

GLASS AND MORE GLASS

Historically, West Virginia has had a major glass industry with hundreds of factories and new techniques that transformed the making of glass. Today only a few major producers remain, as well as fewer than a dozen small studio factories.

Blenko Glass Company is famous for its deep vibrant colors and contemporary designs. They also have the best outlet store with seconds in dozens of popular pieces from $5 up. For serious shopping, come early before the buses arrive.

Blenko's colored glass sheets, blown only at night, make it a mecca for stained glass workers all over the United States and Japan. They come searching for raw material among thousands of sheets in dozens of colors racked in a large warehouse behind the factory. Cheap scraps of brilliantly colored glass are also abundant.

William Blenko came to America from London to produce hand blown glass for stained glass windows. In 1929, he started producing hand blown decorative glassware. Today Blenko proudly claims clients such as the Country Music Awards, St. Patrick's Cathedral, the Pro Football Hall of Fame, the Smithsonian and many more.

For rare collector's pieces such as signed paperweights by Jennings Bonnell, go to **Masterpiece Crystal** in Jane Lew. My favorite glass treasure is a three-dimensional shooting star made by **Hamon Glass** and bought at considerable savings from the studio factory. Bob Hamon is a second generation glass blower with a career that began in 1935 at age ten. Hamon Glass is located in Teays Valley, between Charleston and Huntington. The best selection of West Virginia glass at retail prices is **Carriage House Glass** at Oglebay.

Pilgrim Glass in Ceredo has perfected the arduous job of creating cameo glass. Registered pieces are available for sale at the factory shop. Cameo glass is made by layering various colors of molten glass and then carving through them. Pilgrim artists have succeeded in carving as many as nine layers of glass, resulting in extraordinary pieces of art often worth thousands of dollars. Pilgrim also produces cranberry glass, rare because it requires fusing solid gold with lead crystal.

Free for the Taking

Priced from a nickel on up, West Virginia glass marbles are a favorite purchase at **Tamarack**. The price is even better for souvenir marbles at the source; they are used as mulch at the **Marble King** (left) and you can pick them up, free. The Paden City factory, one of only five in the country that produce marbles, will even give you a bag for collecting. Operating around the clock, Marble King uses mostly discarded glass from nearby glass manufacturers Fenton and Dalzell Viking. The factory can turn out a million marbles a day.

Penny Cures

There is no place like it in the world. In 1991, when **Homeopathy Works** opened in a restored turn-of-the-century building across from the healing waters of Berkeley Springs State Park, it became the only combination manufactory, retail store and homeopathic museum on Earth. What folks buy most when they visit the unique shop are the seventy combination remedies manufactured there, used to relieve common problems like headaches, sinus trouble and bed wetting. The sinus remedy reportedly works for 90% of the people who try it. A new salve has a nearly 100% cure rate for genital herpes. City visitors often leave with a $6 bottle of pills for mental fatigue, while others can't resist Homeopet formulas for pets.

Watching the remedies being produced behind plate glass windows in a gleaming lab filled with exotic machines — some antique, some futuristic — is almost as fascinating as finding a penny cure for lifetime ailments.

Instruction books, assembled kits, poison ivy lotion, various ointments and tinctures, as well as more than 1,600 classic single remedies in varying potencies are all for sale over the counter. One of only six U.S. companies offering a full line of homeopathic products, Homeopathy Works manufactures and markets to nearly 400 pharmacies and hundreds of physicians and veterinarians. "We've put homeopathy back in the towns and cities where it once was," said owner Joe Lillard about his Berkeley Springs shop.

OLD TIMEY STORES

★ There is nothing plastic in **O'Hurley's General Store**, just three rooms crowded with time tested merchandise known for quality and price, ranging from black powder guns and hats to baskets, clothes and wooden toys. Even the shop brochure displays the aggressively traditional nature of the shop and its notable owner, Jay Hurley.

In the rear of the former family gas station, Hurley has a nineteenth-century machine shop where he crafted the working model of James Rumsey's 1787 steamboat. (For more on Rumsey, the hapless inventor, *see* "Historic Oddities.") The latest addition to Hurley's iconoclastic empire in Shepherdstown is the Great Hall, a true timber-frame structure completely hand-done. The working fireplace is floor-to-ceiling nineteenth-century brick, and is used both to heat the room for events as well as to bake johnnycake in its traditional built-in bread oven. Tongue and groove wide oak planks on the floor include some cut from a thirty-three foot oak log. The room is lit by 120 candles held in five foot turned-oak chandeliers made in Hurley's shop.

★ Founded in 1908, **Berdine's** is the oldest, continuously working 5 & 10¢ store in the United States — *the* place for buying all the important stuff like cap pistols, trinkets, West Virginia glass, school supplies, paper dolls and thread. Original oak shelves and display cabinets are chock full of interesting items, including Berdine's specialty, metal mechanized toys. An old timey candy counter laden with new candy is strategically placed.

★ Just down the road in Cairo is **R.C. Marshall Hardware**, complete with its 1902 original tin ceilings, rolling ladders and showcases. The new and usable inventory also fits the period. No electric tools here but you will find plenty of oil lamps, cast iron ware, biking supplies and quality hand tools.

★ **Hillsboro General Store** was established in 1893 and is now in the hands of a young man who loves old things and mountain biking. The store offers aged cheddar, homemade peanut butter and hand-dipped ice cream along with horse plows, mountain bike supplies and fresh bulk spices.

★ The only working business in Thurmond has old timey soda pop, bike rentals, West Virginia books, railroad pins and tools. **Thurmond Supply** continues a tradition dating from the building's construction in 1929 as a railroad commissary. Even when it became the local post office, there was a store in the space. Trains whiz by the front door more than twenty times a day.

Shops that Stand Out in a Crowd

★ The Parkersburg branch of **Trans Allegheny Books** has 150,000 used and rare volumes stashed in the restored 1904 Carnegie Library, complete with spiral metal stairs, brass railings, marble counters and three floors of library stacks with glass floors.

★ Buy something at **Full Moon Rising** in Marlinton and owner Patty Hoover offers a free psychic mini-reading. Hot items you'll find in the occult and antique store are Hoover's huge inventory of Depression glass, handmade jewelry and fortune telling tools. My treasure is a pair of star earrings carved from Pocahontas County rosy quartz.

★ In Wheeling, **Stages** is ideal for costume dressers looking for a good selection. Feather wigs, medieval robes, masks, and a huge vat of stage prop swords await you.

★ An abundant collection of herbs, soaps and teas line the walls of **Root Cellar Herb & Mercantile** on Main Street in Hurricane. Its cunningly draped garden tables and chairs are the setting for traditional, silver service English high tea — scones, breads, desserts and finger sandwiches.

★ For holiday shopping year 'round, the bright red **Greenbrier Christmas Shop at the Depot** offers five rooms overfilled with exquisite ornaments, decorated trees and gifts organized by theme. Located in

White Sulphur Springs across from the Greenbrier, the Depot stocks new items in October.

★ Looking for an Elizabethan ruffle or a flapper headdress? Stop in downtown Beckley at **Brier Rose Studios**, a full-blown costume shop where Susie Sayre sews for Theater West Virginia and your next masked ball.

★ Ask anyone. **Mountain State Muzzleloading** in Boaz is the only place to go for all your early American firearms supply needs, including powder horns and tomahawks.

★ Eddie's signature trucks haul tires from Berkeley Springs to a dozen outlets elsewhere in West Virginia and three other states. But it is the **Eddie's Tires** mother store, south of Berkeley Springs, that draws the customers. They drive from all over for the rock-bottom price, the broad selection from a variety of brands, and most of all for the service. "They can't believe we can get them in and out with new tires, all balanced, in twenty minutes to a half hour," said Debbie Dhayer, daughter of Eddie, the late founder, and one of the pillars of the family-owned empire.

Eddie and Louise Stotler parlayed a roadside gas station into a tire business in 1951. When word was out that Eddie was coming in from a factory run with tires to sell, folks would gather and wait. Almost fifty years and millions of tires later, Eddie's continues to keep the rubber on the road.

GANGS OF SHOPS

Two meticulously restored turn-of-the-century woolen mills in Martinsburg are painted white and sport exposed brick and pipes and highly polished old wood floors. Parking is easy at **Blue Ridge Outlet Center**, where manufacturers' outlets rival the buildings in attracting shoppers. Working women make pilgrimages to Blue Ridge for bargain name-brand hosiery and power clothes.

The **Charleston Town Center Mall** boasts a three-story waterfall, a jungle of greenery, 160 shops and a third floor filled with food stalls. It was America's largest urban mall when built in 1983, and remains the bustling heart of Charleston's downtown shopping.

Sprawled along I-64, the **Huntington Mall** in Ona is West Virginia's biggest mall.

Old Central City in Huntington is focused on West Fourteenth Street. At an average of five antique shops per block, the exhaustive collection numbers more than twenty locations. If your shopping demon wants more, there's a Big Lots nearby.

More than fifty addresses are listed in a handbill for Hurricane's **Citywide Garage Sales** in August. Everyone participates. Also check out Charleston's historic district's **East End Yard Sale**, held annually in May.

Mountain Heritage Arts & Crafts happens twice a year — in mid June and late September — on hundreds of acres of Sam Michael Park outside Harpers Ferry. Nearly 200 artisans are invited to participate, making it one of the top twenty fine arts and craft shows in America. Treasure hunting is enhanced by the presence of the makers. Over the years my personal finds have ranged from a hand-carved bone star pendant and one-of-a-kind pine needle baskets to Wild Woman pins that started a mini-craze in the state.

See "Truly Incredible" for information on Tamarack and the Gendarme Store.

!!!
CHAPTER THIRTEEN

SUPERLATIVES

For a state that perennially turns up at the bottom of lists measuring some sort of economic progress or another, West Virginia also manages to have a number of firsts, biggests and bests to its credit.

BEST BRIDGE

Opened for traffic in 1977, the **New River Bridge** on US 19 is the world's longest single arch steel bridge. Its main span is 1,700 feet long and the total length is 3,030 feet. Suspended 876 feet above the New River, it is the highest bridge east of the Mississippi; second highest in the United States. It is also the site of one of the world's most unique events — Bridge Day, when hundreds come to jump off the span while thousands of others line up to watch. For more on Bridge Day, *see* "Far-Out Festivals."

COASTERS AND CORN DOGS

Camden Park is a stop on the pilgrimage of roller coaster devotees, prized for its two historic wooden coasters. The "Little Dipper" is the only kiddie coaster made of wood still operating in the United States. The younger "Big Dipper" is another classic wooden coaster, ranked in coasterdom's top 100 and included in the American Coaster Enthusiasts Hall of Fame. The classic carousel was the first ride in the park, and has kept spinning since it debuted in 1907.

Camden Park was built at an exchange point on the trolley line with an eye toward boosting streetcar traffic from Huntington. At one time there were prizefights, cockfights and hot air balloon ascensions at the twenty-six acre amusement park which has not missed a summer since it opened in 1903. Today, there are still more than thrilling rides. The park's Pronto Pups are rated by many as the world's best corn dogs, and Camden Park may be the only amusement park with an authentic Indian Mound. Bargain prices are the icing on the cake of West Virginia's sole remaining amusement park.

GOLF HERE FIRST

Russell Montague had a private estate named Oakhurst just down the road from the Greenbrier. In 1884, he added six holes of golf and formed **the first golf club in America** for his rich and fancy friends. The course has been revived and now operates as **Oakhurst Links**, with fairways mowed by grazing sheep. The course is played with replica equipment from St. Andrews, Scotland.

Star-studded golf made its way to the **Greenbrier** by 1913 and President Woodrow Wilson was one of the first to tee-off. He played there often, and other luminaries followed in his trail, including the Duke of Windsor both before and after his abdication as Edward VIII of England. The Greenbrier was one of Dwight D. Eisenhower's favorite golf retreats and JFK's sister, Pat Kennedy, won an amateur tournament there.

Sam Snead began and ended his remarkable career as the Greenbrier's pro, and he and Ben Hogan held repeated match-ups at the course during the 1950s when both were in their prime. In 1957, Snead played the most competitive round of golf in history at the Greenbrier, a feat commemorated in the resort's Sam Snead Museum. Bing Crosby also played there, and Bob Hope shot his best round of golf at the Greenbrier.

Today, Greenbrier guests may choose from three championship golf courses.

GLASS CHAMPS

The **world's largest punchbowl** is in fact the world's largest surviving piece of cut lead crystal and it is no sideshow oddity. The punchbowl stands four feet, ten inches tall, weighs 225 pounds, and holds sixteen gallons of liquid. Lit for dramatic impact by Oglebay Institute's theater designer, it is front and center at Oglebay's Glass Museum. Point and shoot and the story unfolds.

The bowl was called a vase by its designer, Thomas Sweeney, of the noted Sweeney Glass Company. The bowl was made in 1844 by Thomas and his brother Michael. A smaller version, made for Henry Clay, was broken in 1916 and the pieces lost in a 1930 house fire. The Sweeney punchbowl disappeared during a family squabble and did not turn up until 1875, when Thomas found it encased in granite pillars at his brother's grave with an inscription claiming that the bowl was made by Michael alone. It was finally removed from the grave site in 1949 to protect it from vandalism.

There are five pieces to the original punchbowl. In the glass shop above the museum, twelve inch models with removable lids are made for sale by Fenton Glass.

"Run for the Roses" is the **largest cameo glass vase** ever created, and it was made by Pilgrim Glass. Cameo glass is a process of hand carving many layers of different color glass, creating rare patterns. Pilgrim is the only manufacturer in the world to use the process. The record-breaking vase is more than six feet tall and is for sale at Pilgrim's collectors shop for only $10,800.

West Virginia was once the #1 glass producer in America, with its home-turf advantages of white silica sand, limestone and natural gas. Two manufacturing processes invented in Wheeling revolutionized glass making and contributed to the state's ascendancy. William Layton added bicarbonate of soda to the mix of sand in 1864 and Michael Owens invented the bottle-making machine in 1904.

BEST PEOPLE MOVER

Safe, convenient, unique and cute — especially now that the tiny cars are painted in West Virginia University's flashy blue and yellow colors – Morgantown's **Personal Rapid Transit System** is a world champ. In 1997, the New England Electric Railway journal rated the twenty-three-year old system the best overall people mover, beating out Disney World's famed monorail.

Morgantown's PRTS is the first totally automated, computer-operated transportation system in the world. It was formulated in the early 1970s as a joint project of the U.S. Department of Transportation and West Virginia University to solve Morgantown's gridlock, the worst traffic in the state. It was also to serve as a transportation research lab.

The PRTS moves about two million people a year, more than the entire population of West Virginia. Since nightmare traffic remains the most distinguishing characteristic of the state's premier college town, I can only assume that without the PRTS we would be discovering fossilized remains of the Class of '79 still stuck in their cars along University Avenue.

The computer controlled system of mini-cars created by Boeing travels 8.7 miles on elevated guideways. A rider inserts 50¢, pushes a button for one of five stops, and boards a driver-less, electric vehicle that travels up to 30 mph. (WVU students can purchase a "swipe card" with a magnetic strip,  good for unlimited travel during a semester.) A non-stop trip from one end to the other takes not quite twelve minutes.

With a fail-safe system that makes the worst-case scenario being a little late, the PRTS has moved more than fifty million people without an accident since it began regular passenger traffic in 1979. The gravest danger is getting run over, and fences have prevented that to date. Using the PRTS doesn't require much thought and works even with notoriously partying college students like those at WVU. It is demand driven, like an elevator on horizontal tracks. Pay the fare. Push a button. A mini-car appears. Push another button. Tell it where to go.

A standard control room complete with flashing lights, multiple monitors and two-way communication with each of seventy-two cars can manually assign vehicles, maintain a circulation pattern, or set up a schedule as they do during football games. The cars get turned off at night, although individual ones can be sent out at any time. In the morning, the control room gets to wake them all up and send them on their way. A master switch can shut down the entire system, a catastrophic response used only three or four times in twenty years.

As successful as PRTS has been, it has not caught on. It remains one of the few in operation, still ahead of its time. Computer technology has changed dramatically since PRTS was conceived. Mostly off-the-shelf components even then, the fourteen large computers that run the system could be replaced today by six to eight PCs. It's the software that's the problem. The original coding required twenty-three man-years to do and is still in use. They call it "antique hi-tech" around the PRTS control room.

Construction costs in the mid-70s were $120 million. The system is mostly above ground with a few underpasses and off-line stations so traffic does not have to stop. The cars are worth about $200,000 each and have air conditioning or heat as needed. Although there are sanctioned cramming contests during Mountaineer Week, the cars are programmed to shut down if the weight limit is surpassed. Even empty they clear only one inch. Built to hold eight, the record cram is more than a hundred.

There's other neat technology at work in Morgantown. Next door to the PRTS main terminal is a steam plant where **Ciminelli Services Corporation** burns an old slag pile from Preston County, providing the university with electricity and selling extra to the grid.

HOLIDAYS INVENTED HERE

In 1868, Julia Pierpont initiated **Memorial Day** in Fairmont as a means of honoring the Civil War dead.

Forty years later, Anna Jarvis fulfilled her mother's wish for a day to be set aside to honor all mothers and daughters with a public celebration on May 10, 1908, the anniversary of her mother's death. The ceremony was held at Andrew's Methodist Church in Grafton, where Mrs. Jarvis taught Sunday school and **Mother's Day** was introduced to the world. By 1914 it was a national holiday, and today it's the day when more greeting cards are sold and more people eat out than any other. In 1962, the **International Mother's Day Shrine** was erected at the church. Each Mother's Day, special services are held there at 2:30 pm.

The mother-daughter devotion that inspired Mother's Day shines in almost identical faces staring from portraits of the two at the **Anna Jarvis Birthplace House**. Once used as headquarters by General McClellan, the wooden house is now a museum, with Mother's Day festivities and renovation-naming opportunities honoring individual mothers.

Fathers were not forgotten. In 1909, the first **Father's Day** celebration was held in Fairmont.

FAR OUT FIRSTS!

★ **The first motorized plow** was built in Charleston in 1915 from a push plow and Indian motorcycle parts by Benjamin Franklin Gravely. A photographer by trade, Gravely needed to raise food for his family, so he tinkered with garden implements. Local legend claims that Gravely was actually inventing a post hole digger that ran away from him and plowed a furrow in the garden. Eureka! Gravely International remains a major manufacturer of garden implements.

★ The small town of Beverly claims the **first public cemetery west of the Alleghenies** with burials dating from 1768. Soldiers from every American war short of the 1991 Gulf War are buried there.

★ The **first brick paved street** in the United States was done in 1872 by John Hale, a Charleston businessman, at his own expense. Fellow West Virginian, John Porter, had recently perfected the vitrified brick that allowed Capitol Street this singular honor.

★ Arthurdale became the **first resettlement community of the Federal Homestead Act** in 1933 with 165 houses built on 2,400 acres. It was a favorite project of Eleanor Roosevelt. Tours of the community today point out examples of the original structures that remain. Federal funding ran out in the early 1940s, and all are now private homes. Littlepage Terrace and Washington Manor were the **first low-income housing project application**. The buildings still provide housing in Charleston.

★ The notion of delivering mail directly to rural homes occurred to William Wilson, Postmaster General of the United States in 1896. He chose his hometown of Charles Town to launch **the first RFD**, rural free delivery. The Charles Town Post Office is still open for business.

★ Marlinton in 1747 became the **first recorded settlement** west of the Alleghenies.

★ We were mystified. What was an indoor archery range? We stopped at the Corner Mart in Baker on the way to Lost River and "Buster" enlightened us. His was the **first indoor archery range** in the state.

The video disk system set up in a narrow seventy-foot long hall projects nearly 1,800 different wildlife scenes with sound effects onto a screen. The shooter uses a compound bow for speed and accuracy. When the blunt-tipped arrow hits the screen, the picture freezes and a red spot appears to mark the hit and define the kill zone. Even more intriguing is the evidence of "Buster's" real-life prowess. The walls outside the range are hung with an array of mounted game heads, all bagged with a bow.

★ Like George Washington, Thomas "Stonewall" Jackson was everywhere in the state. Born in Clarksburg, he grew up near Weston with his grandfather, who planned the town. As a military professor at Virginia Military Institute, he chose the South and took his cadets to war. Tall, awkward and badly dressed, Jackson was not a romantic general in the vein of Robert E. Lee. He was, however, one of the figures who modernized warfare with his tactical brilliance and battlefield innovations. Wounded by his own troops, Jackson died in 1863. In 1920, Stonewall Jackson's farm in Weston became the **first state 4-H camp in the United States.**

★ Salt making was a prehistoric industry along the Kanawha and Little Kanawha rivers. Indians would boil the brine from salt springs along the rivers to evaporate the salt. Kanawha "red salt," its color derived from iron impurities, was treasured for curing meats and making butter. At the turn of the nineteenth century, the Kanawha Valley was the largest salt production area in the country and in 1817 spawned the country's first trust — the **Kanawha Salt Trust**.

★ The need to power salt furnaces instigated the **first commercial use of natural gas** as fuel at Burning Springs in 1841.

★ When eighteen-year-old George Washington arrived in 1750 with his older brother Lawrence in tow to "take the waters at Bath, " there was already a well established spa society during the summer season around the famous warm springs later known as Berkeley. Today's Berkeley Springs is **the country's first spa**.

★ The **first National Recreation Area** so designated by the U.S. Forest Service was the 100,000 acre Spruce Knob-Seneca Rocks NRA in 1965. It includes both the highest point in West Virginia and the only true rock pinnacle summit east of Devil's Tower, Wyoming.

★ The world's **first golden trout** emerged in the 1950s from the state fish hatchery in Petersburg. From August through October the nature show features the trout in stages from spawning to hatchling to ready-for-the-streams.

BIGGEST! HIGHEST! LONGEST!

★ Mountains ring the fourteen-mile long Canaan Valley; at 3200 feet, it's the **highest valley east of the Mississippi**. With a climate that mimics northern New England and guarantees 150 - 200 inches of snow a season, Canaan Valley is prime ski country. It is also an unusual and fragile Arctic ecology, with the second largest inland wetlands in the United States. Nearby Davis is the **highest incorporated town east of the Mississippi**.

★ Droop Mountain is the site of the **largest Civil War conflict in West Virginia**. Union victory here in 1863 secured most of the state for the duration of the war at a cost of nearly 600 casualties. While the park was under construction by Civilian Conservation Corps members in 1935, workers were unnerved by forests of dead chestnuts and sink holes filled with bodies.

★ The **State Capitol** in Charleston was completed in 1932 after two earlier ones burned in less than a decade. It was designed by the noted architect, Cass Gilbert, and built with a dome taller than the U.S. Capitol and larger than any other state's. In a rash of flagrant display, the 292-foot high lead dome was coated first with copper, and then gold leafed. It keeps flaking off and requires regular replacement. A two-ton chandelier of more than ten thousand pieces of Czech crystal hangs in the dome's Rotunda, reached by climbing 48 steps, one for each state at the time of construction.

• The Greenbrier River is the **longest free-flowing river** in the eastern United States as it flows south from its birthplace along the Continental Divide in Pocahontas County into the New River at Hinton. Fish species unique to the New River watershed make for one-of-a-kind fishing.

Running along much of the river is the seventy-six mile Greenbrier River Trail for hikers, bikers, horseback riders and cross-country skiers. It is considered among the top ten hiking trails in the United States. *See* "Adventure Driving" for more.

• The **world's largest sycamore tree** is on Back Fork Trail one mile east of Webster Springs. The **largest hemlock** east of the Mississippi is in Cathedral State Forest. Named Centennial, it is more than 120 feet tall and is estimated at nearly 500 years old.

• The State Museum in Charleston boasts the **largest male moth** in captivity, captured near Wheeling in 1940.

• Plopped into an intersection just north of downtown Chester, the **world's largest teapot** announces that fact, making it an ideal photo opportunity.

• Wheeling is filled with big things. La Belle is the **largest cut nail plant** in the world. Wheeling Island is second only to Manhattan as the **most heavily populated inland river island** in the United States. Largest of the Ohio River islands, it has 5,000 people, greyhound racing at Wheeling Downs and a wildlife refuge on its point. The incredible Oglebay Resort with panoramic views of its more than 1,500 acres, two 18-hole golf courses, lakes and a 65-acre zoo is the **world's largest municipal park**. More than a million people visit Oglebay's winter long "Festival of the Lights", making it the state's most visited attraction.

★ The **largest cast-iron overshot waterwheel** in the world is located at Thomas Shepherd's gristmill, constructed in Shepherdstown in 1763. The forty foot waterwheel dates to 1891, and can be seen from Mill Street along with the waterfalls of Town Run, a tributary of the Potomac. The mill is privately owned.

★ The **world's longest ribbon stalactite** hangs from the ceiling of Smoke Hole Caverns and weighs six tons. Nearby are unusual side-growing helectites and the second highest ceiling of any eastern cavern — 274 feet. The caverns have always been popular, used by Seneca Indians to smoke meat, by Civil War soldiers to store ammunition, and by moonshiners who appreciated both the abundant supply of spring water and the single entrance cavern. Visitors on guided tours, given every half hour, can watch formations taking shape drop by drop in this still-active cave.

★ Contemporary weddings are held in Seneca Cavern's Grand Ballroom, the **second largest cavern room** in the world.

★ Weirton Steel became the **largest employee-owned plant** in the United States in 1982. It stretches for miles between SR 2 and the Ohio River.

Dam Dams

When huge **Summersville Dam** was built in the mid 1960s by the Army Corps of Engineers, they faced a serious dilemma. Usually the Corps names a dam after the nearest post office. They chose to break tradition and forgo having Gad Dam.

Summersville Dam is 390 feet high and the **second largest rock-fill dam** in the east. It has more than paid its $48 million price tag through the white water epiphany caused when water is released via its twenty-nine-foot wide tunnels. *See* "Fast Living".

The Army Corps of Engineers built its **first concrete-faced dam** at R.D. Bailey Lake on the Guyandotte River. The unusual rock-filled structure is a quarter of a mile across and 310 feet high   the second highest in the state. Perched above the 630-acre lake the dam created, the visitors center provides great views.

Tygart Dam in Grafton is the **oldest and largest concrete dam** east of the Mississippi. Tours are given on Wednesdays in the summer.

It is the Oldest

★ Sitting inside the tiny log building with rough benches and a balcony along two sides, it is easy to imagine Francis Asbury, America's first Methodist bishop, standing on the raised platform and dedicating the space in 1786. **Rehobeth Church and Museum** is the **oldest**

church building in existence west of the Alleghenies. Surrounded by an 18th century cemetery, it is one of ten dedicated Methodist shrines in America.

★ Not far away is the oldest church building in continuous use west of the Alleghenies, the imposing **Old Stone Presbyterian Church** in Lewisburg. The two story native limestone building was constructed in 1796 for a congregation organized in 1783. Tradition claims that women of the congregation carried sand for the building on horseback from the Greenbrier River. The church has an old slave gallery and cemetery.

★ Built in 1770, the **Graham House** between Hinton and Alderson is the **oldest log home** on its original site in West Virginia.

★ Stretching far back into the mists of time, archeological digs have confirmed **St. Albans** as the **oldest continuously inhabited location** in both Americas.

★ **Marsh Wheeling Stogies** have been manufactured since 1840, making the company the **oldest American cigar manufacturer** still operating under its original name in the city where it was founded. Mifflin Marsh started the business by selling his thin, hand-rolled cigars from a basket — four for a penny. By 1879, Wheeling was teeming with nearly a hundred stogie factories complete with "readers" to entertain the workers while they rolled.

JUST PLAIN SPECIAL

★ The only **World War I monument to Black American soldiers** stands in Kimball in McDowell County.

★ Larger than life stone columns, arches and triangles in a play area cut into the hillside earn **Ritter Park** acclaim as **one of the ten best playgrounds** in the United States. The seventy-acre municipal park in Huntington also has a nationally recognized rose garden of more than 1500 bushes.

★ America's **largest indigenous Christian denomination** — Disciples of Christ — developed and thrived in **Bethany** through the Campbell

family. They founded Bethany College, built the historically significant Alexander Campbell Mansion, and lie in state surrounded by spectacular hand-hewn stone block walls (shown above). Today's Bethany is dominated by an early example of American collegiate Gothic architecture — the Old Main with its distinctive bell tower. The tiny town nestled on the campus outskirts is nearly free of recognizable development and modern intrusions.

★ National fraternity **Delta Tau Delta** started at Bethany College.

★ NASA's **Classroom of the Future** is located in the Challenger Learning Center at Wheeling Jesuit College.

★ Bluefield's **Shamrock**, opened in a century-old building in 1964, is a gay and lesbian bar in business at the same spot longer than any in the United States. Helen Compton, the great-grandmother who runs Shamrock, has been honored by gay organizations for her caring and dedication. Located on the main thoroughfare, the Shamrock is known primarily through word-of-mouth. The drag queen Miss Shamrock Pageant brings lots of folks to this neighborhood place on the first weekend in November.

There are other superlatives scattered in other chapters throughout the book. Here are a few of the cross-references to check:

★ *See* "Amazing Architecture" for the Weston State Asylum — largest hand-cut stone building in the United States.

★ *See* "Amazing Architecture" for Our Lady of the Pines — smallest church in United States.

★ *See* "Amazing Architecture" for Camp Washington Carver — 1st African-American 4-H camp in the United States.

★ *See* "Historic Oddities" for more on Indian mounds such as the largest conical earthen mound of its kind — Grave Creek in Moundsville.

★ *See* "Mother Nature's Wonders" for first Grimes golden and first golden delicious apple trees discovered.

★ *See* "Mother Nature's Wonders" for the world's oldest river — the New!

★ *See* "Mother Nature's Wonders" for more on the world's highest coal seam — the Pocahontas Coal Field.

CHAPTER FOURTEEN

THINGS THAT USED TO BE THERE

The importance of things that are no longer is underlined in West Virginia by the commonplace method of giving directions: "turn at the corner where _____ used to be." It happens all the time.

Some of these important, or infamous, buildings, businesses and historic marvels still offer sights to see, others are relegated to photographs or drawings. All play a part in the fabric of life — past, present and future — that is West Virginia. These are a small sample.

MYSTERY HOLE

Since the early '70s, the **Mystery Hole** has been the paramount eccentricity for many visitors. The tiny roadside gift shop covered with signs encouraging you to come in has a gorilla mounted on top and a pre-revival VW bug smashed into its side. On the other side, stairs lead you down into the main attraction — the Mystery Hole. For those who ventured into the narrow hallway lined with fun house mirrors and weird posters, the dollar admission bought creator Don Wilson's tour hustle, a tilted room and berserk gravity tricks. It was virtual reality before the concept was invented, liberally mixed with hillbilly taste and humor.

The gift shop, rated ultimate on the trashy scale, was open to everyone whether they paid for the tour or not.

The Mystery Hole still hugs the side of US 60 just west of Hawks Nest State Park but its life force is gone. Don Wilson, visionary founder and tour guide extraordinaire, died in early 1998 and his twenty-five year creation awaits its fate (re-opened May 1999).

SPRINGS SOCIETY

For more than a century, society took their leisure while they took the waters at a string of resorts that lined the edge of the Blue Ridge. The spas' shared cycles of prosperity and decline were caused by common factors. Blue Ridge spas flourished in the first half of the nineteenth century when they were all in Virginia. The Civil War dealt spa society a disastrous blow and divided the circuit into Virginia and West Virginia. The railroads brought another burst of activity from the 1870s through the early part of the twentieth century. Only three in West Virginia survived the fire, flood and economic bad times to flourish today — Berkeley Springs, Capon Springs and the Greenbrier, and only the latter continues in the grand tradition. All that remain of the others are waters and ruins. *See* the springs tour in "Adventure Driving."

The red brick and white columned splendor of the **Sweet Springs Hotel** — built in 1833 and based on an earlier design by Thomas Jefferson — sits empty and unused, patiently waiting for wise restoration. Three two-story brick guest houses, also from Jefferson's design, remain in varying degrees of disrepair. A long row of chinking-less log lodging rooms with stone fireplaces that resemble a nineteenth century motel are, in fact, remnants of slave and servant quarters. The first hotel built on the spot in 1792 is long gone.

Sweet Springs had notable guests and presidential visitors, from George Washington to Franklin Pierce. The Civil War knocked Sweet Springs from its pinnacle, although the railroad filled the resort with thousands of guests in the 1870s. West Virginia bought the property in 1945, using it successively as a tuberculosis sanitarium and, most recently, a home for the aged.

The exotic bath building, across the lawn from the hotel, would clean up well. All brick, there is a central open air pool where active springs can be seen bubbling. Historically the springs were famous for their acidic briskness and cures for rheumatism and nerve disorders. Today, water from the springs is bottled and sold. It has won repeatedly at the Berkeley Springs International Water Tasting.

Capon Springs originally was a splendid pre-Civil War mountain spa and a favorite part of the summer springs tour. Today, Capon Springs is a pre-World War II family resort, with just a tinge of its illustrious antebellum heritage. When built in 1849, the four-story Mountain House with its long colonnade was one of the largest structures in the South. Its oval outdoor swimming pool was the largest in Virginia. Mountain House burned in 1911; the pool still serves today.

Contemporary Capon Springs has nearly a dozen white Victorian buildings and a comfortable main hotel. It is arranged as a nineteenth century resort village on both sides of a main thoroughfare. The hot, cold and steam bath houses are now residential. Virtually in ruins during the 1920s, today's resort is a registered historic district. For more on Capon Springs, *see* "Unusual Places to Stay."

Nothing remains of the century-old spa that once was a large summer resort with a grand hotel. More than 3,000 acres of the land is now Lost River State Park, and the whitewashed log cabin of original owner Light Horse Harry Lee is a museum. Across the stream, the noted sulphuric spring is captive under glass in a pavilion labeled with the name given it in the 1890s — **Lee White Sulphur Springs**.

Lee, the father of Robert E. Lee, acquired thousands of acres of land and the sulphur springs in 1796 as spoils of war. It was land a young George Washington had surveyed as part of the original Fairfax Grant.

In about 1800, Lee built a boarding house and a white oak cabin on a stone foundation. Later, he reportedly built a large log hotel. The family continued to use the hotel as a resort until the Civil War. The springs and hotel became a commercial resort after the war. The resort was expanded in the 1890s, but destroyed by fire in 1910.

Turn-of-the-century accounts of the water claim it is cooler and medicinally superior to the Greenbrier's sulphur springs. The springs were used in the classic fashion — to relieve the discomfort of excess.

There are three different springs along Indian Creek where once stood the grand resort of **Salt Sulphur Springs**: sweet, salt and sulphur. Thousands came to "take the waters" for brain diseases including headache and mania. The original stone hotel built in 1820 still stands, along with several other stone buildings built at the same time. Now a private home, it is the largest pre-Civil War stone building complex in the state. Gone are the seventy-two room Erskine House on the ridge, brick cottages and legions of guests that continued until the resort finally closed in 1936. Salt Sulphur Springs is located near the town of Union.

Shannondale Springs was founded as an estate on a horseshoe peninsula of the Shenandoah River in the Eastern Panhandle by Lord Summerfield. Summerfield had reportedly fled to America because of a scrape he had gotten into on the Continent. Popular in the first half of the nineteenth century as a haunt of presidents and old world aristocracy, Shannondale claims to have been the unofficial summer White House of Presidents Hayes, Garfield and Arthur. By the early twentieth century, fire and decay had destroyed the large brick hotel and surrounding cottages. There are plans to preserve the sole remaining intact bath house and springs before they are swallowed by development.

HOTELS AND BATHHOUSES IN BERKELEY SPRINGS

A grand 400 room hotel was built by Colonel John Strother between 1845 and 1848 on the south end of the park surrounding the famed warm springs. Strother was replacing an earlier hotel on that spot destroyed by fire in 1844. The hotel was the centerpiece of a golden age for the historic springs and called successively the Pavilion, Strother and finally **Berkeley Springs Hotel**. Strother's noted son, author and illustrator David Hunter Strother – aka Porte Crayon — grew up at the hotel and later operated it. Among the hotel's most memorable guests were the men and horses of Stonewall Jackson's army, who trashed the place when they bivouacked there in 1861. David Hunter Strother had chosen to side with the North.

The Berkeley Springs Hotel was famous for its lavish entertainment and end-of-season balls during another golden age following the Civil War. Those who enjoyed the German musicians in 1898 did not know it would be the last season. The great hotel burned in 1898; its rival the Fairfax Inn succumbed to fire three years later and the town went into decline.

The covered bathhouses of Berkeley Springs, the country's first spa, have also come and gone in successive waves. Grand Victorian baths built in 1888, designed by local inventor Henry Harrison Hunter, were torn down for an outdoor swimming pool in the late 1940s. Two original bath buildings from 1784 and 1815 remain in use at Berkeley Springs State Park. The traditional spot for the grand hotel is occupied by **The Country Inn** built in 1933.

For more photographs and information on the historic springs, *see* "Great Plumbing" and "Historic Oddities."

COAL AND RAILROADS LEFT THEIR MARK

Over 500 small company towns in the southern coal fields did not exist until some railroaders and industrialists in the 1880s brought coal mining to the hills of southern West Virginia. Once the coal was gone, company stores, churches, miners' homes and coal tipples vanished too, leaving ghostly remnants and deserted town sites for hikers and rafters to contemplate.

There are many structures still standing at the huge Kaymoor coal mine which operated from 1899 to 1962. It's not much more than a mile hike to the mine site from the **Kaymoor Trail** head in the New River Gorge.

The town of **Watoga** along the Greenbrier railroad is also gone. Now all that remains of Watoga are a few foundation stones and a bank safe, located along the Greenbrier River Trail eight miles south of Marlinton.

The town of **Thurmond** had no main street. It was created as a steam railroad town in 1873 and the buildings of the business district opened directly onto the tracks. It was a booming place, called by some the Dodge City of the East. More than fifteen passenger trains a day with a 100,000 passengers came to Thurmond in 1916 — more than Richmond and Cincinnati combined.

Across the New River in **Southside**, Thurmond's founder — Thomas McKell — built the fabulous hundred room **Dun Glen Hotel**, home of a legendary fourteen-year poker game. Fire destroyed the hotel in 1931, and the coming of diesel locomotives lessened the demand for coal and water along the route.

Today, the National Park Service displays historic exhibits in the restored **Thurmond Train Station,** which also serves as an Amtrak stop. Ruins of four buildings that were once Main Street await restoration. One of these buildings used to house "Mrs. McLure's Restaurant", world famous for her free dinners to servicemen passing through on troop trains during World War II. The privately-owned Thurmond Supply Company is active in the former post office and sells more root beer than coke to hikers and visitors who venture along the narrow road. The state's smallest incorporated town, today's Thurmond stood-in for the town of **Matewan** in the John Sayles' film of that name.

The coal barons and railroad men who made their fortune off the abundant Pocahontas coalfield decided to create a haven for themselves in a tiny town they called **Bramwell**. Once considered the richest small town in America, Bramwell was home to fourteen millionaires and had three trains a day to Manhattan. The millionaires built opulent mansions for their families and smaller mansions for the coal company physicians on Doctors Row. Extravagant details among the various mansions include a green-toned copper roof and indoor swimming pool, stonework by Italian masters, carved mahogany panels, walls of hand-tooled leather and ebony porch floors.

A quiet town today of historic mansions, brick streets, and the meandering Bluestone River, only the **Corner Shop** remains of the business district. It has more than sixty feet of century-old wood and glass display cases along the wall; ice cream sodas served from an original fountain cost a buck and a quarter. There are regular house tours of Bramwell, and several mansions now operate as B&Bs.

At the turn of the twentieth century, West Virginia's more than 3,000 miles of logging railroads topped all other states. All that remains of **Cass**, a log boomtown developed by lumber interests in 1899, are eleven miles of restored tracks, a few restored buildings, sawmill ruins, an old engine graveyard and big log-hauling locomotives. The state has owned and developed Cass as a historic attraction and train excursion since the early 1960s, when the paper mill closed. For more on the Cass Railroad Excursion, *see* "Tour and Trips."

LAST OF THEIR KIND

Once there were countless ferries crossing the Ohio River from Pennsylvania to Kentucky. Today only one remains. The **Sistersville Ferry**, established in 1817, is now owned by the city. It plies its way back and forth across the river whenever a car or rider appears on the dock between 7 am and 5 pm daily from April through Christmas. The tiny red, diesel-fueled paddle boat holds four cars and has a seating deck. More authentic and less expensive than a carnival ride, the five-minute crossing costs pedestrian riders only 50¢. If you're really lucky, Bib Harmon — who boasts fifty years piloting on the river — will let you hang out in the wheelhouse. Although the Ohio destination has a name — Fry — it's the skyline of Sistersville that draws the eye, with its commemorative oil rig and fine Methodist church tower.

The earliest history of the region was connected to the French and Indian wars of the mid-eighteenth century. During this time, Governor Dinwiddie authorized a chain of forts to protect the western Virginia frontier. George Washington was the young officer entrusted with the task. Today, only **Fort Ashby** remains of Washington's twenty-three wooden palisade forts. Built in 1755, the tiny log fort was restored in 1939, and provides a main attraction in downtown Fort Ashby.

EARLY INDUSTRY

Three notable furnaces are remnants of West Virginia's early 19th century iron industry.

The **Peter Tarr Iron Furnace** in Weirton produced cannonballs in the 1800s, including those used by Commodore Perry in his battles on Lake Erie in the War of 1812. Built in 1794, Tarr was the first blast furnace west of the Alleghenies. It was restored in 1968.

A thirty-foot stone structure is all that remains of the **Henry Clay Iron Furnace**. Once surrounded by a community of log houses, a school and company store, the furnace was built in 1834 to 1836; it operated until 1847. Today's ruins are an attraction of the scenic trail in Coopers Rock State Park.

The **Bloomery Iron Furnace** operated from 1833 to 1881, floating its iron on rafts and flatboats down the Cacapon River to the Potomac. It can be seen in a tiny roadside park near Romney.

Virginius Island in the Shenandoah River at Harpers Ferry was an industrial powerhouse during the nineteenth century, with Hall's Rifle Works and other water-powered factories located along its shores. Along the Potomac on the other side of Harpers Ferry stood the twenty building complex of the U.S. Armory. The Civil War destroyed many of the

industries, while later floods finished off the rest. Today, the pictur-esque ruins shown above are part of hiking and picnicking on Virginius Island.

All phases of Harpers Ferry's long social and industrial history are cap-tured in today's National Historic Park and the thriving tiny town. *See* "Amazing Architecture" and "Historic Oddities" for more on Harpers Ferry.

During World War II, explosives were made in **Point Pleasant** and stored in grass-covered concrete domes. After the war, the explosives were reportedly removed and the domes were given or sold to local government and area chemical companies. Today, they are part of a wildlife station, grown-over with brush and trees.

The rows of concrete igloos captured the imagination of John Keel who reported on UFO and Mothman sightings in what he called "the **TNT area**." Keel further reports that the U.S. Government admitted to storing atomic waste material in the concrete domes. For more on UFOs, *see* "Remarkable Collections."

AMUSEMENTS OF ANOTHER TIME

Three major amusement parks have vanished completely, leaving only Huntington's Camden Park still entertaining visitors.

Preston County's popular **Oak Park** amusements operated from 1905 through the 1930s. Serviced by train, the park was popular for its public promenade, sixty-five foot long polished wooden slide, ferris wheel, merry-go-round, and roller coaster.

Charleston's version — **Luna Park** — was destroyed by fire in 1923.

The granddaddy of them all was **Island Park** in the Potomac River at Harpers Ferry. Built in 1879 by the B&O Railroad, visitors would arrive by train, then cross to the island on a long footbridge just below Hilltop House. A series of devastating floods finally washed away all traces of the park.

E x t i n c t

Bones in Greenbrier County caves demonstrate that woolly mammoths, saber-toothed cats, and giant cave bears called West Virginia home 12,000 years ago. More recently extinct are the once huge herds of buffalo and elk. The last bison were seen in 1825; the elk were gone by 1843.

Mountainsides of giant chestnuts were wiped out by blight in the first part of the twentieth century, remaining only in buildings that used their corpses. Old fenceposts and building materials of chestnut are frequently "recycled" by woodworkers into furniture because of the rarity of the wood.

In 1938, the giant **Mingo Oak** died and was cut down. Ring counters assert that it was 582 years old, the oldest living thing in the state. The 146-foot white oak giant produced 15,000 feet of lumber.

A road marker at an overlook is all that remains of the **Pringle Sycamore** down on Turkey Run. A sprout from the original tree root marks the spot. This giant among the giant sycamores that once populated the state hid the two Pringle brothers from the Indians in an eleven-foot-wide room in the trunk cavity from 1764 to 1767.

CHAPTER FIFTEEN

TOURS AND TRIPS NOT TO MISS

A surprising variety of organized excursions are offered in West Virginia, from industrial tours to train rides. Always worth trying are the numerous quirky local tours — some self-guided — about unique local treasures.

TOURING THE PEN

There is something endearing about exploiting the true soul of a place, even when the soul is as sinister and macabre as **Moundsville** prison's must be.

The **West Virginia Penitentiary tour** is authentic. The horrifying innards of the infamous prison have not been cleaned up and improved by the new occupants — the Moundsville Economic Development Council (MEDC). If anything, the wholesale dismantling of mechanical systems and hardware by the departing correctional authorities makes the graffiti-decorated environment even more bleak. Only the emotional pain is missing from the place inmates called "Blood Alley." However, the tour guides — several of them former guards — add that missing element by recounting day-to-day prison horrors and gory details of past executions like beheadings and hangings. They also point out that serial killer Charles Manson was born just up the road in McMechen.

Once a prison official told me that the worst part of prison was the loss of freedom and that it would be awful even in a hotel. A great theory, but time in a Hilton sounds lots better than time in "the Alamo", the maximum cell block of the maximum security facility and the bottom level in the grotesque stone and steel hell of Moundsville.

The prison was built in 1866 to house the state's most dangerous felons. It was the second public building of the new state of West Virginia. The first was another stone dungeon — Weston's Hospital for the Insane. Moundsville's forbidding block-long Gothic structure was built by convict labor of hand-cut gray sandstone quarried at Grafton and Wheeling. It was located directly across from the Grave Creek Mound on what was then the edge of town. Five acres were captured inside stone walls four feet thick at the base, sunk six feet into the ground, and climbing twenty-four feet in the air. Four towers, parapets and a walkway completed the medieval architecture. It was used for almost 130 years, and is now on the National Historic Register.

Since it costs nearly $2 million annually to heat the place, today's penitentiary tours are often conducted through an unheated building. Sliding along narrow corridors and moving into closed cells scarcely big enough to turn around, it's almost impossible to imagine that the last inmates left this prison as recently as 1995. According to the guide, 2,700 men under the control of 300 guards once crammed the place.

A puff of steam announces hydraulic doors opening and closing as bus tours are herded through the facility, after being fingerprinted and photographed. Being treated like inmates is part of the experience. The tours are the brainchild of Phil Remke, director of MEDC.

One of the final stops is the prison gift shop, where visitors can buy tin cups, handcuffs and prison caps while examining the electric chair. West Virginia couldn't afford to buy an electric chair, so prison officials took two inmates to Ohio to inspect theirs. When they returned, these handy inmates built **Old Sparky**, the deceptively flimsy looking mechanism that killed nine men before being retired in 1965.

In addition to public tours, the prison hosts the country's largest mock riot for law enforcement personnel and equipment manufacturers. The last real riot at Moundsville was in 1986, when 200 inmates held sixteen hostages for two days. Three convicts died, killed by other convicts. It's one of the stories told on the tour.

Remke likes to tell folks that the *L.A. Times* said his tour was better than Alcatraz. I told him I'd been to Alcatraz. "Well, what do you think?" he asked me. "Moundsville doesn't have the boat ride", I said.

CLIFFS AND EAGLES

Some places are made to be seen by train, and the Trough of the South Branch of the Potomac River is one of them.

Up until the train started running between Romney and Moorefield in 1910, the seventeen miles of rocky cliffs and steep canyon known as "the Trough" were inaccessible. Even today it is still just the river and the tracks.

Eagle spotting is the game on the **Potomac Eagle excursion train** that rides back and forth through the Trough from May through November, leaving and returning to Romney's Wappocomo Station. June is the best time for spotting the giant birds as they're raising their young, but spotting is virtually certain on any trip.

Eagles soaring along rocky cliffs above a rippling river are only one part of the scenic package. Passengers also see miles of cattle in lush bottomland, old riverside plantations, stone ruins, fishermen in the river, and historic settings spanning the century from the French and Indian War to the Civil War.

First among the sights from the Potomac Eagle is **Wappocomo**, a large brick colonial house built in 1774. It has a unique orientation, facing the mountains rather than the river. The house has been in Parsons family hands for seven generations and remains a private home today.

Today the path of the Potomac Eagle follows the same route taken by a group of millionaires back in 1910 when they first started passenger service to their exclusive **Hampshire Club**. Since 1945, the club property has become the Peterkin Conference Center of the Episcopal Church, which boasts an altar made from the slate tops of two Romney pool tables.

Passengers ride in standard open window coaches from the 1920s, bought from the Canadian railroad. There's a fifty-two foot open gondola car for the ultimate photo opportunities and a Classic Club Car for high rollers.

Potomac Eagle trips run from three hours to all day. There are extra trains during October leaf season, and special trips include a re-enactment that has the train stopped and mildly terrorized by a group of marauding Civil War troops. Since Romney was a historical battleground in the War Between the States, changing hands a reputed fifty-six times, re-enactors from either side would be accurate.

Facilities are basic, as is the food, with soft drinks, chili and pepperoni rolls leading the list. Bring lots of film and try to arrange to ride on the river side one way and the cliff side the other.

BOATRIDE TO THE PAST

The sternwheel riverboat trip along the broad Ohio River to **Blennerhassett Island Historical State Park** from Point Park in Parkersburg is worth the modest price. Touring the ancient island and reconstructed mansion is a bonus.

Held sacred and inhabited for almost 10,000 years by Native Americans in the Ohio River Valley, the island was the 18th-century home of the famous Delaware Indian, Nemacolin. Cases of ancient artifacts taken from the island are on display in the Blennerhassett Museum back on the mainland. *See* "Remarkable Collections" for details.

The historical romance phase began in 1798. Irish aristocrat, Harman Blennerhassett, married his young niece Margaret and fled to the frontier edge of America in disgrace. They bought the island, called it Isle de Beau Pre, and built a fabulous mansion with a ten-room central section and circular wings for Blennerhassett's extensive library and scientific laboratory.

The pair stuck out like a sore thumb in the isolated outpost, so when Aaron Burr came looking for wealthy partners in his scheme to acquire an empire in the Spanish southwest, Blennerhassett Island was a natural stop. Whatever their involvement, the couple left the island when Burr's scheme crumbled under accusations of treason in 1806. The mansion was plundered soon after and finally burned to the ground in 1811.

Archaeologists uncovered the mansion site in 1973. It was faithfully rebuilt on its foundations, furnished and established as the centerpiece of Blennerhassett State Historical Park during the 1980s. The boat ride, tour of the mansion and entry to the mainland museum for less than $10 is one of my favorite West Virginia bargains.

TAMING GLASS

Glass factories share three qualities — they're hot, metal and male. Nowhere was this more obvious than at Fenton Glass where I watched their master blower tame molten glass with his breath. He had the attitude of an Olympic athlete.

I was shocked when the tour at **Fenton** took us directly onto the expansive factory floor, close enough to wilt under the heat of huge furnaces filled with molten glass. Deafening noise, glass, dust and heat met the tour group as we moved within touching distance of the men working the floor. There were no warnings or guard rails.

Shock turned to fascination as we moved into place on the perimeter of the blow shop and watched a lean, intense man turn, twist and blow gobs of molten glass into art forms. The team of gatherers, blockers and assorted "boys" served the master blower, who stood on the traditional blowers' platform, hand on hip, staring a challenge at the crowd, waiting to blow the next phase. He was heat personified and obviously a star; he's even on Fenton's postcards.

Traditional tools and processes are used at Fenton, where the first piece of glass was blown in 1907, two years after the factory opened. All the painted pieces are still done by hand, almost exclusively by women, and signed by the artist. Fenton's most well-known contribution to the glass industry was the development of gaily colored **carnival glass**. Fenton continues to introduce new colors and pieces each year, which are available for sale by subscription.

Fenton's shop is filled with preferred seconds and glass items at bargain prices. The forty-minute factory tour, complete with blower's show, is free and available on weekdays, except in late June and early July when the whole factory closes for vacation.

CONGRESS GOES UNDERGROUND

When the "big one" fell, the President of the United States would give the word and 1,100 members of Congress, staff and top government officials would be whooshed by jumbo jet to the **Greenbrier**. There they would enter the **Government Relocation Center**, a secret bunker below the world-famous resort hotel, and proceed to run the government using stored documents for payroll, retirement and health benefits.

A full electronic media production room allowed the buried members to stay in touch with whatever constituents survived. The Capitol dome backdrop for televised messages had both a fall and spring version. No one considered what the audience would think about the uniform green jumpsuits all the Members of Congress would be wearing in their contamination-free hideaway.

Part Cold War-paranoia and part golfing fantasy, the bunker was built in the late 1950s by **President Dwight D. Eisenhower** at a cost of $10 million. Although the world disappointed planners by never going up in mushroom clouds of flame and radiation, that was never an issue at the bunker, which was maintained at top readiness for thirty-four years. Magazines in each of four lounges were replaced constantly. A single Greenbrier employee received all the subscriptions, making him a world class junk mail magnet. The complex mechanical systems that provided water, heat and the cleanest air on the planet were turned on and run for six hours every Wednesday. Sixty days of freeze dried K-rations, wine and alcohol were stored and rotated. There were no cigarettes; bunker world was smoke-free.

Accommodations were expensive, but not posh: a bathroom for every 120 people, mass bunk rooms with a locker for every four bunks, a twelve-bed hospital ward with lab and dental chair. There were plenty of clocks to help keep people regular and 800 active phone lines. The trash incinerator was set so it could double as a crematorium. For thirty years, every piece of new technology that remotely fit the purpose of life after nuclear war was installed at the bunker.

One deception led to another. A jet airport with the longest runway in West Virginia and a control tower chock full of instruments most cities don't have was plausible pork. Cable television was brought into the tiny, rural valley to provide a cover occupation for the shadowy Forsythe Associates, who had the only key to the bunker's gun room and therefore were the guys in charge. The infamous "television repairmen" from Forsythe were also in control of straight jackets stored in the "jail."

Parts of the top secret bunker were used by the Greenbrier regularly. The meeting room set up to mimic the floor of the House of Representatives served as the resort's theater. The hall planned for congressional staff was used for exhibitions; the abundance of pillars needed to shore up the 70 feet of dirt piled on top of the secret structure was explained away as an architectural quirk. The famous **Dorothy Draper** decor, with its busy patterns and bright colors, worked perfectly to hide doors and cuts in concrete.

The party line claims the bunker was top secret, not even showing up in Soviet intelligence files. Hundreds of Greenbrier County residents, hotel workers, and other personnel have years of bunker stories that show local folk knew what was hidden in plain sight. They just saw no need to tell the outside world.

The Greenbrier was paid well for being the only hotel in the world with a contingency plan for the destruction of civilization. Tax dollars built the West Virginia wing, literally the cover for the bunker buried under Kate Mountain, which was then leased to the Greenbrier for a modest annual fee of no more than $50,000. When the bunker was conveniently revealed in mid-1992, in time to be placed on a base closing list, it was given to the hotel. The cafeteria and fully equipped kitchen are now the site of the Greenbrier's world famous cooking school, and tours are conducted regularly with fees used to cover maintenance. Plans are afoot to transform the underground paradise from a bet on life after nuclear holocaust to more mundane but profitable casino gambling.

Tours begin as a twenty-five ton steel door, cut into the side of the mountain and perfectly balanced to be moved by the hand of a single person, shuts behind the group. A well-informed guide — ours was a former Central Intelligence Agency employee — leads us down a 433-foot tunnel lined with food supplies to the first stop and begins the incredible tale.

MOVE OVER, CASPER

Ghosts — and **ghost tours** — are popular in the Eastern Panhandle.

For more than twenty years, Shirley Dougherty has been giving tours of the scariest places in **ghost-ridden Harpers Ferry**, from April through November. Her stories are collected in her book, *Ghosts of Harpers Ferry*.

Susan Crites collects ghost stories and turns them into pamphlet-sized books. She's published more than a dozen, with themes ranging from Civil War spooks to romance. During the fall, she conducts tours of a dozen ghost-visited sites in and around **Martinsburg**, accompanied by a talented psychic. A favorite stop is the **actively haunted graveyard** near the Blue Ridge Outlet Center, with a glowing tombstone and resident male ghost. Another is the historic **Apollo Theater** and Harry, the original cigar-smoking owner.

"People come unhinged," said Crites. "I tell them not to come on my ghost tour if they don't want to see a ghost."

Crites points to locations where quick, violent deaths have occurred as prime ghost territory. Civil War battlefields are ideal. There are regular sightings of Civil War ghosts at a dilapidated mansion off I-81 near the Springs Mill exit in Berkeley County. Lines of cars often come to hear the ghostly sounds of cannon fire and galloping horses.

DAILY BREAD

Wandering through Huntington's Old Central City, my nose suddenly caught the scent of fresh bread as I saw hundreds of loaves rolling past at eye level in the windows of a large concrete building painted brick red. I tracked down the entryway and attached myself to a group of schoolkids just departing on a regular hour-long tour of **Heiner's Bakery**.

From the moment I slipped on the required white hairnet, I was swept back to childhood memories of bakery tours in my hometown.

Heiner's Bakery started in 1905. The aroma and recipe are unchanged. Piles of flour are still turned into bread dough and stacks of pans still stand at the ready. Even with new silicon chip-directed machines, the process remains a mechanical wonder of breaking down every step needed to make bread and inventing a machine to do it. Little balls of dough zoom around at just the right speed, getting rolled then dropped into a pan. The measured rising time complete, mechanical arms lift gangs of pans into huge fifty-eight tray bread ovens. A young man watches the wall of dials, lights and chalk boards filled with loaf counts. The purpose of staff is realized mostly when the mechanical and silicon systems fail. Human hands will reach in and reload plastic bags or straighten a loaf of bread as needed.

Each day 100,000 loaves of Heiner's bread accumulate countless miles of travel time sailing around on conveyor belts just under the ceiling of the building. Every loaf travels for an hour to cool off before slipping into its plastic wrapping at the rate of eighty-four each minute.

Heiner's Bakery is a cog in several local economic wheels, providing rolls for the famous Stewart hot dogs on other side of town, (*see* "Local Food") and giving away waste dough to a man who feeds it to his hogs.

SECRET METHODS

The company's ever-popular **Fiestaware** has earned the daily bread for the **Homer Laughlin Factory** for more than half a century. It is made within the more than mile-long compound in a building separate from the main factory. No tours of this area are allowed, presumably to protect the trade secrets surrounding the prized Fiestaware pottery.

A fourth generation family-owned business, Homer Laughlin is the world's largest pottery plant, and during most years the largest manufacturer of dinnerware. It was the first American pottery to be totally lead free, and the innovator of tunnel kilns. There are regular tours of the enormous main factory, and I was fortunate enough to have noted studio potter Pam Parziale along as a companion.

We watched their newest machine molding a perfect plate from raw clay in six seconds. "It takes me twenty minutes," said Pam. The rest of the operation is just as streamlined, with new twelve-hour kilns that allow the pottery to turn a piece of china around in twenty-four hours.

The tour ends in a museum room filled with rare and historic Fiestaware pieces, where everyone is given a small commemorative plate and released into the outlet shop. To learn more about buying the product, *see* "Shopping Treasures".

DIG DEEP

Jeff Moorefield is a robust and rollicking former miner who delights in tales of methane gas burning off eyebrows and rats eating unprotected lunch pails. He was our guide at the **Beckley Exhibition Coal Mine**, taking us through a gaping hole in the mountain into 1,500 feet of dark tunnels only slightly larger than the standard three-foot seam of coal once mined there. We were riding in a man-trip mine trolley pulled by a battery powered locomotive. This is not an excursion for those who avoid close spaces.

The exhibition mine was worked by a local family around the turn-of-the-century; it closed in 1910. The exhibition mine is an authentic example of what coal mining once was; when working in ankle deep water to move three or four tons of coal a day with a pick and shovel was the norm. It does not represent today's mechanized industry, where miners suit up like astronauts and direct "continuous miners" by remote control to chew up and move several tons of coal a second. Only the maze of low tunnels and the usefulness of the product remains unchanged.

There's a self-guided tour of other authentic coal camp buildings reconstructed above the mine, including a church, miner's house, superintendent's house and a tiny single man's shed.

NATURE TOURS

★ The Spotted Salamander is the paved, level trail with Braille interpretive nature stations in **Kanawha State Forest** at the edge of Charleston.

★ **River House B&B** has a fortuitous location on a horseshoe bend of the Cacapon River that allows its guests downstream/upstream round trip tube floats with a short portage walk and no car planting. Tubes are available.

★ The state publishes a **fall color map** allowing folks to follow the leaves, beginning with the Highland counties in late September, rolling west in early and mid-October, and finishing with the southern tier and Eastern Panhandle in late October. The map is a thoughtful gesture, but one that will not stop repeated calls in June or July by potential leaf peepers asking which day the leaves will peak.

★ Governor William MacCorkle built and lived in **Sunrise**, a mansion atop a hill across the river from downtown Charleston. He often welcomed visitors at the train station, located at the bottom of the hill along the river. To accommodate the traffic, MacCorkle built the **Carriage Trail**. Today, the trail is a favorite city walk through dense woods switching back and forth around giant rocks. A marker designates the spot where two women tried as spies by a drum head court martial in 1863 were brought, shot and buried. Speculation has it that the two were probably prostitutes someone wanted to discard. **Tramps' Walk** is a parallel sidewalk down the hill.

★ Llamas are gentle and obedient, humming while they walk. They are ideal pack animals for the sensitive New River Gorge, making less environmental impact than most hiking boots. **New River Llama Trekking Company** offers popular four hour gourmet lunch treks, as well as pairing the trek with a day of white water rafting.

Dolly Llamas provide the animals for trekking Dolly Sods Wilderness near Canaan.

★ Thoroughbreds, quarter horses and Irish Connemara ponies are the animals of choice at **Swift Level**, near Lewisburg. Guests can stay at the 1827 plantation-style historic mansion, bunkhouse or log cabin, and choose from various rides, including a three-day, 125 mile mountain trek to Cass in Pocahontas County.

Odd Rides

★ Besides mountain bikes, rubber rafts, kayaks, trains, horses and ATVs, there are a couple of odd things to ride. You can hail a horse-drawn trolley behind shelter # 3 on the **North Bend Trail** on weekends.

★ Weekdays in season, **West Virginia Northern Railways** offers excursions on a 4-wheel open air track car for small groups of as few as two. The caboose can be rented for private parties.

★ The 3,600 foot aerial tram is often obscured by morning mists, as it drops nearly 1,100 feet from the rim of Bluestone Canyon to Mountain Creek, Pipestem's lodge along the Bluestone River at the canyon bottom.

"I had no idea it would be so aerial," said my pilot husband as we rode up and down through the clouds. He was clearly impressed with the expansive windows of the four-person gondola. Doing the trip in the dark is another adventure highlighted by the heritage comedy of a well-lit still nestled in an overhang on the side of the mountain.

The tram ride is free to guests of Mountain Creek, a bonus for staying down in the canyon. For more, *see* "Unusual Places to Stay."

★ Frank Thomas is a working artifact. For more than fifty years his **"Poor Man's Flying School"** has been turning out pilots from the dog-leg runway he literally hacked out of the Fayetteville countryside. In his seventies, Frank still flies folks around the New River Gorge. The bargain price earns him the title of "Five Dollar Frank". His distinctive voice guides pilots through the gorge with terse replies. Once on the ground, his stories and flying museum keep him talking.

★ The extensive forests of West Virginia once supported a booming timber industry and 3,000 miles of logging railroad line. **Cass Scenic Railroad** is the last whistle-screaming, smoke-pouring eleven miles left.

Some of the last steam-powered Shay locomotives invented to haul logs down the steep curves now take folks up a sheer climb through red spruce forests to the million dollar view at Bald Knob, second highest peak in the state at 4,800 feet. Traveling at five miles per hour in red and green open-window passenger cars renovated from old logging cars, the trip to the top takes more than four hours and requires a stop at a spring for water. A shorter trip to Whittaker Station takes two hours. There are dinner trains and a special fall color schedule. The brakemen will answer your questions.

CHAPTER SIXTEEN

TRULY INCREDIBLE

A handful of places transcend any category and can only be described as truly incredible. Each of them could serve as the centerpiece of an advertising campaign entitled: "Surprise! It's West Virginia."

MUMMIES IN PHILIPPI

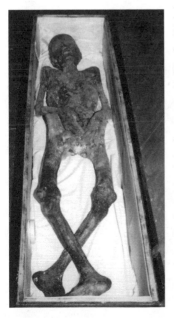

It was the #1 choice for weird from online insiders when I posted the call for "way out" suggestions. There was no background information, only the intriguing mention of the **mummies in Philippi**. I could not imagine how that could be. Visiting became a top priority.

The mummies are housed in the small **Barbour County Historical Museum** next to the famous Philippi covered bridge. Purely by chance, we arrived on the first day the museum was opened for the 1997 season, and there was a major crisis. The mummies had grown mold over the winter from water leaks in the building. Town employees were consulting a museum curator about the best method for cleaning them. "They're a hundred years old," she warned the men who were planning to wash the mummies down with bleach. "Wear gloves."

While the cleaning crew deliberated on what to do, I slipped into the back room where the mummies were. Two tiny wooden boxes lay on the floor. Feeling like a tabloid journalist, I opened them and quickly snapped pictures of two leather dolls with splotches of green mold. Then I set out to gather their story.

Graham Hamrick was a Philippi man with a hankering to develop and patent a mummification process. After trials with vegetables and animals, he needed to test it out on humans. In 1888, Hamrick obtained two unnamed female corpses from the Hospital for the Insane in nearby Weston, and tried out his formula. According to records, he also mummified a hand, a head and a baby; all three are now gone. His pair of females, called **the Hamrick mummies** after their creator, became famous world travelers touring Europe with P.T. Barnum in 1891.

Hamrick received patent #466,524 for an intricate formula including water, saltpeter and sublimed sulfur set afire. In his patent request, he identified the process as a simple and economic way for anyone "without special skill" to effectively preserve a body in its natural condition for a long time. Fumigating the bodies in a closed box, Hamrick gave the two corpses immortality — and a permanent leather complexion.

Barnum returned the mummies to Philippi, and sporadic sightings were reported through the years. Pearl Buck was fascinated with the mummies, and anyone over fourteen could pay to see them at the Philippi Street Fair in the mid-1960s. They then disappeared until the flood of 1985, when they were found under the piano of "Bigfoot" Byrer, the owner of the mummies prior to the town of Philippi.

Hamrick's mummies are not the only bizarre attraction in this small college town along the Tygart River. There is also the limb amputation.

In June 1861, a minor skirmish took place in Philippi, identified by some as the first land battle of the Civil War. The Federal troops routed the Confederates who retreated so fast the battle has been called the "Philippi Races." Among the few wounded was **James Hanger** of Virginia.

Dr. James Robinson of Ohio amputated Hanger's cannonball shattered leg that fateful day in June. It was the first limb amputation of the Civil War. Hanger made himself an artificial leg of wood, and then began fashioning them for other amputees. The Confederate army kept Hanger busy, eventually contracting with him to manufacture artificial limbs. After the war, he invented an organization to continue producing the wooden limbs. Today, J.E. Hanger Inc. is one of the world's largest manufacturers of artificial limbs. Its macabre beginning is recognized by a plaque on the Crim Memorial Church, just off the main square of Philippi.

NATURE TRAINING

The **National Conservation Training Center** in Shepherdstown, completed in 1997, is the best of its kind in the world. In fact, it may be the only one of its kind. Developed by the Fish and Wildlife Service of the U.S. Government, it is working on the future of education by offering a civic version of temple training for environmental servants.

Hidden on 125 acres of the 538 acre former Hendrix Farm, the campus view is filled with giant hay biscuits, rather than the upscale housing developments crowding the area near Shepherd College. Mrs. Hendrix still lives on a five acre life estate near the entrance of the facility. Former governor Gaston Caperton lives next-door in a newly-built showplace home.

The architecture of the training center is a successful example of ecological resonance, both physical and cultural. A dozen buildings with

the look of barns on steroids are linked by walkways through sycamore groves rather than parking lots. Low-maintenance design favored stone walls, recycled steel roofs and brick floors. Concern for "outdoor" folk who spend more time with trees than people dictated lots of light and single rooms with private baths for housing.

The Commons offers a cafeteria dining room that compares with the Greenbrier's facility at Tamarack, minus the arty tabletops. There's even a wine pub with the only mounted head in the place — a rare Tule elk shot by poachers and captured by Fish and Wildlife cops who tracked the evildoers down.

Walls in all the buildings are shrines to conservation heritage, displaying countless photographs of Fish and Wildlife employees and other conservation professionals doing the sacred work — saving rivers, forests and animals.

The long list of "gee whiz" items at the Center includes both education and technology wonders. In the Geographical Information Systems lab, digital maps with varying information overlays are created on drafting tables that are, in reality, computer screens. Production facilities are state-of-the-art, including television and audio studios, a digital editing suite and satellite uplink. Live distance learning to the field is planned, although the facility is designed to be a training "home" for the Fish and Wildlife Service's far-flung employees; a place where they can return every three years for "touchstone" courses and "roots" development through re-exposure to the Center.

The facility is equipped for the development of conservation education materials, with a professional design staff and a special hands-on lab where kids can come in and play with the stuff that turns into classroom courses. For outdoor studies, they move just outside the large glass doors to a pond that hatched literally millions of frogs one day. " The frogs poured out of that pond for hours," said my tour guide. I asked what happened. "They headed for the woods," he replied.

An existing storehouse of public domain conservation film footage and still images for information use by anyone, anywhere, is being expanded daily.

Folks who go to lots of training sessions obviously had a hand in designing the education space. Informal break-out areas are flooded with light and pastoral views, chalkboards are placed by the phones for messages, and abundant techie toys fill each of the nineteen classrooms. There are four state-of the art labs — two "wet" and two "dry" — for training state and local officials in testing standards and techniques. The labs are wired so individual students can watch the teacher from their own video screen.

Conservation professionals are the student body — men and women working for the government on every level from federal to local, or for their corporate and private sector organization partners in the work of conserving the Earth's resources. The ninety-page training catalog outlines more than 150 classes including Principles and Techniques of Electrofishing, Advanced Land Acquisition, Oil Spill Response, and Habitat Planning for Endangered Species. Field personnel teach most of the offerings.

For The Fish and Wildlife Service, the National Conservation Training Center is a prize, a source of pride for the often-overlooked bureau. Already, conservation officials from all over the planet are clamoring to train at the facility. Biotech conferences bring international CEOs to the conservation table and corporate jets to the Martinsburg airport.

The world-class working laboratory of continuous education is also a good neighbor, preserving farmland and boosting educational opportunities for Shepherd College students. With an unusual financial deal that will allow NCTC to pay its own way, the facility is a shining example of how well spent $134 million can be.

HAND-CRAFTED HEAVEN

No other state in America has attempted what West Virginia has — jamming all the state's hand crafted art under one very unique roof. Both the roof and the assemblage of art at **Tamarack** are truly incredible.

The cultural center's most prominent external feature is its roof — twenty red-shingled glass-front peaks rising from a huge circular core, exploding above the Beckley exit on I-77. According to Tamarack's architect, it was inspired by traditional quilting patterns and the surrounding mountain peaks. The surreal roofline not only provides abundant daylight for the interior, but also creates waterfalls when it rains. The center of the building is an open courtyard ideal for displaying large sculptures.

Once inside, there is no escaping the art of Tamarack. The "retail avenue" is a circle under the pointy roof, moving the shopper around and around through the 60,000 square feet of art, before they may recognize a piece of what they've seen before. The rule for wise shopping becomes: buy it when you see it, you may never find your way back. There is so much to see.

Filled with literally tens of thousands of art objects all created by more than 1,300 West Virginia artists juried into the system, Tamarack's biggest sellers are the noted West Virginia marbles, ranging in price from 5¢ – 25¢. What a deal for art! There are also one-of-a-kind pieces with four-figure price tags, displayed both in living pods, that blend objects in real-life room displays, as well as in traditional gallery-type spaces. Everywhere else are display sections filled with wood, glass, pottery, jewelry, fabric, books, music and other art forms too many to name.

Part of the attraction of hand crafted art is the personal connection with the artist through their work. The name and address of any artist producing a piece is available from the section clerk who will print it out on a register slip.

Food is another art practiced at Tamarack. It offers more than a thousand food items produced in the state; the foodstuffs often compete with glass to be Tamarack's biggest seller. Apple butter is the most popular item on a list that includes jams, wines, sauces, chocolate, honey, syrup and vinegars.

Turning the food court over to the noted **Greenbrier** was an inspired decision. The food court provides five star eating in a cafeteria setting, at prices that compete with the fast food chains surrounding Tamarack at the interstate exit. The special of the day for our visit was pork barbecue, the sliced not shredded kind, with a tangy sauce that did not contain fake smoke. It was paired with crispy sweet and sour cole slaw. The new red potatoes were served, skin on, in country-style chunks almost as large as the chunks of chicken in my pot pie.

Tabletops in the food court were designed by a variety of state artists, and we had the serendipitous treat of sitting at a table that turned out to be a grid of metal art vegetables made by our friends at Hsu Studios in Berkeley Springs.

It's not all shopping at Tamarack. The theater offers entertainment from all over the state. There's a gallery for ever-changing art exhibitions, and studios for resident artists and demonstrations. Occasionally, the largest continuous art and craft fair in the state stages a weekend festival that somehow finds even more art to add to the mix.

Tamarack appears to be fulfilling its plan of becoming a major tourist attraction. Hundreds of cars with license plates from all over the United States and Canada often fill the parking lot, advertising Tamarack's appeal as a must-see stop on the road south — or back.

Although Tamarack was named for an obscure West Virginia tree, its impact since opening in 1996 has been enormous, and not simply for the artists whose work is being sold. It has also raised the perception of

West Virginia hand crafts to a new level. And now, throughout the state, there are shops advertising themselves as offering Tamarack-like sections and buying from the Tamarack distribution system. "The Best of West Virginia" is selling well.

PALACE OF GOLD

It's the most startling view in the state.

Traveling north to Moundsville, there's a small sign indicating the turn onto a typical back road — narrow, rough, twisting repeatedly around tree-covered hills. Suddenly, after one more curve, the **Palace of Gold** appears, beamed down directly from a Himalayan village. Gold encrusted domes peek over the red and pink brick colonnade; a wide brick thoroughfare leads down from the Palace to the temple, lodge and lake. Krishna's pet peacocks strut around the lake, paying homage at the feet of thirty-foot-tall statues representing Hindu aspects of divinity. Ritual swan boats nestle in an elaborately domed boat house or skim the lake with blissful passengers. Redwood chalets surround the lake, putting visitors in mind of a surreal state park that happens to have larger-than-life elephant and sacred cow sculptures.

In fact, the scene is the 3,000 acre mountaintop home of the **New Vrindaban** community of **Hare Krishnas**, largest of their farm communities in the world, and the location of America's largest goshalla (cow shelter) at its Govardhan Dairy. The sign by the lodge spells out its unique destiny: "You are entering a sacred place. No smoking, intoxicants. No non-vegetarian foods. Please keep grounds clean."

The sacred complex was the brainchild of Srila Prabhupada, who came to America in 1965. He invented the Hare Krishnas and their signature chanting as a path to higher consciousness. America, the world and countless airport travelers have felt the impact of Prabhupada's vision.

According to the New Vrindaban party line, the head swami selected Bhaktipada, a young American he met in New York, to create a special Hare Krishna center on an abandoned farm outside Moundsville. It was named after the place in India where Lord Krishna reportedly spent his childhood. When Prabhupada visited the West Virginia site in 1969, there were a dozen or so devotees living in primitive conditions, walking groceries in two miles from the county road. The guru left his disciples with a vision of seven temples built on seven hills.

Prabhupada was a humble teacher who died before the splendor of the Palace of Gold was completed. He never lived in the east gallery, where ornately paneled and inlaid rooms are described as his study and living rooms. He never turned on the gold plated fixtures with rosy quartz handles on the marble sink in "his" bathroom. He never saw the lifelike idol of himself, mounted on a golden throne under a crystal dome, dressed luxuriously in a way the live saint would never have allowed. He never sat through the homage paid to his idol in a daily ceremony called "worshipping the guru."

In its heyday of the mid-1980s, when more than 600 devotees called the huge compound home and more than 200,000 visitors passed through, the *New York Times* dubbed New Vrindaban and its Palace of Gold, "America's Taj Mahal." Built specifically to attract public attention to the teachings of Krishna, the Palace is a wonder of West Virginia appropriately located in an area selected by the ancients for one of their largest mounds, and by the state for its Gothic prison.

Bhaktipada's devotion drove unskilled devotees to do-it-yourself books where they learned to cut marble, mix cement, landscape and assemble crystal chandeliers. Masters appeared to carve, sculpt, paint and create stained glass. For seven years they struggled in the hills and the result is stunning — a tribute to the power of devotion.

The Palace of Gold is 8,000 square feet, with ten rooms of rare materials inside a shining black and gold trimmed structure, framed by two levels of extensive terraces. A twenty-five foot dome has 4,000 crystals in a ceiling mural of Lord Krishna. There are thirty-one stained glass windows, including four of peacocks glowing and shimmering in tones of blue and gold. Other windows have ornate scrollwork under a halo of colored glass jewels. Antique French chandeliers illuminate elaborate hand-painted murals. More than fifty-two varieties of imported marble and onyx decorate walls, floors and ceilings. Intricately carved teakwood doors lead to the main hall, which is dazzling with gold marble pillars and more than 20,000 pieces of polished marble. All of the gold leaf tracery, inside and out, is twenty-two carat — and it covers thousands of square feet of surface. A vegetarian restaurant, lounge and gift shop complete the floor plan. Chatras, elaborately painted and inlaid open domes that are covered sitting places for prayer, mark the corners of the lower terrace, which is interspersed with flowers, lions and fountains. Ornate gardens tumble across the landscape from the palace terraces culminating in huge sitting statues.

Where the Indian holy man Prabhupada envisioned New Vrindaban as a tribute to Lord Krishna, the renamed American follower, Bhaktipada, built it to honor Prabhupada. The hubris proved lethal. As guru, Bhaktipada eventually was consumed by the dangerous doctrine that the position made him all powerful.

Bhaktipada began altering the traditional rituals and practices of the Hare Krishnas and earned New Vrindaban expulsion from the international organization in 1987. By 1994, the community was in near total collapse, with resources drained by legal trials and fines. The life of a cow was held sacred at New Vrindaban; unfortunately for its development, the lives of its members were not. After two trials, Bhaktipada received a twenty-year federal jail sentence for racketeering in 1996; his henchmen were convicted of murder. One of his appeals was handled by noted attorney Alan Dershowitz. Because of the ongoing hostility of Moundsville residents and officials, he compared the case to a "witchcraft trial."

Having severed ties to Bhaktipada, the community struggles to return from near destruction. Current plans chart the path back through selling off more than 2,000 acres of the property to member families, and revitalizing New Vrindaban as a resort community with a spiritual flavor.

Fewer than a hundred devotees currently live at New Vrindaban, where they sustain the intricate daily rituals of worshipping Krishna and maintaining the farm and school. Introducing the culture to visiting tourists remains a major part of the project, and the complex is open for tours or just to wander around at will. The Palace of Gold still gleams in its gardens and terraces, with domes outlined against the mountains of three states, and signature chanting filling the air. Whatever else is true, the Hare Krishnas have always had the best beat.

WORLD FAVORITE

Mention rich, famous and luxury in one sentence in West Virginia and you have to be talking about **The Greenbrier**. A historic landmark before the Civil War, the Greenbrier has dominated the "best resorts in the world list" for the past century and a half; and for just cause — it has everything. There are thousands of pristine acres and expansive gardens, a European-style spa, the luxury of more staff than guests, matchless food, elegant fixtures and a rambling collection of white buildings, including the aristocratic main hotel. Guests have

COURTESY THE GREENBRIER

long shared the three golf courses with the Greenbrier's famous pro, Sam Snead, and come for unique diagnostic vacations at the hotel's medical clinic.

Unlike any other five-star resort in America, the Greenbrier had contingency plans for nuclear Armageddon. The U.S. Government built and maintained a secret bunker for Congress under the West Virginia wing, to which they could escape when "the big one" dropped. *See* "Tours" for more.

History reigns supreme at the Greenbrier, bestowing a timeless quality on "Old White." Annual pilgrimages for the 400 ruling families of the South were the order of the day in antebellum times when the Greenbrier and White Sulphur Springs were in Virginia, and Henry Clay was its unofficial host. After the war, as part of the new state of West Virginia, railroads blended the prevailing southern society with northern wealth for a new sparkling society that lasted through the rest of the century. Revered as a summer retreat, Old White was a must for Europeans on the "American Grand Tour."

The Treadmill, invented at the resort, defined the primary purpose of 19th century visitors — and it was not health. Every evening, splendidly dressed guests indulged in a fashion and matchmaking parade around the huge dining room, which could seat 1,200! Being on display at the Greenbrier virtually guaranteed a young girl a husband. Irene Langhorne was a Greenbrier belle who became immortalized as "The Gibson Girl" by her husband, artist Charles Dana Gibson.

Greenbrier's tenure as America's premier resort was broken only twice in its long history. It served as a military hospital, first for the Confederacy and then later for Union forces, after a Captain DuPont of Delaware persuaded his general from burning it to the ground. During World War II, the U.S. Army commandeered it to serve as Ashford General Hospital for military personnel.

Following both interruptions, private owners recovered the resort and it continued with an undiminished reputation. The post-World War II grand reopening was marked by the famed party of the time, and hosted by the Duke and Duchess of Windsor. It was a nostalgic return for the Windsors. She had been there for her first honeymoon, he for a holiday while King of England. Other notables included the Kennedy family with their son, John, the young Congressman from Massachusetts. Bing Crosby broke a lifetime rule for the party and sang for his fellow guests.

During the 1950s and '60s when the historic hotel industry was at its lowest, the Greenbrier hosted guests like Dwight D. Eisenhower, Princess Grace and the Kennedys in luxury suites. The sumptuous Presidential Suite is a virtual private residence in the Virginia wing of the hotel with a grand piano, large dining room and curved stairs that lead to seven bedrooms on the suite's second floor. Outside the main hotel, the Colonnade Estate House dates to 1838, when it was President Martin Van Buren's summer retreat. Renovated in 1989, Colonnade has a dining room that can seat twenty-two for Gold Service private dinners.

That legends beget legends is commonplace wisdom at the Greenbrier. Twenty-six U.S. Presidents, royalty, movie stars, and other millionaires and celebrities have visited, creating memories that are the stuff of legend. Countless thousands of obscure guests, including this author, have their own magical Greenbrier stories.

It was an improbable trip from the beginning. A friend and I had been hired to "tell fortunes" at a '60s party planned for the Blockbuster video store convention. We negotiated a minimal fee and lodging at the Greenbrier. It was the opportunity of a lifetime. We recruited my pilot-husband and arrived like many of the rich and famous do — flying into the sophisticated, jet-accepting Greenbrier Valley Airport.

As we checked in, the improbable ascended to mythic. Juliana was at the front desk. She recognized my name, knew our purpose, and was waiting for us. "Read my cards," she said, "and we'll upgrade you at no charge to a Paradise Row Cottage." A free, $650-a-night room was impossible to decline.

Cottages are the most traditional housing available at the Greenbrier, which began its life as a cottage resort in the first decade of the 19th century. Paradise Row cottages were among the first built at the resort and long served as honeymoon lodging — hence their name. Renovated in the 1980s, they offer amenities common to all of the sixty-nine guest houses: privacy, comfort, fireplaces, and complimentary limo service to the main hotel, an easy stroll away. Our cottage in Paradise Row had the biggest bed in the largest bedroom I've ever seen, let alone slept in. The porch had a stunning view of the historic main hotel, framed by green West Virginia mountains and acres of flowers and manicured lawns attended to constantly by armies of gardeners.

Beginning life as a Georgian antebellum masterpiece, today's main hotel has been altered and rebuilt nearly half a dozen times, currently reflecting its colonial Virginia roots, and having more than 500 rooms and fifty suites. A Gilbert Stuart painting of George Washington hangs in the entrance and the staff historian is on hand for tours and lectures. Dorothy Draper's famous redecorating splashed bright color, wicker furniture and harmonious prints in all the rooms and exhilarating black and white marble floors in the lobby.

Along with social position, health has always been a primary commodity at the Greenbrier. In the 1840s, Dr. John Moorman, the resort's first resident physician, began a lifelong study of the effects of mineral water, especially the Greenbrier's sulphur variety. His findings a century ago mimic those recently touted by alternative practitioners extolling the benefits of taking natural minerals — it cures everything and makes you feel great. The bath wing — with mud baths, a huge mosaic encrusted Roman-style indoor pool, and poolside lounge — was expanded in 1987, providing nearly 30,000 square feet in spa area and an extensive menu of treatments.

Golf and spa facilities are enhanced by fly fishing, outdoor and indoor tennis courts, and nearby white water rafting. For those seeking more unusual recreation, falconry is available with both instruction and demonstrations. Outstanding conference capacity includes magnificent lobbies and huge assembly rooms designed for their Doomsday use to mimic the halls of Congress. Romantics enjoy tea in the Wisteria Room and carriage or sleigh rides around the resort. The traditional exclusive shops now include the "Best of West Virginia", with products from Tamarack.

In a world approaching the next millennium at warp speed, the Greenbrier remains true to its roots. The view of the most ancient mountains in North America remains unchanged, and travelers are still enchanted by the contrast of emerging from rough wilderness and dense forests to a swirl of fashionable society and the enclave of neat white cottages surrounding the majestic white hotel. For more on special aspects of the Greenbrier, *see:* "Local Food", "Great Plumbing", "Amazing Architecture", "Superlatives" and "Tours Not to Miss".

COSMIC EARS AND ANCIENT ROCKS

The time continuum from ancient past to unforeseeable future runs south through the West Virginia mountains from **Seneca Rocks** to the **National Radio Astronomy Observatory** in Green Bank. The connection was made astonishingly obvious by two events between October 1987 and November 1988.

For the past 400 million years or so, natural forces have eroded away a geologic fold so nothing but the root of the mountain remains. As long as anyone knew, the root was three-pronged. Called Seneca Rocks after the native tribes who introduced the place to early settlers, it is over 900 feet of Tuscarora sandstone jutting up from the North Fork

River. At 3:27 p.m. on October 22, 1987, the twenty ton third prong of the great rock — the Gendarme — fell. The twenty-five foot chimney of hard rock gave no warning. Its disappearance will forever divide Seneca Rocks time into before and after.

John Maxwell, founder of the Gendarme Climbing School and Store, characterized the event as "the peak of fall and fall of peak." The astrological position of the stars indicates that the fall took place at a moment of almost pure balance and harmony, under the Libra New Moon.

Thirty miles south and a year later, at 9:43 p.m. on November 15, 1988, one of the world's largest radio telescopes — 300 feet — crashed to the ground in an instant. The cause cited was sudden failure of a key structural item. Its collapse tore a hole in the fabric of the astronomical community.

There was no discernible pattern — no harsh weather or measurable earth changes — linking these two extraordinary events so close in time and space. Postulating a cosmic message, both could have been affected by the Harmonic Convergence claimed by millions around the world in August 1987 as the beginning of a new cosmic vibration.

Walking around the array of scientific ears in the form of giant white telescopic dishes listening to outer space at the National Radio Astronomy Observatory, I could feel the remarkable confluence of unusual energy. Intent listening seemed to be drawing cosmic force to the spot surrounded by friendly, spruce-covered mountain peaks in remote West Virginia. If the Harmonic Convergence, derived from Mayan calendars, depicted an actual shift in the fabric of time, they would have heard about it in Green Bank. That's the type of pattern in the space chatter they're listening for as the telescopes focus cosmic radio waves. Sometimes too much focus on too strong a force can knock a giant telescope down, it seems. The theory is easy to accept when you feel the energy and hear the hum of the radio waves drawn to Green Bank.

The 2,700-acre depression on top of a mountain — a natural bowl for listening — was selected by officialdom in 1954 for its isolation from man-made interference with radio waves. Even to the naked eye, the uncluttered West Virginia night sky provides almost unmatchable opportunities to view the stars. On satellite maps of light pollution, there's a black hole over much of the state. A facility of the National Science Foundation, the Observatory was in place by 1958. It is one of only four in the world, and is part of a global array of radio telescopes that observe quasars and measure the motion of continents.

For a place where such astounding work is being done, the site is remarkably open. It is an extraordinary experience to walk up and touch the huge mechanical wonders and hear them hum. Wandering along the roads and paths is permissible as long as you move on foot. Only special vehicles without the common motorized systems that disturb the telescopes' energy field are allowed to drive beyond a gate on the road. The staff uses bicycles.

The replacement for the fallen telescope is even larger, and will be the largest, most advanced and fully steer-able telescope in the world. The reflector — 100 x 110 meters — has a unique surface that can be adjusted to maintain a perfect shape for focusing radio waves. Able to listen in on a much wider band of waves, the new Green Bank Telescope will revolutionize radio astronomy. Huge cranes and derricks, miles of wire, and the erector set modules of the offset arm gleaming white against the green meadow and vibrant blue sky define a construction site straight out of a science fiction show. The finished telescope will weigh in at sixteen million pounds, stand 480 feet high and be level to within a few thousandths of an inch.

Old jokes about the satellite dish being West Virginia's state flower fade when confronted with the array of enormous telescope dishes tucked along a typical twisting mountain road, which draw astronomers and space scientists from across the globe. By listening to the universe, the scientists of Green Bank explore the profound truths of the structure of space, the nature of time and eternal radio hiss. They are taking an ongoing census of cosmic noise.

In addition to the soon-to-be **Green Bank Telescope**, there are other notable instruments to be seen in the Green Bank compound. The 200 foot high, 140 foot dish is the largest equatorially mounted radio telescope in world. The 85 foot Tatel Telescope is the oldest built at the Observatory. In 1960, the OZMA Project that became the now nearly mythical search for extraterrestrial intelligence (SETI) was launched from here. A forty-foot telescope is used for student projects.

There are even historic landmark instruments, including an exact replica of the antenna used in 1933 to discover radio waves from space, as well as the backyard-built first parabolic radio telescope used in the 1940s to produce the first maps of the radio sky.

From space aliens roaming along the Ohio in the western part of the state (*see* "Remarkable Collections") to the scientific world listening to space chatter in the east, West Virginia has an assured place in a galactic community.

CHAPTER SEVENTEEN

UNUSUAL PLACES TO STAY

T he ads promoting West Virginia to potential visitors inevitably feature the state's matchless natural beauty or outdoor adventure possibilities. Strangers can be forgiven if they think there's no place to sleep here except under the stars. What a surprise it is to find more than enough lodging, some of it quite unforgettable.

HISTORIC HOSPITALITY

Metal bars and poetic graffiti still mark the four maximum security cells on the third floor, all that's left of the former Grand Hotel's incarnation as the **State Prison for Women** from 1947 to 1983. Once a choice destination with its sixty rooms filled every season, the Grand was saved from the wrecker's ball by a former correctional officer's son, who resurrected it as the **Pence Springs Hotel**.

Ashby Berkeley grew up at Pence Springs. His mother worked at the women's prison and he played ball on the lawn beneath the cell block; inmates would referee from above.

Ashby's exuberance fills the gracious brick hotel the way light fills the white sun porch, where he can often be found serving feather-light silver dollar pancakes with real maple syrup, substantial but light home-made biscuits and plates of still-firm cooked apples to guests for break-fast. Trained as a chef, Ashby's dinner menu includes eighteenth century Berkeley family specials like chicken and peanut pie and peach up-side-down cake.

The twenty-six plain but spacious rooms date to the hotel's peak years in the 1920s. Third floor restoration is underway for more guest rooms. There are fresh cookies in every room, along with claw foot bathtubs and old iron radiators, modified with individual thermostat control. The prison years added three inch peepholes to the doors so guards could check on inmates. Reconfigured and decorated, the peep holes now aim out. There are no phones in the rooms; calls are announced by a knock on the door and can be taken on the sun porch lounge.

Ashby loves talking about the stories that haunt various parts of the hotel. Noted for its blind eye to prohibition rules, the hotel boasted brick-lined hidey holes joined by a tunnel under the front porch to keep the bootleg liquor flowing. The holes now open from the under-ground Cider Press Lounge. Even the bar's piano has a story. It belonged to the notorious **Bricktop**, a jet-setting Alderson native well known on the international club circuit, and reputed to be Charles DeGaulle's mistress.

Herds of prehistoric buffalo searching out the unique water left their indelible mark on the trace cutting along one side of the hotel's 400 acres to the springs at the base of a steep hill. With the coming of the railroads in 1872, shopkeeper Andrews Pence acquired the land around the notable springs and sank a primitive pipe. He began bottling and selling the water. Soon there was a bottling house — today filled with antiques — and train cars filled with Pence Springs water flowed out of the valley.

Pence built a hotel in 1897 which burned in 1912. In spite of the tragedies and the new focus of the United States on mobilization for World War I, Pence was able to rebuild, opening the **Grand Hotel** in June 1918. By the 1920s there was a casino, as well as the arrival of fourteen passenger trains a day.

Today, Pence Springs is a popular wedding setting and is listed on the National Register of Historic Places. A hearty country brunch every

Sunday compliments the huge flea market held next to the Victorian spring house. The Hinton-Alderson airstrip across the road along the Greenbrier River can accommodate small planes.

Only Tell Your Friends

Originating as a pre-war summer resort — that's pre-Civil War — the family-operated **Capon Springs** wants prospective guests to understand what the cultural environment is. The fashionable nineteenth century resort with a huge hotel and bathing colonnade is gone. The current incarnation boasts first-rate Victorian buildings in excellent condition and a pre-war — this time World War II — family orientation.

At **Capon Springs and Farms**, the farms are real. Organic strawberries and tomatoes are grown by resort staff and find their way onto dining room tables, where they are joined by Capon Springs eggs and resort-raised and cured ham and bacon. There's an 11 p.m. curfew, a volunteer flag raising each morning, regular songfests and talent shows in the activities hall. Guests can even add their own slides and films to evening programs. Alcoholic beverages are BYO and confined to guest rooms and porches.

There is no town at Capon Springs in modern terms — no post office, courthouse, mini-mart or other hallmarks of town life. Instead, you'll find a registered historic district filled with gracious cottages and the main hotel for guests; it was all built in the 1880s. Monumental cliffs and eccentric shaped rock outcroppings frame the 5,000 acre scenic resort.

Once a country getaway for presidents and notables, Capon Springs stood in virtual ruins during the 1920s from fire, flood and hard economic times. Lou Austin revived it as an offshoot of his quest to bottle the spring water. Today, Austin grandkids, known as the "Thirds," manage Capon Springs with an enduring dedication to the face-to-face charm of the place. The deep narrow valley where the springs bubble forth is now filled with hammocks, water fountains, tennis, badminton, a golf course, pools, hiking trails and children with grandparents.

Life is casual and reminiscent of a big family camp that happens to have grown up around noted springs. When the hundred rooms are full, 250 guests of all ages dine family-style in a light-filled dining room, called there three times a day by an old iron bell. Ties and dress-up clothes are considered unfashionable, and there are no limits placed on appetites, which is fortunate when the homemade bread and baked goods emerge fresh from huge, coal powered, brick ovens. Hotel chefs can often be cajoled into following the tradition of cleaning and cooking a guest's catch for breakfast, and outdoor barbecues happen regularly. There's a rack of black umbrellas at the ready and a free place to do the laundry.

People know each other here. Summertime finds a list of all guests coming for the week posted at the desk for all to see. Many names are familiar. Guests return each year, same time, same rooms, same fellow guests. "Sometimes they call to let us know," chuckled Jonathan Bellingham, an Austin grandson. Some guests haven't missed a year in half a century and more than fifty families have annual reunions there. Newcomers are quickly absorbed into the extended resort family of the moment.

As befits a unique place, there are unique souvenirs to take home along with memories. Lou Austin was a philosopher, who transmitted his understanding of personal responsibility and the spiritual connection both through the resort, and through his books and "Little Me/Great Me" dolls. Former U.S. Labor Secretary Willard Wirtz is a longtime regular who wrote **Capon Valley Sampler** about the region. The books and dolls are available at the resort shop; the day-to-day experience of an honorable life is available to all who visit. Water is free for the taking.

Summer is traditionally the most active time, when the resort is filled with families and served by more than 120 staff members. Open from May 1 to November 1, spring and fall offer an almost idyllic private getaway into a genteel past.

Tradition is not exorbitantly priced at Capon Springs and best of all, there are no nickel and dime annoyances. One personal check at the end of a guest's stay covers everything. The memories are up to you. The resort joins Berkeley Springs and the Greenbrier as the only remaining operative springs resorts in West Virginia.

It's a tough act to balance — being friendly but reclusive. So, don't scream Capon Springs to the world; share it as a special secret.

NO ELVIS SIGHTINGS AT THIS GRACELAND

Stylish Grace Davis was her father's Washington hostess for the years **Henry Gassaway Davis** served as U.S. Senator from West Virginia. The lavish Victorian summer house Davis built overlooking Elkins was named in her honor and often filled with famous guests. Newly restored as an inn by Davis & Elkins College, **Graceland** has been renting rooms to the public since late 1996.

Walking out of a guest room suite in the middle of the night onto wide halls, sweeping staircases with seating areas on the landings, and a wide angle view of the Great Hall and massive fireplace on the floor below, I felt like I was staying in Grace Davis' Victorian mansion. The lights of Elkins twinkled through large windows decorated with opulent tie-back drapes, and soft shadows gleamed in the corners of elegant West Virginia hardwood floors and walls.

Railroads and timber made Henry Davis rich. Political power accompanied the wealth and in 1904, Davis lived up to his title of Grand Old Man and became the oldest man to ever run for U.S. Vice President. He was eighty and ran on the unsuccessful Democratic ticket against Teddy Roosevelt.

The Queen Anne style mansion with turrets and wrap-around porches was the height of fashion in 1893, and filled with every innovation Davis could find. He and son-in-law Steven Elkins, who built the twin mansion of Halliehurst, (see "Amazing Architecture") put in electricity and maintained their own power generating plant. The exterior of Graceland was made of local sandstone; the roof, red Vermont slate. The family last occupied the house in 1939.

After Graceland was used for thirty years as a fraternity house and a few years more for storage, the college had plans to tear the mansion down. Fate, private supporters and Senator Robert Byrd intervened.

It took three years and $2 million to restore Graceland to its Victorian splendor — and it was done to the highest standards of excellence. One father and son team spent nearly a year properly hanging more than ninety doors; most were original with reconfigured hardware. Sliding counterweighted pocket doors were refurbished and original shutters, with wall insets where the shutters "disappear," were remounted on floor to ceiling windows. In the two-story entry hall, a huge original painting of Blackwater Falls hangs once again.

Heirloom treasures are mostly in wood. There's cherry wood in the library, a floor-to-ceiling wood billiard room, and a music room entirely of bird's eye maple, including the cabinets. The Inn's restaurant in the Mingo Dining Room is red oak with a glass conservatory. All the original fireplaces have hand carved mantles.

Fabulous stained glass windows dominate the front of the house. They were saved from destruction and hidden away by folks at the Augusta Heritage Center when there was talk of demolition. When the restoration began, the windows were revealed. They've been totally reconstructed to last another century or two.

I stayed in Ellen Bruce Lee's room, now a luxurious guest suite. The lace canopy bed was a climb and Oriental throw-rugs were strewn on original wood floors. Along with her husband, journalist John Kennedy, Bruce traveled the world. Later she lived at Sunrise in Charleston, the notable mansion of former Governor MacCorkle.

Bruce apparently loved a soak. Her deep claw foot tub with a thick gray marble cap around the top edge and gleaming chrome fixtures is set in a small bathroom lined with original marble.

Grace's Suite was in the turret and is now filled with lush, rich furnishings. Every guest room is different, but all are filled with period furnishings, and have a private bath.

The magnificent oak at the entrance to Graceland grew from an acorn Grace Davis picked up on her honeymoon — at a party in the Emperor's garden in Japan.

WWW.AVALON-NUDE.COM

Clothing is optional on the lawn, at volleyball games, Saturday night dances (usually only the band is clothed) or in the dining room. It's forbidden in the hot tub and swimming pool. **Avalon** is a family-style naturalist resort tucked away in the hills of Hampshire County near Paw Paw. Undistinguished from other members of the local Chamber of Commerce at group meetings, the folks from Avalon don't recruit.

There's an eighteen-room lodge, dance barn and campgrounds with plans for more development on the 250 acre site. Nudism is growing in America by leaps and bounds with its own Washington action committee. Avalon memberships are available, although non-members may visit.

According to one Avalon neighbor, skinny dipping is nothing new in these hills. Another reports that it's like a big family picnic with lots of nice people, except nobody wears clothes.

There are local dissenters. When the Berkeley Springs newspaper ran a thoughtful feature on the nearby resort, it sparked three times as many column inches in responding letters, including one calling Avalon "the shame of Hampshire County."

CENTURY-OLD BEDS

There are ghosts, old time water fountains in the halls, corkscrews mounted on bathroom walls and no bed less than a century old at the **General Lewis Inn**.

We checked in with a lovely woman at the tiny front desk. Both Patrick Henry and Thomas Jefferson reportedly stood and checked in at that same hand-built desk in its previous incarnation at the once grand Sweet Chalybeate Springs Hotel nearby. We were directed to wander the halls and select from any room with the door open. We tried a few beds and checked the views. We selected a corner room with windows on two sides, from which we could see both the rooftops of historic Lewisburg and folks playing croquet on the inn's clipped lawns.

There are antiques everywhere, authentic remnants of the frontier Lewisburg once was. An enormous but organized collection of antique tools and household items — many made from covered wagon parts — cover the walls in Memory Hall. Other caches are tucked away in old cupboards throughout the inn. The comfortable parlor has games, puzzles and a lovely fire in season.

Breakfast was served in the dining room, located on what was once the first floor of the original 1834 home. Sunlight flooded the windows and baroque music played. The breakfast potatoes were an abundant assemblage that included mushrooms, scallions, tomatoes, banana peppers, cheese, salsa and sour cream. Belgian waffles with real maple syrup and delicious omelets held their own with the potatoes.

As for the ghosts — those in the know ask for rooms 206 and 208, both part of the original house. The ghosts are an adult and two children. Innkeeper Jim Morgan is skeptical as befits a former research scientist for DuPont and inventor of one segment of the Polaroid process. He attributes the reports to mistaken identity, pointing to the old steam heat as source for thumps and groans as the wood dries out. "No one ever sees the ghosts in summer," said Jim.

CABIN FEVER

The remote location did not protect the mountains of **Kumbrarow State Forest** from being stripped of their fine hemlock and spruce forests early in this century. The excessively wet climate — the wettest place around even in the last Ice Age — accelerated the second growth forest, which now envelops the small clearing where the park's five rustic cabins sit around a central courtyard near the picturesque well house.

Built by the **Civilian Conservation Corps** in the late 1930s, the cabins have no electricity or running water. They do have a fireplace, gas appliances, pit toilets and the well. Light is provided by Coleman-type lanterns, including one ingeniously rigged as a five-pod chandelier. The screened porch backs up to a very loud, rock-strewn Mill Creek. Lush vegetation and abundant rhododendron are everywhere along the walking trails. One direction leads easily downstream to a series of falls, riffles and rapids. Although it is the state's highest forest at 3,855 feet, the area around the cabins is the relatively flat Mill Creek streambed.

A favorite with hunters, each cabin is equipped out back with hanging racks for game.

Visit soon. The timber industry has designs on hundreds of giant oaks, cherry and maple missed in the early twentieth century harvests and grown extra big because of the moist climate.

ROOM WITH A RIDE

There's only one way down and up at **Mountain Creek Lodge** — an aerial tram that connects the thirty-room hideaway deep in the Bluestone Gorge to Pipestem State Park's main hotel on the rim. Rooms are undistinguished except for the balcony overlooking the rock-strewn

Bluestone River. Easy walks along the riverbank may stir up over-friendly wildlife. I was shadowed for miles by a fawn who didn't get that I consider all deer potential garden wreckers and candidates for the road kill bill. Closed through the winter season, Mountain Creek has the added distinction of harboring the only first-rate restaurant in the state park system. *See* "Tours and Trips" and "Local Food" for more on Pipestem.

MILLENNIUM LODGING

Adventure-based camps like **Elk River Touring Center** are the evolving face of West Virginia lodging. There's a ten-room B&B and restaurant as well as cabins and a campground. Established in 1985 as one of the first mountain bike touring companies in the United States, Elk River is an outfitter for day, weekend and week-long guided trips, mostly through the Monongahela National Forest. They rent an assortment of camping gear, tents, and sleeping bags, and arrange for meals in the wilderness. They also offer mountain bike riding camps and fly fishing trips.

NOTABLE BED TIME

★ There is no finer lodging experience in America than West Virginia's **Greenbrier Hotel**. Read about it in "Truly Incredible."

★ I spotted the turret as we approached the **Blennerhassett Hotel's** modest entrance on Parkersburg's main thoroughfare, and immediately began plotting how to get whatever room was hidden in its round walls. One-of-a-kind guest quarters are a trait of old hotels and examining the outside is an almost infallible way of discovering where those special rooms may be. What I found in the turret at the Blennerhassett was Room 315, oversized, with a view from the curved window of the Smoot, a historic vaudeville theater. It became my room of choice.

The century-old hotel that re-opened at double the size in 1986 also offers rooms with the distinction of frontage on a tropical atrium filled with sunlight and a jungle of greenery. The street-level lounge is dark and inviting; the dining room is dress-up with white linen.

★ **Cheat Mountain Club** is a former hunting lodge with wood paneled walls and floors, spartan rooms and gender-separated gang bathrooms. It was built in the 1890s for a guest list that included Henry Ford and Thomas Edison. Family-style dining comes with the room, and Shavers Fork River offers great fishing and swimming.

★ **Mountaineer Hotel** in downtown Williamson was built in 1925 and is being restored to its grand railroad hotel past. It boasts a snazzy cigar bar and walk-in humidor.

★ Walker and Jody Boyd received History Hero awards for their work in reviving the historic **Wells Inn**. Built as the Wells Hotel in 1894, its thirty-six guest rooms were targeted for genteel travelers to Sistersville, an oil and gas boom town along the Ohio.  Restored to that Victorian time, today's Inn receives rave reviews for special touches, affordable gourmet food and a bakery.

★ Once the site of an important stagecoach stop on the old Kanawha Turnpike, the **Glen Ferris Inn** is famous for its spectacular view of Kanawha Falls, especially from an executive suite.

★ There are unique touches in many of the state's B&Bs, often in beautiful, rescued historic homes. On the walls of **Boydville** in Martinsburg, important wallpaper in near perfect condition was discovered. Its pattern happened to be "Views of North America", by Jean Zuber et Cie in Rheim Alsace, first printed in 1834. This is the same wallpaper uncovered in the White House Diplomatic Room by Jacqueline Kennedy. Boydville does the White House one better with its hand painted English wallpaper in the foyer, dating from 1812.

No Ogres in this Bavarian Fable

A visit to **The Bavarian Inn** is certain to stir childhood memories of *Grimm's Fairy Tales* — one with a beautiful princess and a happy ending. Chalets of distinctive stucco, dark timbered Alpine architecture and individual balconies perched high above the rushing Potomac River recall Hansel and Gretel's town before they were lost in the woods. Our room behind the balcony had a high four-poster canopied bed and a gilded mirror above the whirlpool bath. I was Sleeping Beauty, fantasy floating in a nobleman's fantasy castle high above the Danube.

Time shifted back to reality. I was a guest with my husband at the Bavarian Inn. And the cliffs of the Potomac at the edge of Shepherdstown marked the rise of the Alleghenies, not the Alps. Still,

I remembered Snow White and wondered about the gleaming red apples on the table.

The entry road marked Bavarian Inn curves up to an unexpected world of tidy Alpine structures outlined against the forested mountain across the river. The subdued hum of historic Shepherdstown seems far away.

Authentic Old World charm intensified at dinner in the original gray stone mansion. We ate near the stone fireplace in the hardwood-trimmed Hunt Room. A three-foot chandelier of twisted deer horn lit our table; matching antler sconces were scattered around the handsome room. The extensive menu featured an entire column of schnitzels and wursts, an unpronounceable selection of German cordials, and an invitation to slip downstairs to the Rathskeller. Casual and comforting, the Rathskeller offers the welcoming closeness of a richly-paneled hideaway — with benches before the fireplace ready for comrades sipping brandy or clicking steins of German beer.

The Alpine setting comes naturally for "the Bavarian man with an English wife and two blond boys in *liederhosen*," as Erwin Asam and his wife Carol were described when they first arrived in the late 1970s Both are dapper, courtly, and obviously the European spirits that inhabit the place and generate its flavor. And it is just as natural for the rustic eleven-acre spot above the Potomac to be where 200 years earlier there had been a thriving German community, known as Mecklenburg.

The chalets were built using the images on Bavarian postcards as models. Rounded bathrooms fill the turrets in one chalet; and each building has several private entrances for clusters of rooms. Foundations were blasted from the solid rock cliffs on which they sit. An appealing gallery of Alpine frescoes are featured on the exterior walls of chalets and the outdoor garden wall of the new lodge.

The Bavarian Inn was one of the first places in the area to have rooms with fireplaces and private whirlpools. Most of the seventy guest rooms are equipped with both, as well as European bidets. The gas fireplace, igniting at the flick of a switch, is especially luxurious for those of us who live with hauling logs and sitting by the stove waiting for the fire to catch. Many rooms have a large sitting area with a comfortable couch; all rooms are furnished with irons, hair dryers and coffee makers. The opulent suites display polished antiques against the river view.

Twenty years have treated the Asams and their vision of Continental hospitality kindly. They celebrated the Inn's anniversary in 1997, comfortable in their three-year old expansion — the thirty room Black Forest lodge. The towheads in liederhosen are now young men, college educated and gaining needed experience at other resorts for the career of providing continuity to the Bavarian Inn.

APPENDIX
WAY OUT BY COUNTY

The best place to obtain detailed information is the local convention and visitors bureau (CVB) in each area. They are listed below with the county or counties they serve. For West Virginia in general call 1-800-CALL WVA. They will send "West Virginia It's You!," a glossy travel magazine published by Bell Atlantic. It's a gold mine of useful information.

Towns and Cities and their Counties:

Beckley — *see* Raleigh
Berkeley Springs — *see* Morgan
Bluefield — *see* Mercer
Buckhannon — *see* Upshur
Charleston — *see* Kanawha
Clarksburg — *see* Harrison
Elkins — *see* Randolph
Fayetteville — *see* Fayette
Harpers Ferry — *see* Jefferson
Huntington — *see* Cabell
Lewisburg — *see* Greenbrier
Martinsburg — *see* Berkeley
Morgantown — *see* Monongalia
Parkersburg — *see* Wood
Philippi — *see* Barbour
Romney — *see* Hampshire
Shepherdstown — *see* Jefferson
Wheeling — *see* Ohio

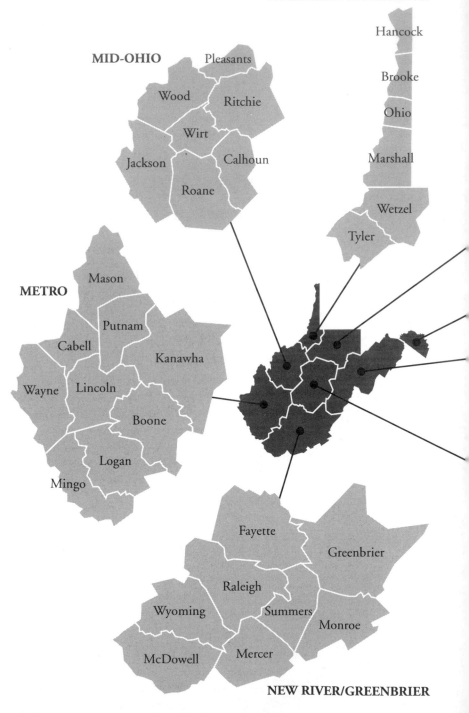

NORTHERN PANHANDLE

Hancock

Brooke

Ohio

Marshall

Wetzel

Tyler

MID-OHIO

Pleasants

Wood

Ritchie

Wirt

Jackson

Calhoun

Roane

METRO

Mason

Putnam

Cabell

Kanawha

Wayne

Lincoln

Boone

Logan

Mingo

Fayette

Greenbrier

Raleigh

Wyoming

Summers

Monroe

McDowell

Mercer

NEW RIVER/GREENBRIER

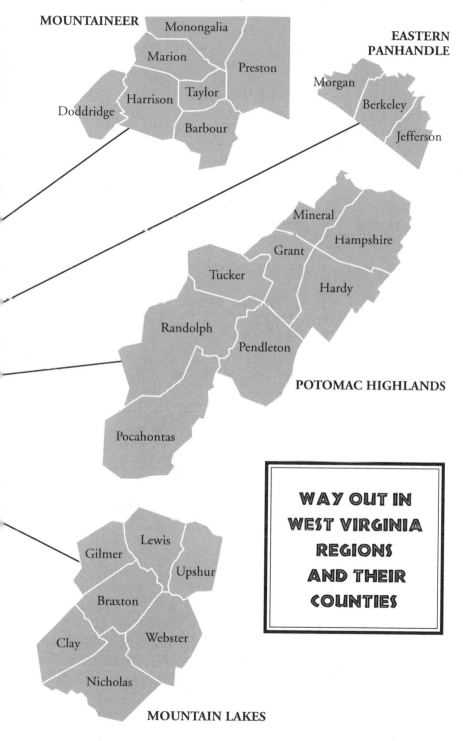

MOUNTAINEER

Monongalia

Marion

Preston

Doddridge

Harrison

Taylor

Barbour

EASTERN
PANHANDLE

Morgan

Berkeley

Jefferson

Mineral

Grant

Hampshire

Tucker

Hardy

Randolph

Pendleton

POTOMAC HIGHLANDS

Pocahontas

WAY OUT IN
WEST VIRGINIA
REGIONS
AND THEIR
COUNTIES

Lewis

Gilmer

Upshur

Braxton

Clay

Webster

Nicholas

MOUNTAIN LAKES

The attractions for each county and the chapter in which they can be found are listed below.

Barbour County
> Philippi CVB
> 124 N. Main St, Philippi 26416
> 304-457-1225

Carrollton Covered Bridge • Amazing Architecture • Philippi
Mummies • Truly Incredible • Philippi
Philippi Covered Bridge • Amazing Architecture • Philippi

Berkeley County
> Martinsburg CVB
> 208 S. Queen St., Martinsburg 25401
> 800-4WVA-FUN

Apollo Theater • Art Wonders • Martinsburg
Asian Gardens • Local Foods • Martinsburg
Belle Boyd House • Historic Oddities • Martinsburg
Blue Ridge Bank • Amazing Architecture • Martinsburg
Blue Ridge Outlet Center • Shopping Treasures • Martinsburg
B&O Roundhouse Complex • Amazing Architecture/Historic Oddities
  • Martinsburg
Boydville • Unusual Places to Stay • Martinsburg
Buck's Hill • Million Dollar Views
Bunker Hill Mill • Historic Oddities • Bunker Hill
The Ghost Line • Tours • Martinsburg
Snyder's Gourmet Hams • Local Foods • Martinsburg
Vanmetre Ford Bridge • Amazing Architecture • Martinsburg

Braxton County
> Braxton CVB
> 245 Skidmore Lane, Sutton 26601
> 304-765-3300

Flatwoods Monster • Remarkable Collections • Flatwoods

Brooke County
> Wellsburg Chamber of Commerce
> 600 Colony Center, Wellsburg 26070
> 304-737-2787

Bethany College • Superlatives • Bethany
Grimes Golden • Mother Nature's Wonders • Wellsburg

Cabell County
> Cabell/Huntington CVB
> 210 11th St. #13, Huntington 25708
> 800-635-6329

Blenko Glass • Shopping Treasures • Milton
Camden Park • Historic Oddities/Superlatives • Huntington
East Huntington Bridge • Amazing Architecture • Huntington
Fortification Hill • Historic Oddities • Barboursville
Heiner's Bakery • Tours • Huntington
Huntington Mall • Shopping Treasures • Huntington
Huntington Museum • Amazing Architecture/Remarkable Collections
   • Huntington
Keith Albee Theater • Art Wonders • Huntington
Museum of Radio & Technology • Remarkable Collections • Huntington
Old Central City • Shopping Treasures • Huntington
Ritter Park • Superlatives • Huntington
Summerfest • Fast Living • Huntington
Stewart's Original Hot Dogs • Local Food • Huntington

Calhoun County

Heartwood in the Hills • Art Wonders • Five Forks

Clay County

Elkhurst Bridge • Adventure Driving • Clay

Doddridge County

Center Point Covered Bridge • Amazing Architecture
North Bend Rail Trail • Adventure Driving/Tours

Fayette County
         Fayetteville Visitors Center
         120 Windsor Lane, Fayetteville 25840
         888-574-1500

Ace Adventure Center • Great Plumbing • Oak Hill
African-American Heritage Family Tree Museum • Remarkable Collections
   • Ansted
Bridge Day • Far Out Festivals • Fayetteville
Camp Washington Carver • Amazing Architecture/Superlatives
Canyon Rim Visitors Center • Million Dollar Views/Mother Nature's Wonders
Cathedral Cafe and Bookstore • Art Wonders • Fayetteville
Class VI River Runners • Fast Living • Lansing
Country Road Cabins • Great Plumbing • Hico
Fayetteville Visitors Center • Amazing Architecture • Fayetteville
Glen Ferris Inn • Unusual Places to Stay • Glen Ferris
Hawks Nest Diversion Tunnel • Historic Oddities • Ansted
Hawks Nest State Park • Million Dollar Views • Ansted
Jet boats at Hawks Nest • Fast Living • Ansted
Kaymoor Mine Trail • Things That Used to be There
Midland Trail Scenic Highway • Adventure Driving
Mill Creek Cabins • Great Plumbing • Lansing

Mystery Hole • Things That Used to be There • Ansted
New River/New River Gorge • Fast Living/Festivals/Mother Nature's Wonders
New River Gorge Bridge • Amazing Architecture/Festivals
New River Llama Trekking Co. • Tours • Edmond
Poor Man's Flying School • Tours • Fayetteville
Red Dog Saloon • Fast Living • Fayetteville
Thurmond • Adventure Driving/Things That Used to be There
Thurmond Supply • Shopping Treasures • Thurmond

Grant County

> Grant County Chamber of Commerce
> PO Box 1366, Petersburg 26847
> 304-257-2722

Harman's North Fork Cottages & Cabins • Great Plumbing • Petersburg
North Fork Mountain Inn • Great Plumbing
Petersburg Fish Hatchery • Superlatives • Petersburg
Smoke Hole Cabins • Great Plumbing • Petersburg
Smoke Hole Caverns • Superlatives/Mother Nature's Wonders • Petersburg
Smoke Hole Road • Adventure Driving

Greenbrier County

> Lewisburg CVB
> 105 Church St., Lewisburg 24901
> 304-645-1000 or 800-833-2068

Alderson • Historic Oddities
Carnegie Hall • Art Wonders • Lewisburg
The Coal House & Gift Shop • Amazing Architecture • White Sulphur Springs
General Lewis Inn • Great Plumbing/Unusual Places to Stay • Lewisburg
The Greenbrier • Truly Incredible/Superlatives/Great Plumbing/Unusual Places
    to Stay • White Sulphur Springs
Greenbrier Bunker Tour • Tours • White Sulphur Springs
The Greenbrier Christmas Shop at the Depot • Shopping Treasures •
    White Sulphur Springs
Greenbrier River • Superlatives
Greenbrier River Trail • Adventure Driving/Superlatives
Gwen's Kitchen • Local Food • Lewisburg
Herns Mill Covered Bridge • Amazing Architecture • Lewisburg
Hokes Mill Covered Bridge • Amazing Architecture • Ronceverte
Lake Sherwood • Mother Nature's Wonders
Lay over roads • Adventure Driving
Leland's Small World • Remarkable Collections • Alderson
Lewisburg • Great Plumbing/Mother Nature's Wonders
Lost World Caverns • Mother Nature's Wonders • Lewisburg
Midland Trail Scenic Highway • Adventure Driving
Oakhurst Links • Superlatives • White Sulphur Springs
Old Stone Presbyterian Church • Superlatives • Lewisburg
Organ Cave • Historic Oddities/Mother Nature's Wonders • Ronceverte
Savannah Lane Shooting Association • Fast Living • Lewisburg

Shanghai Parade • Far-Out Festivals • Lewisburg
Swift Level Guest House • Tours • Lewisburg

Hampshire County

> Hampshire County Chamber of Commerce
> HC63-Box 3550, Romney 26757
> 304-822-7221

Avalon • Unusual Places to Stay
Bloomery Iron Furnace • Things That Used to be There
Capon Springs and Farms • Great Plumbing/Unusual Places to Stay/
  Things That Used to be There • Capon Springs
Coca Cola Bottling Works Museum • Remarkable Collections • Romney
Fort Mill Ridge Trenches • Historic Oddities • Romney
Ice Mountain • Mother Nature's Wonders
Potomac Eagle • Tours • Romney
Raven Rocks • Million Dollar Views
Indian Mound Cemetery • Historic Oddities • Romney

Hancock County

> Hancock County CVB
> RD2 - Box 17B, Weirton 26062
> 304-723-3408

Homer Laughlin • Shopping Treasures/Tours • Newell
Peter Tarr Iron Furnace • Things That Used to be There • Weirton
World's Largest Teapot • Superlatives • Chester

Hardy County

Baker Indoor Archery Range • Superlatives • Baker
Hanging Rocks • Mother Nature's Wonders • Baker
Lee White Sulphur Springs • Things That Used to Be There • Mathias
Lost River • Mother Nature's Wonders • Wardensville
South Branch Inn • Great Plumbing • Moorefield
Trout Pond • Mother Nature's Wonders

Harrison County

> Bridgeport/Clarksburg CVB
> 109 Platinum Dr. - Suite B, Bridgeport, 26330
> 304-842-7272 or 800-368-4324

Bonnie Belle Bakery • Local Foods • Nutter Fort
Clarksburg • Adventure Driving
Fletcher Covered Bridge • Amazing Architecture • Wolf Summit
Gray Barker UFO collection • Remarkable Collections • Clarksburg
Italian Heritage Festival • Far-Out Festivals • Clarksburg
Julio's • Local Foods • Clarksburg
North Bend Rail Trail • Adventure Driving/Tours
Oak Mound • Historic Oddities • Clarksburg
Oliverio's Cash and Carry • Local Foods • Clarksburg

Simpson Creek Covered Bridge • Amazing Architecture • Bridgeport
Tomoro's • Local Food • Clarksburg

Jackson County
Jackson County Chamber of Commerce
104 Miller Dr., Ripley 25271
304-273-5367

Mountain State Art and Craft Fair • Far-Out Festivals • Ripley
Rankin Octagonal Barn • Amazing Architecture • Ravenswood
Sarvis Fork Covered Bridge • Amazing Architecture • Sandyville
Staats Mill Covered Bridge • Amazing Architecture • Ripley
Washington Western Lands Museum • Historic Oddities • Ravenswood

Jefferson County
Jefferson County CVB
PO Box A, Harpers Ferry 25425
304-535-2627

Bavarian Inn & Lodge • Great Plumbing/Unusual Places to Stay • Shepherdstown
Beallair • Historic Oddities • Charles Town
Charles Town • Historic Oddities/Mother Nature's Wonders
Charles Town Post Office • Superlatives • Charles Town
Claymont/Blakeley • Historic Oddities • Charles Town
Contemporary American Theater Festival • Art Wonders • Shepherdstown
Election of 1860 • Far-Out Festivals • Harpers Ferry
George Tyler Moore Center for the Study of the Civil War • Historic Oddities
    • Shepherdstown
George Washington Cave • Historic Oddities • Charles Town
German Street • Amazing Architecture • Shepherdstown
Ghost Tours of Harpers Ferry • Tours • Harpers Ferry
Happy Retreat • Historic Oddities • Charles Town
Harewood • Historic Oddities • Charles Town
Harpers Ferry National Historical Park • Amazing Architecture/
    Historic Oddities/Things That Used to Be There • Harpers Ferry
Hillbrook Inn • Historic Oddities • Charles Town
Hilltop House • Great Plumbing/Million Dollar Views • Harpers Ferry
Jefferson County Courthouse • Historic Oddities • Charles Town
Jefferson County House and Garden Tour • Historic Oddities
Jefferson Rock • Million Dollar Views • Harpers Ferry
John Brown's Fort • Amazing Architecture • Harpers Ferry
Mountain Heritage Arts and Crafts Festival • Shopping Treasures •
    Harpers Ferry
National Conservation Training Center • Truly Incredible • Shepherdstown
O'Hurley's General Store • Great Plumbing/Shopping Treasures •
    Shepherdstown
Rumsey Monument • Historic Oddities • Shepherdstown
Rumsey Boathouse • Historic Oddities • Shepherdstown
Shannondale Springs • Things That Used to be There • Charles Town

Shepherdstown Opera House • Art Wonders • Shepherdstown
Storer College • Historic Oddities • Harpers Ferry
Summit Point Raceway • Fast Living • Summit Point
Thomas Shepherd Gristmill • Superlatives • Shepherdstown
Virginius Island • Things That Used to be There • Harpers Ferry
Yellow Brick Bank • Art Wonders • Shepherdstown
Zion Episcopal Church Cemetery • Historic Oddities • Charles Town

Kanawha County

Charleston CVB
200 Civic Center Dr. Suite 002, Charleston 25301
800-733-5469

South Charleston CVB
PO Box 8595, South Charleston 25303
800-238-9488

Badlands • Adventure Driving • Jefferson
Cabin Creek Quilts • Shopping Treasures • Malden
Capitol Theater • Art Wonders • Charleston
Carriage Trail • Tours • Charleston
Charleston Town Center • Shopping Treasures • Charleston
Dutch Hollow Wine Cellar Park • Historic Oddities • Dunbar
East End Yard Sale • Shopping Treasures • Charleston
Historic Charleston B&B • Great Plumbing • Charleston
Island Sunset • Local Foods • Charleston
Kanawha State Forest Braille Trail • Tours • Charleston
Mountain Stage • Art Wonders • Charleston
South Charleston Mound • Historic Oddities • South Charleston
Southern Kitchen • Local Foods • Charleston
State Capitol • Superlatives • Charleston
The Strand • Fast Living • Charleston
University of Charleston • Amazing Architecture • Charleston
Vandalia Festival • Art Wonders/Far-Out Festivals • Charleston
WV Archives and History Library • Remarkable Collections • Charleston
West Virginia State Museum • Historic Oddities/Remarkable Collections/
   Superlatives • Charleston
Yeager Airport • Adventure Driving • Charleston
Yeager Monument • Adventure Driving • St. Albans

Lewis County

Lewis County CVB
PO Box 379, Weston 26452
304-269-7328

Jackson's Mill • Superlatives • Weston
Masterpiece Crystal • Shopping Treasures • Jane Lew
Walkersville Covered Bridge • Amazing Architecture • Walkersville
Weston State Asylum • Amazing Architecture/Superlatives • Weston

Logan County

Chief Logan State Park • Historic Oddities
Devil Anse Hatfield Statue • Historic Oddities • Sarah Ann
Morrison's Drive-in • Local Food • Stollings

Marion County
Marion County CVB
110 Adams Street, Fairmont 26554
304-368-1123 or 800-834-7365

Barrackville Covered Bridge • Amazing Architecture • Barrackville
Colacessino's • Local Foods • Fairmont
Country Club Bakery • Local Foods • Fairmont
Round Barn • Amazing Architecture • Mannington

Marshall County
Moundsville Economic Development
818 Jefferson St., Moundsville 26041
304-845-6200

Cresap Mound • Historic Oddities
Grave Creek Mound • Historic Oddities/Superlatives • Moundsville
Ohio River Islands Wildlife Refuge • Mother Nature's Wonders
Palace of Gold • Truly Incredible • Moundsville
WV Penitentiary Tours • Tours • Moundsville

Mason County
Mason County Tourism
305 Main St., Point Pleasant 25550
304-675-8799

Battle Monument State Park • Historic Oddities • Point Pleasant
Cornstalk • Historic Oddities • Point Pleasant
Robert Byrd Locks Visitor Center • Million Dollar Views
TNT area • Things That Used to be There • Point Pleasant
WV State Farm Museum • Remarkable Collections • Point Pleasant

McDowell County
City of Welch
88 Howard St., Welch 24801
304-436-3113

Kimball • Superlatives
McDowell County Courthouse • Amazing Architecture • Welch
Panther State Forest • Mother Nature's Wonders

Mercer County
Bluestone CVB
500 Bland St., Bluefield 24701
304-325-8438

Bluefield • Mother Nature's Wonders
Bluefield Arts & Science Center • Amazing Architecture • Bluefield
Bramwell • Amazing Architecture / Things That Used to be There
Chicory Square Park • Art Wonders • Bluefield
Concord United Methodist Church • Art Wonders • Athens
Cooper House • Amazing Architecture • Bramwell
East River Mountain Overlook • Million Dollar Views • Bluefield
East River Mountain Tunnel • Adventure Driving • Bluefield
Eastern Regional Coal Archives • Remarkable Collections • Bluefield
Natural gravity railyards • Amazing Architecture • Bluefield
Pinnacle Rock State Park • Mother Nature's Wonders
Pocahontas coal fields • Mother Nature's Wonders/Superlatives
Ramsey School • Amazing Architecture • Bluefield
Shamrock • Superlatives • Bluefield
University Club • Historic Oddities • Bluefield

Mingo County
>Tug Valley of Commerce
>2nd Ave. & Court St., Williamson 25661
>304-235-5240

Coal House • Amazing Architecture • Williamson
Dingess Tunnel • Adventure Driving
Matewan Development Center • Historic Oddities • Matewan
Mountaineer Hotel • Unusual Places to Stay • Williamson

Mineral County
>Mineral County CVB
>75 S. Mineral St., Keyser 26726
>304-788-2513

Fort Ashby • Historic Oddities/Things That Used to be There • Keyser
Saddle Mountain • Adventure Driving/Million Dollar Views

Monongalia County
>Greater Morgantown CVB
>709 Beechurst Ave., Morgantown 26505
>800-458-7373

Dents Run Covered Bridge • Amazing Architecture
Gabriel Brothers • Shopping Treasures • Morgantown
The Met • Fast Living • Morgantown
Nite Glow • Far-Out Festivals • Morgantown
Personal Rapid Transit System • Superlatives • Morgantown
West Virginia and Regional History Collection • Remarkable Collections
   • Morgantown

Monroe County
>Monroe County Historical Society Museum and
>   Tourism Information Center
>304-772-3003

Alderson • Historic Oddities
Cheese n' More • Adventure Driving/ Local Foods • Gap Mills
Creekside • Great Plumbing • Greenville
Indian Creek Covered Bridge • Amazing Architecture • Salt Sulphur Springs
Kitchen Creek Bakery • Local Foods • Gap Mills
Laurel Creek Covered Bridge • Amazing Architecture
Marie Road • Adventure Driving
Monroe County • Adventure Driving
Monroe County Confederate Monument • Historic Oddities • Union
Peter's Mountain • Adventure Driving/Great Plumbing
Rehobeth Church and Museum • Superlatives • Union
Salt Sulphur Springs • Things That Used to Be There
Scott Hollow Cave • Mother Nature's Wonders • Sinks Grove
Sweet Springs • Adventure Driving/Things That Used to be There
Union • Adventure Driving/Amazing Architecture

Morgan County
>Travel Berkeley Springs
>304 Fairfax St., Berkeley Springs 25411
>800-447-8797

Apple Butter Festival • Far-Out Festivals • Berkeley Springs
Arts Kiosk • Art Wonders • Berkeley Springs
Atasia Spa • Great Plumbing • Berkeley Springs
Berkeley Castle • Amazing Architecture • Berkeley Springs
Berkeley Springs • Historic Oddities/Superlatives/Things That Used to Be There
Berkeley Springs International Water Tasting • Far-Out Festivals
   • Berkeley Springs
Berkeley Springs Roman Baths • Great Plumbing • Berkeley Springs
Berkeley Springs State Park • Historic Oddities/Great Plumbing
   • Berkeley Springs
Coolfont Resort • Great Plumbing • Berkeley Springs
The Country Inn • Great Plumbing • Berkeley Springs
Eddie's Tires • Shopping Treasures • Berkeley Springs
Highlawn Inn • Great Plumbing • Berkeley Springs
Homeopathy Works • Remarkable Collections/Shopping Treasures •
   Berkeley Springs
The Manor B&B • Great Plumbing • Berkeley Springs
Maria's Garden and Inn/Marian Museum • Great Plumbing/Remarkable
   Collections • Berkeley Springs
O'Brien's Cabins • Great Plumbing • Hedgesville
Panorama Overlook • Million Dollar Views • Berkeley Springs
Paw Paw Tunnel • Amazing Architecture • Paw Paw
River House B&B • Tours • Great Cacapon
Star Theatre • Art Wonders • Berkeley Springs

SR 9 • Adventure Driving
Tari's Premier Cafe • Local Foods • Berkeley Springs

Nicholas County
  Summersville CVB
  411 Old Main Dr., Summersville 26651
  304-872-3722

The Gauley River Festival • Far-Out Festivals/Fast Living • Summersville
Feast of the Ransom • Far-Out Festivals • Richwood
Kirkwood Wineries • Local Foods • Summersville
Summersville Bluegrass Festival: Music in the Mountains • Far-Out Festivals
 • Summersville
Summersville Lake & Dam • Fast Living/Superlatives • Summersville

Ohio County
  Wheeling CVB
  1401 Main St., Wheeling 26003
  800-828-3097

Bonnie Dwaine B&B • Great Plumbing • Glen Dale
Big Bertha's Gentlemen's Club • Historic Oddities • Wheeling
Bugsy's • Local Food • Wheeling
Capitol Music Hall • Art Wonders • Wheeling
Carriage House Glass • Shopping Treasures • Wheeling
Centre Market • Amazing Architecture • Wheeling
Coleman's • Local Foods • Wheeling
Festival of Lights • Far-Out Festivals • Wheeling
Jamboree USA • Art Wonders • Wheeling
Kruger St. Toy & Train Museum • Remarkable Collections • Wheeling
Mount de Chantal Academy • Art Wonders • Wheeling
National Road • Historic Oddities • Wheeling
Oglebay Institute • Art Wonders • Wheeling
Oglebay Institute's Glass Museum • Remarkable Collections/Superlatives
 • Wheeling
Oglebay Resort • Superlatives • Wheeling
Ohio River Islands Wildlife Refuge • Mother Nature's Wonders
Point Overlook Museum • Million Dollar Views • Wheeling
Stages • Shopping Treasures • Wheeling
Stifel Fine Arts Center • Art Wonders • Wheeling
Stratford Springs • Great Plumbing • Wheeling
Undo's • Local Food • Wheeling
Upper Market House • Amazing Architecture • Wheeling
Victoria Vaudeville Theater • Art Wonders • Wheeling
Victorian Wheeling Landmarks Foundation • Amazing Architecture
 • Wheeling
Wheeling Island • Superlatives • Wheeling
Wheeling Jesuit College • Superlatives • Wheeling
Wheeling Suspension Bridge • Amazing Architecture • Wheeling
Wymer's General Store and Museum • Remarkable Collections • Wheeling

Pendleton County
>Pendleton County Visitors Commission
>PO Box 602, Franklin 26807
>304-358-7573

Gendarme and Seneca Rocks Climbing School • Million Dollar Views/
  Shopping Treasures • Seneca Rocks
Seneca Caverns • Mother Nature's Wonders/Superlatives
Seneca Rocks • Truly Incredible/Million Dollar Views/Mother Nature's
  Wonders
Spruce Knob • Mother Nature's Wonders
Yokum's Stables • Million Dollar Views • Seneca Rocks

Pleasants County

Ohio River Islands Wildlife Refuge • Mother Nature's Wonders

Pocahontas County
>Pocahontas County Tourism Commission
>PO Box 275, Marlinton 24954
>304-799-4636

Beartown State Park • Mother Nature's Wonders
Cass Scenic Railroad State Park • Tours/Thing That Used to Be There • Cass
Cranberry Glades • Mother Nature's Wonders
Droop Mountain Battlefield State Park • Superlatives
Elk River Touring Company • Unusual Places to Stay • Slatyfork
Elk River Trout Ranch • Local Foods
Falls of Hill Creek • Mother Nature's Wonders
Full Moon Rising • Shopping Treasures • Marlinton
Gaudineer State Forest • Mother Nature's Wonders
Greenbrier River • Superlatives
Greenbrier River Trail • Adventure Driving/Superlatives
Highland Scenic Highway • Adventure Driving
Hillsboro General Store • Shopping Treasures • Hillsboro
Locust Creek Covered Bridge • Amazing Architecture • Hillsboro
National Radio Astronomy Observatory • Truly Incredible • Green Bank
Opera House • Amazing Architecture • Marlinton
Pearl Buck Birthplace • Remarkable Collections • Hillsboro
Red Fox Inn • Local Foods • Snowshoe
Roadkill Cook-off • Far-Out Festivals • Marlinton

Preston County
>Preston County CVB
>PO Box 860, Arthurdale 26520
>304-864-4601

Arthurdale • Superlatives • Kingwood
Buckwheat Festival • Far-Out Festivals • Kingwood
Cathedral State Park • Mother Nature's Wonders • Aurora
Henry Clay Iron Furnace • Things That Used to be There

Cool Springs Park • Remarkable Collections • Fellowsville
Coopers Rock State Forest • Million Dollar Views
Luminaria • Far-Out Festivals • Bruceton Mills
Our Lady of the Pines • Amazing Architecture/Superlatives • Silver Lake
Tunnelton • Amazing Architecture
West Virginia Northern Railways • Tours • Kingwood

Putnam County

Putnam County CVB
1 Valley Park Dr., Hurricane 25526
304-562-0518

City-wide Garage Sale • Shopping Treasures • Hurricane
Hamon Glass • Shopping Treasures • Scott Depot
Hurricane Fire Hall • Art Wonders • Hurricane
Maiden of the Rock petroglyph • Historic Oddities • Hurricane
Museum in the Community • Remarkable Collections/Amazing Architecture
  • Hurricane
Root Cellar Herbs and Mercantile • Shopping Treasures • Hurricane
Village site • Historic Oddities • Buffalo
War Memorial Museum • Remarkable Collections • Nitro
WV Flintlock Championship • Far-Out Festivals • Hurricane

Raleigh County

Southern WV CVB
PO Box 1799, Beckley 25802
800-VISIT-WV

Beckley Exhibition Coal Mine • Tours • Beckley
Brier Rose Studio • Shopping Treasures • Beckley
Country Inn and Suites • Great Plumbing • Beckley
Peace Totem • Art Wonders • Beckley
Take-in Creek • Fast Living • Beckley
Tamarack • Local Food/Art Wonders/Shopping Treasures/Truly Incredible
  • Beckley

Randolph County

Randolph County CVB
200 Executive Plaza, Elkins 26241
800-422-3304

Augusta Heritage Center • Art Wonders/Remarkable Collections • Elkins
Beverly Cemetery • Superlatives • Beverly
Cheat Mountain Club • Unusual Places to Stay • Durbin
Cheat River Lodge & Inn • Great Plumbing/Local Foods • Elkins
Darby Collection • Remarkable Collections • Elkins
Fasnacht • Far-Out Festivals • Helvetia
Gaudineer State Forest • Mother Nature's Wonders
Graceland • Amazing Architecture/Unusual Places to Stay • Elkins
Halliehurst • Amazing Architecture • Elkins

Hutte Restaurant • Local Foods • Helvetia
Hutton House • Great Plumbing • Huttonsville
Kumbrabow State Forest • Unusual Places to Stay
Maple Syrup Festival • Far-Out Festivals • Pickens
Pickin' in the Park • Art Wonders • Elkins
International Ramp Cook-Off and Festival • Far Out Festivals • Elkins
Richter's Maplehouse • Local Foods • Pickens
Sinks of Gandy • Mother Nature's Wonders • New Italy
Warfield House • Great Plumbing • Elkins
Wimpy's Pool Hall • Great Plumbing • Elkins

Ritchie County

Berdine's • Shopping Treasures • Harrisville
The Edge Horseshoe and Carriage Company • Tours • Cairo
R.C. Marshall Hardware • Shopping Treasures • Cairo
Natural Wonder Wildfoods Weekend • Far-Out Festivals • Harrisville
North Bend Rail Trail • Adventure Driving/Tours
Pennsboro Speedway • Fast Living • Pennsboro
West Virginia Marble Festival • Far-Out Festivals • Cairo

Summers County
Summers County CVB
206 Temple St., Hinton 25951
304-466-5420

Alderson • Historic Oddities
Bargers Springs • Adventure Driving
Bluestone Canyon • Mother Nature's Wonders
Graham House • Superlatives
John Henry Collection • Remarkable Collections • Hinton
John Henry Statue and Park • Historic Oddities • Talcott
Mountain Creek Lodge & Restaurant • Local Foods/Unusual Places to Stay
  • Pipestem
Pence Springs Hotel • Amazing Architecture/Great Plumbing/Unusual Places
  to Stay • Pence Springs
Pipestem Resort State Park & Observation Tower • Million Dollar Views/Tours/
  Unusual Places to Stay • Pipestem
Sandstone Falls • Million Dollar Views • Hinton
St. Patrick's Church • Art Wonders • Hinton
Star House • Amazing Architecture • Hinton
State Water Festival • Fast Living • Hinton

Taylor County
Grafton/Taylor CVB
214 Main St., Room 205, Grafton 26354
304-265-3938

Anna Jarvis Birthplace • Superlatives • Webster

International Mother's Day Shrine • Superlatives • Grafton
Tygart Dam • Superlatives • Grafton

Tucker County
Tucker County CVB
PO Box 565, William Ave., Davis 26260
800-782-2775

Blackwater Falls State Park • Million Dollar Views
Canaan Valley • Mother Nature's Wonders/Superlatives
Davis • Superlatives
Dolly Llamas • Tours • Canaan
Dolly Sods • Mother Nature's Wonders
Fairfax Stone • Historic Oddities
24 hours of Canaan • Far-Out Festivals • Davis

Tyler County
Sistersville City Hall
200 Diamond St., Sistersville 26175
304-652-6361

Ben's Run Fortifications • Historic Oddities • Ben's Run
Marble King • Shopping Treasures • Paden City
Ohio River Islands Wildlife Refuge • Mother Nature's Wonders
Sistersville Ferry • Things That Used to be There • Sistersville
The Wells Inn • Unusual Places to Stay • Sistersville

Upshur County
Buckhannon CVB and Chamber of Commerce
16 S. Kanawha St., Buckhannon 26201
304-472-1722

Donut Shop • Local Food • Buckhannon
Little Hungary Farm Winery • Local Food • Buckhannon
Pringle Sycamore • Things That Used to be There • Buckhannon
West Virginia Weslyan • Amazing Architecture • Buckhannon

Wayne County

Pilgrim Glass • Shopping Treasures/Superlatives • Ceredo

Webster County

Holly River State Park • Historic Oddities
Tecumseh • Historic Oddities
Webster County Woodchopping Festival • Far-Out Festivals • Bakers Island

Wetzel County

Fish Creek Covered Bridge • Amazing Architecture • Hundred
Ohio River Islands Wildlife Refuge • Mother Nature's Wonders
Thistledew Farms • Far-Out Festivals • Proctor

Wood County
> Parkersburg/Wood County CVB
> 215 First St., Parkersburg 26101
> 800-752-4982

Artsbridge • Art Wonders • Parkersburg
Blennerhassett Hotel • Unusual Places to Stay • Parkersburg
Blennerhassett Island State Park • Historic Oddities • Parkersburg
Blennerhassett Museum • Historic Oddities/Remarkable Collections
  • Parkersburg
Blennerhassett Island Tour • Tours • Parkersburg
Fenton Glass • Tours • Williamstown
Henderson Hall • Historic Oddities/Remarkable Collections • Williamstown
Holl's Chocolates • Local Foods • Vienna
Julia-Ann Square Historic District • Amazing Architecture • Parkersburg
Mountain State Muzzleloading • Shopping Treasures • Boaz
North Bend Rail Trail • Adventure Driving/Tours
Ohio River Islands Wildlife Refuge • Mother Nature's Wonders
Oil and Gas Museum • Remarkable Collections • Parkersburg
Smoot Theater • Art Wonders • Parkersburg
Transallegheny Books • Shopping Treasures • Parkersburg
West Virginia Honey Festival • Far-Out Festivals • Parkersburg
WV Motor Speedway • Fast Living • Mineral Wells

Wyoming County
> Wyoming County CVB
> PO Box 906, Pineville 24874
> 304-294-5151

R.D. Bailey Lake & Dam • Superlatives
Burning Rocks • Mother Nature's Wonders • Pineville
Itmann Company Store • Amazing Architecture • Itmann
Mullens • Art Wonders

Statewide
> WV Division of Tourism
> 2101 Washington Ave., E., Charleston 25305
> 800-CALL-WVA

Coffindaffer Cross Clusters • Adventure Driving • statewide
Fall Color Map • Tours
Graffiti • Art Wonders
Hatfield and McCoy Trail • Adventure Driving
Interstates • Adventure Driving
Mountain biking • Adventure Driving
US 50 • Adventure Driving
US 219 • Adventure Driving
US 250 • Adventure Driving
WV Crafts Map • Art Wonders
White water rafting • Fast Living

WAY OUT INDEX

A

Ace Whitewater and Adventure Center, p. 60
   Fayette Co. P.O. Box 1168, Oak Hill 25901. Along the New River two miles from Oak Hill. 800-787-3982.

African-American Heritage Family Tree Museum, p. 120
   Fayette Co. On US 60 2 miles east of Hawks Nest State Park. Open Thu-Sat 11-5, Sun 1-5, May 15-Oct. 15. 304-658-5526.

Alderson, p. 72
   Summers/Greenbrier/Monroe Co. From I-64, take Alta exit, then go south on SR12.

Apple Butter Festival, p. 46
   Morgan Co. Chamber of Commerce, 304 Fairfax Street, Berkeley Springs 25411. On Columbus Day weekend in the parks and streets. Held annually since 1974. 800-447-8797.

Apollo Theater, pgs. 30, 164
   Berkeley Co. East Race Street, Martinsburg 25401. 304-263-6766.

Arthurdale, p. 138
   Preston Co. Driving tour. Located on SR 92, 10 miles west of Kingwood in Preston County. Visitor Center open Sat 12-5, Sun 2-5 in the summer. 304-864-3959.

Artsbridge, p. 33
   Wood Co. P.O. Box 1706, Parkersburg 26102. 304-428-3988.

Arts Kiosk, p. 33
   Morgan Co. Morgan Arts Council, at corner of Washington and

Congress Sts. in front of Star Theatre in Berkeley Springs 25411.
304-258-2300.

Asian Gardens, p. 90
Berkeley Co. 748 N. Foxcroft Avenue, Martinsburg 25401, in North
Mall Plaza just off I-81 and SR 45. Open daily for lunch and dinner.
Closed Tuesdays. 304-263-8678.

Atasia Spa, p. 55
Morgan Co. 206 Congress Street, Berkeley Springs 25411.
Open daily 9am-6pm. Toll free: 877-258-7888.

Augusta Heritage Center, pgs. 14, 26, 119
Randolph Co. 100 Campus Drive, Elkins 26241. 304-637-1209.

Avalon, p. 195
Hampshire Co. P.O. Box 369, Paw Paw 25434. From SR29 at the
Hampshire/Morgan Co. line, go west on Critton Hollow Rd. for 2 miles.
304-947-5600.

B

Badlands, p. 3
Kanawha Co. Jefferson, on US 60 west of Charleston.

R.D. Bailey Lake & Dam, p. 143
Wyoming Co. New Visitors Center, P.O. Drawer 70, Justice, 24851.
On US 52. 304-664-3229.

Baker Indoor Archery Range, p. 139
Hardy Co. Corner Mart at intersection of SR 55 & 259 in Baker.
304-897-5908.

Barbour County Historical Museum, p. 171
Barbour Co. 200 North Main Street, Philippi 26416. 304-457-4846.

Bargers Springs, p. 2
Summers Co. Marie Rd. at junction of SR 122 and SR 12, approximately
6 miles from Talcott.

Barrackville Covered Bridge, pgs. 20, 22
Marion Co.

Battle Monument State Park, p. 65
Mason Co. 1 Main St., Point Pleasant 25550. Open daily, year 'round.
304-675-3330.

Bavarian Inn and Lodge, pgs. 56, 59, 89, 199
Jefferson Co. Rt. 1, Box 30, Shepherdstown 25443. SR 480 north.
304-876-2551.

Beallair, p. 68
Jefferson Co. North of US 340 near Halltown. 304-876-2242.

Capon Springs, pgs. 58, 149, 191
 Hampshire Co. P.O. Box 0, Capon Springs 26823. SR 259 north from
 Wardensville, right on CR 16. 304-874-3695.

Carnegie Hall, p. 28
 Greenbrier Co. 105 Church St., Lewisburg 24901. One block off
 Washington St. 304-645-7917.

Carriage House Glass, p. 127
 Ohio Co. At Oglebay Park. Take US 40 east from Wheeling, go north on
 SR 88. 304-243-4000.

Carriage Trail, p. 167
 Kanawha Co. Sunrise Museum.

Carrollton Covered Bridge, p. 20
 Barbour Co.

Cass Scenic Railroad State Park, pgs. 153, 169
 Pocahontas Co. P.O. Box 107, Cass 24927. SR 28/92 between Dunmore
 and Green Bank in Pocahontas County or SR 66 from US 219 at
 Slatyfork. Open May through Nov.; four trips a day. Reservations available. 304-456-4300.

Cathedral Cafe and Bookstore, p. 32
 Fayette Co. 134 S. Court St., Fayetteville 25840. Open daily 9-7
 except Tues. 304-574-0202.

Cathedral State Park, pgs. 104, 141
 Preston Co. US 50 at Aurora. 304-735-3771.

Cedar Lawn, p. 68
 Jefferson Co. SR 51, 4 miles west of Charles Town. Private.

Center Point Covered Bridge, p. 20
 Doddridge Co.

Centre Market, p. 18
 Ohio Co. Market St. between 20th and 22nd in Wheeling. Open Mon-
 Sat. 304-234-3878.

Charleston Town Center, p. 131
 Kanawha Co. Corners of Clendenin, Court, Lee and Quarrier Sts.
 304-345-9525.

Charles Town, pgs. 67, 108
 Jefferson Co. US 340 & SR 51 & 9. Jefferson Co. CVB. 800-848 TOUR
 or 304-535-2627.

Charles Town Post Office, p. 74
 Jefferson Co. 101 W. Washington St., Charles Town 25414. Open year
 'round Mon-Fri 8:30-5. 304-725-2421.

Cheat Mountain Club, p. 198
 Randolph Co. Off US 250 on Shavers Creek near Cheat Bridge.
 304-456-4627.

D

Dancing Outlaw, p. 29
Part of "The Different Drummer" series. Order from WNPB-TV.
191 Scott Ave., Morgantown 26505. 304-293-6511.

Darby Collection, pgs. 14, 117
Randolph Co. Halliehurst. Davis and Elkins College, 100 Campus Dr.,
Elkins 25241. Open by reservation. 304-637-1980.

Davis, p. 140
Tucker Co. SR 32 off US 219.

Dent's Run Covered Bridge, p. 20
Monongalia Co.

Devil Anse Hatfield Statue, p. 76
Logan Co. Off SR 44 near Sarah Ann.

Dingess Tunnel, p. 7
Mingo Co. SR 65.

Dolly Llamas, p. 167
Tucker Co. 304-866-4359 or 304-574-1117.

Dolly Sods, p. 104
Tucker Co. Take SR 28/55 west from Petersburg to Jordan Run Rd.
Turn right and proceed 1 mile to FR 19. 304-257-4488.

Donut Shop, p. 81
Upshur Co. US 33 and SR 20 south in Buckhannon. 304-422-9328.

Droop Mountain Battlefield State Park, p. 140
Pocahontas Co. US 219 near Hillsboro. 304-653-4254.

Dutch Hollow Wine Cellar Park, p. 71
Kanawha Co. From I-64 take exit 63. In Dunbar go right on SR 25 and
follow signs. 304-766-0223.

E

East Huntington Bridge, p. 19
Cabell Co. Connects US 60 and SR 2 with Ohio SR 7.

East River Mountain Overlook, p. 98
Mercer Co. US 460 to SR 598 to top of mountain. Bluefield.

East River Mountain Tunnel, p. 3
Mercer Co. I-77 in Bluefield.

Eastern Regional Coal Archives, p. 119
Mercer Co. 600 Commerce St., Bluefield 24701. Mon-Fri 9:30-5.
304-325-3943.

Eddie's Tires, p. 131
    Morgan Co. US 522 south of Berkeley Springs. Mon-Fri 8-5, Sat 8-3.
    304-258-1368.

Election of 1860, p. 43
    Jefferson Co. The Saturday of Columbus Day weekend in mid-October.
    Harpers Ferry National Historic Park. $5 per car to park; bus available.
    US 340 at the WV/MD/VA border. 304-535-6029.

Elk River Touring Company, p. 198
    Pocahontas Co. US 219 at Slatyfork. 304-572-3771.

Elk River Trout Ranch, p. 84
    Pocahontas Co. SR 15 near Monterville. 304-339-6455.

Elkhurst Bridge, p. 6
    Clay Co. From I-79 take exit 40, go south on SR16 through Clay.

F

Fairfax Stone, p. 71
    Tucker Co. About 2 miles from US 219 north of Thomas. (Not where
    the mile marker is.)

Fall Color Map, p. 167
    1-800-CALL-WVA.

Falls of Hill Creek, p. 109
    Pocahontas Co. SR 55/39 east of Richwood and 6 miles west of
    Cranberry Mountain Visitor Center. 304-846-2695.

Fasnatch, p. 43
    Randolph Co. Celebrated the Saturday before Ash Wednesday. 34 miles
    from Buckhannon: SR 20 to French Creek then SR 46, follow signs; or
    from Elkins: US 250 S., right at Mill Creek & SR 46 to Helvetia.
    304-924-6435

Fayetteville Visitors Center, p. 16
    Fayette Co. Old Fayette County Jail, 120 Windsor Lane, Fayetteville
    25840. 888-574-1500.

Fenton Glass, pgs. 135, 161
    Wood Co. I-77 to SR14/31 west to 3rd St. Go south approx. four blocks.
    Open Mon-Fri 8:30am-4:15; tours 40 minutes. Closed late June-early
    July. 304-375-7772.

Festival of Lights, p. 41
    Ohio Co. Oglebay and city of Wheeling. Located just off I-70 or US 40
    east from Wheeling, north on SR 88. Open daily from Nov. to Jan.;
    weekends through Feb.1. One time donation per car. 800-624-6988.

Fiddles, Snakes & Dog Days, p. 30
    Available on 60 minute VHS from Augusta Heritage Center.
    304-637-1209.

Caldwell. From I-64 take US 60 W exit; north onto CR 38 1.6 miles. Northern terminus at Cass in Pocahontas County. 304-799-4087.

Grimes Golden, p. 105
Brooke Co. Take SR 27 2.5 miles east of Wellsburg.

Gwen's Kitchen, p. 88
Greenbrier Co. Clingman's Meat Market, 102 E. Washington St., Lewisburg 24901. 304-645-1990.

H

Halliehurst, pgs. 14, 117, 194
Randolph Co. Davis and Elkins College, 100 Campus Drive, Elkins 26241. 304-637-1900.

Hamon Glass, p. 127
Putnam Co. 102 Hamon Dr., Scott Depot 25560. Back into housing area, small sign for Hamon Glass. 304-757-9067.

Hanging Rock Observatory, pgs. 2, 95
Monroe Co. From SR3 go left at Gap Mills on CR 15, Waiterville Rd. Look for Allegheny Trail parking area at crest of Peter's Mountain. 304-722-3003.

Happy Retreat, p. 68
Jefferson Co. Blakely Place and Mordington Ave., Charles Town 25414. Private.

Harewood, p. 68
Jefferson Co. Visible from SR 51, 3 miles west of Charles Town. Private.

Harman's North Fork Cottages and Cabins, p. 59
Grant Co. SR 55 10 miles west of Petersburg. 800-436-6254.

Harpers Ferry National Historic Park, pgs. 12, 43, 73, 155
Jefferson Co. US 340 at WV/MD/VA border. Buildings opened until 5 pm year 'round except Christmas and New Year's Day. 304-535-6371.

Hatfield and McCoy Trail, p. 9
Check on progress with the Hatfield-McCoy Scouts. 304-727-7441.

Hawks Nest Diversion Tunnel, p. 76
Fayette Co. On US 60 6 miles west of US 19 at Ansted.

Hawks Nest State Park, pgs. 50, 96
Fayette Co. On US 60 6 miles west of US 19. 304-658-5212.

Heartwood in the Hills, p. 34
Calhoun Co. 1 mile off SR 16 at Five Forks midway between Smithville & Grantsville. 304-354-7874.

Heiner's Bakery, p. 165
Cabell Co. 14th and Washington Sts., Huntington. Call for tours: 304-523-8411.

Henderson Hall, p. 120
Wood Co. Take SR 14 from Parkersburg to Williamstown. 4.5 miles past Vienna line; look for River Rd. and sign. Sundays May-Oct 1-4 pm. Fee. 304-375-2129.

Herns Mill Covered Bridge, p. 21
Greenbrier Co. CR 40.

Highland Scenic Highway, p. 3
Pocahontas Co. SR 55 from Richwood to US 219 north of Hillsboro. The Parkway section is SR 150 from SR 55 to 219 at Marlinton. Call for map: 304-636-1800.

Highlawn Inn, p. 58
Morgan Co. 304 Market St., Berkeley Springs 25411. 304-258-5700.

Hillsboro General Store, p. 129
Pocahontas Co. In Hillsboro on US 219. Open daily three seasons; weekends only in winter. 304-653-4414.

Hillbrook Inn, p. 67
Jefferson Co. Route 2, Box 152, Charles Town 25414. On CR 13, 5 miles west of Charles Town. 304-725-4223.

Hilltop House, pgs. 59, 93
Jefferson Co. P.O. Box 930, Harpers Ferry 25425. 304-535-2132.

Historic Charleston B&B, p. 59
Kanawha Co. 110 Elizabeth St., Charleston 25311. 304-345-8156.

Hokes Mill Covered Bridge, p. 21
Greenbrier Co.

Holl's Chocolates, p. 83
Wood Co. 2001 Grand Central Ave., Vienna 26105. 304-295-6576.

Holly River State Park, p. 65
Webster Co. On SR 20 in Hacker Valley. 304-493-6353.

Homeopathy Works, pgs. 119, 127
Morgan Co. 124 Fairfax St., Berkeley Springs 25411. Open daily 10-5. 304-258-2541.

Homer Laughlin, pgs. 125, 165
Hancock Co. Take SR 2 north of Weirton to Newell. Factory tours: Mon-Fri at 10:30 and 1. Outlet open Mon-Sat 9:30-5; Sun 12-5. 800-452-4462.

Holy Cow, Swami!, p. 29
Broadcast on WNPB-TV.

Huntington Mall, p. 131
Cabell Co. Take exit 20 off I-64 at Mall Road. 304-733-0492.

Huntington Museum, p. 18
Cabell Co. 2033 McCoy Rd., Huntington 25701. From I-64 take exit 8. Follow Museum of Art signs. 304-529-2701.

Anna Jarvis Birthplace, p. 138
>   Taylor Co. Take US 250/119 north of Philippi to Webster. Open Tue-
>   Sun 10-6. Admission: $4 adults; $2 students. 304-265-5549.

Jefferson County Courthouse, p. 74
>   Jefferson Co. Located at the corner of N. George and Washington Sts.,
>   Charles Town 25414. 304-725-9761.

Jefferson Rock, p. 92
>   Jefferson Co. At US 340, just past St. Peter's Church in Harpers Ferry.
>   304-535-6371.

Jet boats at Hawks Nest, p. 50
>   Fayette Co. Operated by New River Jet Boats, Inc. at Hawks Nest State
>   Park. Take US 60 6 miles west of US 19 to Ansted. 304-658-5212.

John Brown's Fort, pgs. 15, 73, 75
>   Jefferson Co. Harpers Ferry Historic Park. Open until 5 pm year 'round
>   except Christmas and New Year's Day. At US 340 at the WV/MD/VA
>   border. 304-535-6223.

John Henry Collection, p. 114
>   Summers Co. Summers County Visitors Center, 206 Temple St.,
>   Hinton 25951. 304-466-5420

John Henry Statue and Park, p. 72
>   Summers Co. Off SR 3 between Hinton and Alderson in Talcott.

Julia-Ann Square Historic District, p. 11
>   Wood Co. For walking tour contact Parkersburg Chamber of Commerce,
>   8th and Juliana Sts., Parkersburg 26101. 800-752-4982.

Julio's, p. 87
>   Harrison Co. 501 Baltimore Ave., Clarksburg 26301. 304-622-2592.

K

Kanawaha State Forest Braille Trail, p. 167
>   Kanawha Co. From I-64, in Charleston take exit 58A, travel south on
>   US 119, go left at second light, follow signs to Forest. 304-346-5654.

Kaymoor Mine Trail, p. 151
>   Fayette Co. US 19 N from Oak Hill, go right on Fayette Station Rd., the
>   last right before the New River Gorge Bridge. Railhead is 1 mile on the right.

Keith Albee Theater, p. 30
>   Cabell Co. 925 4th Ave., Huntington 25701. 304-523-0185.

Kimball, p. 144
>   McDowell Co. On US 52.

Kirkwood Wineries, p. 82
>   Nicholas Co. Route 1, Box 24, Summersville 26651. Take US 19 north
>   of Summersville to CR 8. Open Mon-Sat 9-7, Sun 1-7. 304-872-7332.

M

Museum of Radio and Technology, p. 120
Cabell Co. 1640 Florence Ave., Huntington 25701. Open Fri and Sat
10-4, Sun 1-4. 304-525-8890.

Mystery Hole, p. 147
Fayette Co. US 60 just east of Hawks Nest State Park near Ansted.
Open noon-8 daily except Tues and Weds. 304-658-9101.

N

National Conservation Training Center, p. 173
Jefferson Co. Route 1, Box 166, Shepherdstown 25443. Take SR 45 to
SR 480 north 2 blocks, then left on CR 5, Shepherdstown Grade Road.
Travel approx. 3 miles, following signs. 304-876-7200.

National Radio Astronomy Observatory, p. 184
Pocahontas Co. Take SR 92/28 26 miles northeast of Marlinton.
P.O. Box 2, Green Bank 24944. Daily tours hourly from 9-4 mid-June
through Labor Day, or call 304-456-2011.

National Road, p. 73
Ohio Co. US 40.

Natural Gravity Railyards, p. 18
Mercer Co. Bluestone CVB in Bluefield. 304-325-8438.

Natural Wonder Wildfoods Weekend, p. 44
Ritchie Co. North Bend State Park in Harrisville. Third weekend in Sept.
1-800-CALL-WVA.

New River/New River Gorge, pgs. 49, 96, 101
Fayette Co. New River Gorge National River, P.O. Box 246, Glen Jean
25846. 304-465-0508.

New River Gorge Bridge, pgs. 19, 133
Fayette Co. US 19.

New River Llama Trekking Co., p. 167
Fayette Co. P.O. Box 697, Edmond 25837. Reservations required.
304-574-1117.

New Vrindaban, p. 178
See "Palace of Gold."

Nite Glow, p. 40
Monongalia Co. In Morgantown, at Mountaineer Mall. Take I-68, exit 1,
go north on SR 119, right on SR 857. Nite Glow is held at 7:30 pm on
Thursday during the Balloon Festival. Balloon Festival held at Hart Field.
Take Sabraton exit off I-68. Follow the airport signs. 304-296-8356.

North Fork Mountain Inn, p. 59
Grant Co. Smoke Hole near Petersburg. 304-257-1108.

North Bend Rail Trail, pgs. 7, 168
Wood/Ritchie/Doddridge/Harrison Co. Trail runs from Parkersburg to

Wolf Summit. Trail headquarters are in Cairo, open weekends and holidays 11-7. 304-643-2931.

⊚

Oak Mound, p. 63
Harrison Co. On US 19 2 miles south of Clarksburg, on a hill near Veterans Hospital.

Oakhurst Links, p. 134
Greenbrier Co. P.O. Box 639, White Sulphur Springs 24986. 304-536-1884.

O'Briens Cabins, p. 60
Morgan Co. Off SR 9 about 12 miles east of Berkeley Springs in Hedgesville. 304-754-9128.

Oglebay Institute, p. 28
Ohio Co. Take US 40 east from Wheeling, go north on SR 88. 304-242-4200.

Oglebay Institute's Glass Museum, pgs. 114, 135
Ohio Co. See directions above. 304-242-7272.

Oglebay Resort, p. 142
Ohio Co. See directions above. 800-624-6988.

Ohio River Islands National Wildlife Refuge, pgs. 66, 110, 142
Wood/Pleasants/Tyler/Wetzel/ Marshall/Ohio Counties. Open daily for visitors from sunrise to sunset. 304-420-7568.

O'Hurley's General Store, pgs. 56, 128
Jefferson Co. Turn on SR 230 .25 mile south of Shepherdstown. Open Tue-Sat 10-7; Sun 12-6; closed Mondays. 304-876-6907.

Oil and Gas Museum, p. 120
Wood Co. 119 Third St., Parkersburg 26101. Open regularly on weekends. 304-485-5446.

Old Central City, p. 132
Cabell Co. Take I-64, exit 6. Huntington. W. 14th St. from Madison to Washington Sts. 304-429-3900.

Old Stone Presbyterian Church, p. 144
Greenbrier Co. 200 Church St., Lewisburg 24901. Open daily 9-4. 304-645-2676.

Oliverio's Cash and Carry, p. 83
Harrison Co. 4th and Wholesale Sts. in Glen Elk section of Clarksburg. 800-296-4959.

Opera House, p. 17
Pocahontas Co. Off SR 39 in center of Marlinton on 3rd Ave. 800-336-7009.

Organ Cave, p. 71
>   Greenbrier Co. 417 Masters Rd. From US 60 east of Lewisburg take SR
>   63 south about 9 miles to Ronceverte. 304-645-7600.

Our Lady of the Pines, p. 17
>   Preston Co. US 219, 8 miles north of Thomas at Silver Lake.
>   Mass celebrated by mission priests in season.

P

Palace of Gold, p. 178
>   Marshall Co. Take US 250 about 5 miles south of Moundsville to Limestone
>   Ridge and Palace Road, then about 4 miles. Tours available. 304-843-1812.

Panorama Overlook, p. 94
>   Morgan Co. On SR 9 3 miles west of Berkeley Springs. 800-447-8797.

Panther State Forest, p. 103
>   McDowell Co. Take US 52 to CR 1 north to Panther then CR 3-2.
>   304-938-2252.

Paw Paw Tunnel, p. 23
>   Morgan Co. Take SR 9 west to SR 29 north to Paw Paw. Cross Potomac
>   River and is .5 mile on right. Allow 45 min. from Berkeley Springs.
>   301-678-5463.

Peace Totem, p. 33
>   Raleigh Co. Youth Museum of Southern West Virginia, 2 miles north on
>   SR 3 from exit 44 of I-77. Left on Ewart Ave. to New River Park.
>   304-252-3730

Pearl Buck Birthplace, p. 119
>   Pocahontas Co. On US 219 in Hillsboro. Tours Mon-Sat 9-5, Sun 1-5.
>   304-653-4430.

Pence Springs Hotel, pgs. 16, 57, 189
>   Summers Co. P.O. Box 90, Pence Springs 24962. Take SR 3 & 12 south
>   of Alderson for 10 miles. Closed Jan-March. 800-826-1829.

Pennsboro Speedway, p. 51
>   Ritchie Co. Dirt Track World Championship. US 50 in Pennsboro.
>   304-659-2976.

Personal Rapid Transit System, p. 136
>   Monongalia Co. 99 8th St., WVU, P.O. Box 6565, Morgantown 26506-
>   6565. 304-293-5011.

Petersburg Fish Hatchery, p. 140
>   Grant Co. Take SR 220 south of Petersburg. Turn onto Fish Hatchery/
>   Airport Rd. Take to end of paved area — less than 2 miles from town.
>   Open daily 7:30 am-3:30 pm. 304-257-4014.

Peter's Mountain, pgs. 2, 57, 87, 95
>   Monroe Co. Take SR 3 at Gap Mills, go left on CR 15, Waiterville Rd.

Allegheny Trail parking area at crest of Peter's Mountain. 304-772-3003.

Philippi Covered Bridge, pgs. 21, 22
Barbour Co.

Pickin' in the Park, p. 33
Randolph Co. Elkins City Park. 304-637-1209.

Pilgrim Glass, p. 127
Wayne Co. Take I-64, exit 1 in Ceredo. Take US 52 south to CR3-2. Follow Tri-State airport signs; is about 3 miles on left. Mon-Sat 9-5, Sun 1-5. 304-453-3553.

Pinnacle Rock State Park, p. 109
Mercer Co. Take US 52 just east of Bramwell. 304-589-5307.

Pipestem Resort State Park & Observation Tower, pgs. 87, 98, 105, 168, 197
Summers Co. P.O. Box 150, Pipestem 25979. Take I-77 to SR 20; travel approx. 20 miles. 304-466-1800.

Pocahontas Coal Fields, pgs. 98, 106, 152
Mercer Co. Bluestone CVB. 800-221-3206.

Point Overlook Museum, p. 98
Ohio Co. From I-70 take Oglebay exit, go west on US 40; 1.4 miles up Wheeling Hill, left past Indian Monument, on Grandview St. Open daily 10-3. 304-232-3010.

Poor Man's Flying School, p. 169
Fayette Co. Fayette Airport. US 19 two miles SW of Fayetteville. 304-574-1035.

Potomac Eagle, p. 159
Hampshire Co. US 50 to SR 28, 1 mile north of Romney. P.O. Box 657, Romney 26757. May through Oct. 800-22-EAGLE.

Pringle Sycamore, p. 156
Upshur Co. US 119 and SR 20, 1.6 miles north of Buckhannon.

R

Ramps, pgs. 45, 82
Festivals held mid-April when first ramps peek out at:
Nicholas Co.: Feast of the Ransom, Richwood High School, Richwood. 304-846-6790;
Randolph Co.: International Ramp Cook-Off and Festival. Elkins City Park. Free. 800-422-3304;

Ramsey School, p. 18
Mercer Co. 300 Ramsey St., Bluefield 24701. 304-327-9218

Rankin Octagonal Barn, p. 18
Jackson Co. On Wilding Rd. visible from I-77 just north of Ravenswood/Silverton exit.

Raven Rocks, p. 95
Hampshire Co. Nature Conservancy tours to Ice Mountain leave from
Slanesville Post Office, SR 29 east of Romney on the third Thursday and
second Saturday. Reservations recommended. 304-345-4350.

Red Dog Saloon, p. 50
Fayette Co. Take SR 82, Fayette State Rd. in Fayetteville. 800-879-7483.

Red Fox Inn, p. 90
Pocahontas Co. Snowshoe Mountain Resort. US 219, 26 miles north of
Marlinton. Closed April, May and Nov. 572-5252.

Rehobeth Church and Museum, p. 143
Monroe Co. SR 3, 2 miles east of Union. Open Memorial Day to Labor
Day, 10 am-5 pm. 304-772-3003.

Richters Maplehouse, p. 83
Randolph Co. Take US 219/250 to SR 15. At Monterville, go west 11
miles on Pickens Rd., right at the Richters sign and proceed 3 miles to
the Maplehouse. 304-924-5404.

Ritter Park, p. 144
Cabell Co. From I-64, take exits 8 or 11. Near 12th St., Huntington.
304-696-5954.

River House B&B, p. 167
Morgan Co. Take SR 9 west to Great Cacapon, go left on Rock Ford Rd.,
B&B is about .5 mile on left. 304-258-4042.

Roadkill Cook-off, p. 45
Pocahontas Co. Held in Marlinton in September. 304-799-4636.

Robert Byrd Locks Visitor Center, p. 97
Mason Co. P.O. Box 9, Apple Grove 25502. Take SR 2 approximately 12
miles south of Point Pleasant. Open Mon-Fri 8-3:45; observation deck
open daily 8 am-9 pm. 304-576-9901.

Root Cellar Herbs and Mercantile, p. 130
Putnam Co. 2739 Main Street, Hurricane 25526. Store open Mon-Sat
10-5; Tea Room open Tue-Sat 11 am-3 pm. 304-562-4139.

Round Barn, p. 18
Marion Co. West Augusta Historic Society. Take US 250 west of
Fairmont to SR 11 for less than a mile to Mannington. Open
Sun 1:30-4:30 or by appointment. 304-986-2636.

Rumsey Monument, p. 75
Jefferson Co. Go right at end of North Mill St., Shepherdstown.

Rumsey Boathouse, p. 75
Jefferson Co. Located behind Entler Hotel on German Street,
Shepherdstown. 304-876-6907.

S

Saddle Mountain, pgs. 5, 99
Mineral Co. US 50 west of Romney.

Salt Sulphur Springs, p. 150
Monroe Co. US 219, 3 miles south of Union. 304-772-3003.

Sandstone Falls, p. 97
Summers Co. From I-64, take exit 438, south on SR20 approximately 3 miles; near Hinton. 304-466-0417.

Sarvis Fork Covered Bridge, p. 21
Jackson Co.

Savannah Lane Shooting Association, p. 51
Greenbrier Co. Contact: Free Spirit Adventures and Bike Shop in Lewisburg. 800-877-4749.

Scott Hollow Cave, p. 108
Monroe Co. Take SR 3 just north of Union to CR 5 (Fort Springs Rd.) past Sinks Grove Post Office. Immediately turn right onto the gravel Scott Hollow Rd. Marked entrance is across from the rounded barn with llamas. 800-814-5218.

Seneca Caverns, p. 142
Pendleton Co. Take SR 33/28, 3 miles southwest of Riverton. Open daily, April 1 thru Labor Day; other times by appointment. 304-567-2691.

Seneca Rocks, pgs. 99, 110, 184
Pendleton Co. From SR 33 & 55, go approx. 15 miles west of Franklin on SR 33. 304-567-2827.

Shamrock, p. 145
Mercer Co. Bluefield.

Shanghai Parade, p. 42
Greenbrier Co. Held in Lewisburg on Jan 1. 800-833-2068.

Shannondale Springs, p. 150
Jefferson Co. Take SR 9 4 miles east of Charles Town, south CR9-5. 304-725-6423.

Shepherdstown Opera House, p. 30
Jefferson Co. German Street, Shepherdstown. 304-876-3704.

Simpson Creek Covered Bridge, p. 21
Harrison Co.

Sinks of Gandy, p. 106
Randolph Co. Take CR 29 approximately 5 miles south of New Italy.

Sistersville Ferry, p. 153
Tyler Co. Charles and Catherine St., Sistersville 26175. Open Mon-Fri 7 am-5:30 pm; Sun 7 am-4 pm.

T

U

V

W

War Memorial Museum, p. 118
Putnam Co. 21st St. and 2nd Ave., Nitro 25143. Take SR 25 west, one block past Nitro Bridge. Call before 9 am or after 5 pm to arrange a tour. 304-755-1173.

Warfield House, p. 59
Randolph Co. 318 Buffalo St., Elkins 26241. 888-636-4555

Washington Western Lands Museum, p. 66
Jackson Co. Washington St., 1 mi. south of downtown Ravenswood. Open only Sunday afternoons from Memorial Day to Labor Day.

Webster Springs Woodchopping Festival, p. 43
Webster Co. Held in May. 304-847-7666.

The Wells Inn, p. 199
Tyler Co., 316 Charles St., Sistersville 26175. 304-652-1312.

West Virginia Crafts Map, p. 35
To obtain a copy, call 800-CALL WVA.

West Virginia Flintlock Championship, p. 43
Putnam Co. Held in Hurricane. 304-727-6194.

West Virginia Honey Festival, p. 46
Wood Co. Held mid-Sept. in Parkersburg at the Wood County 4-H campgrounds. 800-752-4982.

West Virginia Marble Festival, p. 42
Ritchie Co. Held the 1st Sat. in May in Cairo. 304-628-3321.

West Virginia Motor Speedway, p. 51
Wood Co. Off I-77 in Mineral Wells. 304-489-1889.

West Virginia Northern Railways, p. 168
Preston Co. 156 Sisler St., P.O. Box 424, Kingwood 26537. Excursions May through Oct. 800-253-1065.

West Virginia Penitentiary Tours, p. 157
Marshall Co. 818 Jefferson Ave., Moundsville 26401. Take I-70 or 470 to SR 2/US 250. Go south on US 250/Jefferson Ave. Open April-Dec., 10-5 Tue-Sun, closed Mon. 304-843-1993.

West Virginia and Regional History Collection, p. 116
Monogalia Co. Colson Hall, West Virginia University, Morgantown 26505. 304-293-3536.

West Virginia State Archives and History Library, p. 119
Kanawha Co. Cultural Center at Capitol Complex, Kanawha Blvd., Charleston 25305. Mon-Fri 9-5; Sat 1-5. 304-558-0230.

West Virginia State Farm Museum, p. 121
Mason Co. Rt 1, Box 479, Point Pleasant 25550. Adjacent to Mason County Fairgrounds near Pt. Pleasant. Take SR 62 north, east on Fairgrounds Rd. 304-675-5737

Y

Z

Zion Episcopal Church Cemetery, p. 67
    Jefferson Co. 300 E. Congress St., Charles Town 25414. 304-725-5312.

BIBLIOGRAPHY

Adams, Charles. *Roadside Markers in West Virginia*. Shepherdstown, WV: Charles Adams, 1998.

Anderson, Colleen. *The New West Virginia One-Day Trip Book*. McLean, VA: EPM Publications, 1998.

Braley, Dean. *Shaman's Story: West Virginia Petroglyphs*. St. Albans, WV: St. Albans Publishing, 1993.

Charleston Gazette. Charleston, WV.

Cohen, Stan. *Historic Springs of the Virginias*. Charleston, WV: Pictorial Histories Publishing Co., 1997.

Cohen, Stan. *West Virginia's Covered Bridges*. Charleston, WV: Pictorial Histories Publishing Co., 1992.

Conte, Robert. *The History of the Greenbrier, America's Resort*. Charleston, WV: Pictorial Histories Publishing Co., 1989.

David Hunter Strother. Morgantown, WV: WVU Press, 1997.

Davidson, Paul, Ward Eister, Dirk Davidson, and Charlie Walbridge. *Wildwater West Virginia*. Birmingham, AL: Menasha Ridge Press, 1996.

Goldenseal. Charleston, WV: The State of West Virginia.

Graffiti. Charleston, WV.

Hudson, Jim. *Rail Trails along the Greenbrier River*. Charleston, WV: Quarrier Press, 1998.

Hutchins, Frank. *Mountain Biking in West Virginia*. Charleston, WV: Quarrier Press, 1995.

Keel, John. *The Mothman Prophecies*. Avondale Estastes, GA: IllumiNet Press, 1991.

Lowry, Terry. *Last Sleep: Battle of Droop Mountain*. Charleston, WV: Quarrier Press, 1998.

Newbraugh, Fred. *Bath, That Seat of Sin*. Berkeley Springs, WV: 1993.

Soltis, Stephen and Stacy. *West Virginia: Off-the-Beaten-Path*. Old Saybrook, CT: The Globe Pequot Press, 1998.

Teets, Bob. *West Virginia UFO's: Close Encounters in the Mountain State*. Terra Alta, WV: Headline Books, 1995.

Travel Through Time: David Hunter Strother. Washington, DC: Porte Crayon & Co., 1996.

West Virginia Atlas and Gazetteer. Yarmouth, ME: DeLorme Pub., 1997.

West Virginia, It's You! Charleston, WV: Bell Atlantic.

Williams, John Alexander. *West Virginia: A History for Beginners*. Martinsburg, WV: Appalachian Editions, 1997.

Wonderful West Virginia. Charleston, WV: West Virginia Dept. of Natural Resources.

ABOUT THE AUTHOR

Jeanne Mozier has lived in Berkeley Springs since 1977 where she and her husband, Jack Soronen, own and operate the Star Theatre.

A prize-winning writer of fiction and non-fiction, **Way Out** is her first book.

Jeanne was named West Virginia Woman of the Year for Volunteer Services in 1996 for her work in arts, tourism and local history.